T0060103

TRUE DEVOTION
to MARY
with PREPARATION FOR
TOTAL CONSECRATION

Imprimi Potest
A. Josselin, S.M.M.
Superior General

Nihil Obstat
John M. A. Fearns, S.T.D.
Censor Librorum

Imprimatur
✠ Francis Cardinal Spellman, D.D.
Archbishop of New York
September 26, 1949

TRUE DEVOTION
to MARY
with PREPARATION FOR
TOTAL CONSECRATION

SAINT LOUIS-MARIE GRIGNION
DE MONTFORT

Translated from the Original French by
Father Frederick William Faber, D.D.
PRIEST OF THE ORATORY

Edited and Annotated by
The Fathers of the Company of Mary

*"Jesus Christ is not known as He ought to be
because Mary has been up to this time unknown."*
—St. Louis De Montfort

TAN·CLASSICS

Copyright © 2010 TAN Books.

TAN Books, a division of Saint Benedict Press, LLC.

Copyright © 1941 by the Fathers of the Company of Mary. Retypeset in 2010 by TAN Books.

All rights reserved. With the exception of short excerpts used in articles and critical reviews, no part of this work may be reproduced, transmitted, or stored in any form whatsoever, printed or electronic, without the prior written permission of the publisher.

Published with the assistance of The Livingstone Corporation. Cover and interior design by Mark Wainright, The Livingstone Corporation. Typeset by TAN Books.

Cover Image: *The Virgin Annunciate* by Pompeo Girolamo Batoni (1708-87) (after), Private Collection. Photo: Bonhams, London, UK/The Bridgeman Art Library.

ISBN: 978-0-89555-154-2

Printed in India

14 13 12 11 10 9 8 7 6 5

www.TANBooks.com

TAN·CLASSICS

"*The more we honor the Blessed Virgin,
the more we honor Jesus Christ,
because we honor Mary only that
we may the more perfectly honor Jesus,
since we go to her only as the way
by which we are to find the end
we are seeking, which is Jesus.*"
—St. Louis De Montfort

FROM THE POPES

Pope Pius IX declared that St. Louis De Montfort's devotion to Mary was the best and most acceptable form of devotion to Our Lady.

Pope Leo XIII granted a plenary indulgence to those who make St. Louis De Montfort's act of consecration to the Blessed Virgin. On his deathbed he renewed the act himself and invoked the heavenly aid of St. Louis De Montfort, whom he had beatified in 1888.

Pope St. Pius X: "I heartily recommend *True Devotion to The Blessed Virgin*, so admirably written by Blessed De Montfort, and to all who read it grant the Apostolic Benediction."

Pope Benedict XV: "A book of high authority and unction."

Pope Pius XI: "I have practiced this devotion ever since my youth."

Pope Pius XII: "The greatest force behind all his [St. Louis De Montfort's] apostolic ministry and his great secret for attracting and winning souls for Jesus was his devotion to Mary." (*From Canonization address, July 20, 1947*).

Pope Paul VI: "We are convinced without any doubt that devotion to Our Lady is essentially joined with devotion to Christ, that it assures a firmness of conviction to faith in Him and in His Church, a vital adherence to Him and to His Church which, without devotion to Mary, would be impoverished and compromised."

Pope John Paul II: "The reading of this book was a decisive turning-point in my life. I say 'turning-point,' but in fact it was a long inner journey. . . . This 'perfect devotion' is indispensable to anyone who means to give himself without reserve to Christ and to the work of redemption." "It is from Montfort that I have taken my motto: '*Totus tuus*' ('I am all thine'). Someday I'll have to tell you Montfortians how I discovered De Montfort's *Treatise on True Devotion to Mary*, and how often I had to reread it to understand it."

Vatican Council II: "The maternal duty of Mary toward men in no way obscures or diminishes this unique mediation of Christ, but rather shows its power. All her saving influence on men originates not from some inner necessity, but from the divine pleasure. It flows forth from the superabundance of the merits of Christ, rests on His mediation, depends entirely on it and draws all its power from it." ". . . the practices and exercises of devotion to her recommended by the Church in the course of the centuries [are to] be treasured. . . ." (*Lumen Gentium*: 60, 67).

CONTENTS

PART ONE
Devotion to the Blessed Virgin Mary

PART TWO

Perfect Devotion to the Blessed Virgin Mary or
Perfect Consecration to Jesus Christ

SUPPLEMENT

ABOUT ST. LOUIS DE MONTFORT

St. Louis Marie Grignion de la Bacheleraie, who abandoned his family name for that of his birthplace, was born on January 31, 1673 in the little town of Montfort-la-Canne, which is located in Brittany, France. He studied for the priesthood at St. Sulpice in Paris, having made the 200-mile journey there on foot. He was ordained a priest in 1700, at the age of 27.

St. Louis De Montfort had wanted to become a missionary in Canada, but he was advised to remain in France. There he traveled around the western part of the country, from diocese to diocese and from parish to parish, instructing the people, preaching, helping the poor, hearing confessions, giving retreats, opening schools and rebuilding church buildings. His labors were almost miraculously fruitful. He stated that never did a sinner resist after being touched by him with a Rosary.

But because he encountered great opposition from religious authorities—in particular, being forbidden by the Bishop of Poitiers to preach in his diocese—he decided to travel to Rome to ask the Holy Father if he was doing God's Will and whether he should continue as before. St. Louis De Montfort walked to Rome—a thousand miles—and put his case to Pope Clement XI. The Pope told him to continue his traveling missionary work, and named him Missionary Apostolic, but told him always to be sure to work under obedience to the diocesan authorities. One of St. Louis De Montfort's greatest problems was the opposition he encountered from propagators of the Jansenist heresy, which was then very active in France. The Jansenists spread an atmosphere of harshness and moral rigorism, claiming that human nature was radically corrupted by Original Sin (as opposed to the Catholic teaching that human nature is still essentially good, though fallen, and although it has suffered a darkening of the intellect and weakening of the will). The Jansenists denied that God's mercy is available to all, and they allowed only infrequent reception of the Sacraments of Penance and the Holy Eucharist, and only after long and severe preparation—with Holy Communion being looked upon as a reward rather than a remedy. Also, they taught that God should always be addressed with fear and trembling. These tenets resembled those of Calvinism. Although Jansenism had been condemned by the Church twice even before St. Louis De Montfort's birth, its teachings continued to spread and to influence people for a century. In contrast, St. Louis De Montfort preached confidence in Mary and union with her Divine Son.

St. Louis De Montfort founded two religious orders: the Daughters of Wisdom, begun in 1703 from a number of poor and afflicted girls at the Hospital of Poitiers, where he was temporary chaplain, and the Missionaries of the Company of Mary (Montfort Fathers and Brothers), founded in 1715. The Brothers of St. Gabriel, a teaching order, also claim St. Louis De Montfort as their spiritual father.

St. Louis De Montfort left several writings, the most famous being *The Secret of the Rosary*, *True Devotion to Mary*, and *The Secret of Mary*. These books were based on sermons he had given when traveling around France. By spreading devotion to the Blessed Virgin Mary, St. Louis De Montfort was teaching souls to love the devil's great enemy. (In *True Devotion to Mary*, he states that the devil fears Mary more than all angels and men, and in a sense more than God Himself—see no. 52). At the Saint's beatification investigation, many witnesses testified that during his life they had heard struggles between him and the devil, including the sound of fist blows and the swish of whips.

St. Louis De Montfort exhausted his great physical strength by his apostolic labors. On his deathbed in Sainte-Laurent-sur-Sèvre, at age 43, he kissed the crucifix and a statue of the Blessed Mother. Apparently speaking to the devil, he exclaimed: "In vain do you attack me; I am between Jesus and Mary! I have finished my course: All is over. I shall sin no more!" Then he died peacefully on April 28, 1716. His feast day is April 28, the day of his birth in Heaven. St. Louis De Montfort's writings were examined by the Holy See, which pronounced that there was nothing in them to hinder his beatification and canonization. He was canonized a Saint in 1947.

ABOUT TRUE DEVOTION TO MARY

St. Louis De Montfort himself prophesied regarding *True Devotion to Mary*: "I clearly foresee that raging beasts shall come in fury to tear with their diabolical teeth this little writing and him whom the Holy Ghost has made use of to write it—or at least to smother it in the darkness and silence of a coffer, that it may not appear. They shall even attack and persecute those who shall read it and carry it out in practice." (T.D., no. 114). This prediction was fulfilled to the letter. Throughout the whole 18th century, the spiritual sons of St. Louis De Montfort were persecuted by the Jansenists for their zeal in spreading this devotion; the precious manuscript of De Montfort remained hidden during the troubled times of the French Revolution and was brought to light only in the year 1842, when it was found in a chest of old books by a Montfort Father.

The title page from *True Devotion* was missing, and the book has been variously known as *True Devotion to the Blessed Virgin*, *Treatise on True Devotion to Mary*, and *True Devotion to Mary*—the phrase "true devotion" being drawn from chapter III of Part 1, wherein St. Louis De Montfort distinguishes between true devotion and false devotion to Mary. Over the years, however, the phrase "true devotion" has come to be used in reference to the *Perfect* Devotion to Mary which is expounded on in Part 2 of the book.

St. Louis De Montfort was the one to whom it was given to explain thoroughly the path "to Jesus through Mary" and to shape it into a definite method of spiritual life. He does not propose some special or "extra" prayers, but rather, a devotion which essentially consists of one single act which, under various forms and conditions, we apply to our whole life, both interior and exterior. This devotion leads to a permanent disposition of living and acting habitually in dependence on Mary; it embraces one's entire life, not just one's prayer times or specifically religious acts.

St. Louis De Montfort knew that Mary is the pathway to her Son, leading souls quickly and securely to Jesus Christ, the Eternal Wisdom.

Inflamed with holy love St. Louis De Montfort wrote many poems to the Divine Wisdom, including the following fervent lines:

Divine Wisdom, I love Thee unto folly.
I am Thy lover.
Thou alone in this world I seek,
Thou alone I desire.
I am a man gone mad with love,
Forever chasing Thee.

Tell me who Thou art,
For I am half blind.
I can discern only
That Thou art a secret I must fathom.
Show Thyself fully to my soul
Which dies for love of Thee.

Where dost Thou live,
Wisdom Divine?
Must I cross continents or seas
To find Thee,

Or fly across the skies?
I am ready to go wherever Thou art,
Not counting the costs, to possess Thee.

To Jesus through Mary: This is the sublime secret of holiness set forth by St. Louis De Montfort in *True Devotion to Mary*—a book which ranks among the greatest spiritual masterpieces ever penned, a book which seems to have been inspired by the Holy Ghost Himself. May this book lead many souls to a deep and faithful love of Our Lord Jesus Christ.

PREFACE

by

Cardinal O'Connell

The doctrine of St. Louis Marie Grignion De Montfort needs neither introduction nor explanation to those who are conversant with the spiritual life. It is well known that the practice of the Perfect Devotion to the Blessed Virgin which he taught is widespread among priests, religious and even lay people throughout the world. It is gratifying to note that its beneficial influence is felt in many sections of our own country.

This widespread propagation of the Perfect Devotion in many respects resembles the growth of the mustard seed spoken of in the Gospel: It had a humble beginning, grew without great exterior display, and, by the grace of the Holy Ghost, spread throughout the entire Church. This new edition of the manual will contribute toward making it still better known. It is my happy privilege to recommend it to everyone, following therein the example of our late Holy Father of blessed memory, Pius X.

I have known this form of devotion for many years and I have never hesitated to recommend it to those in whom the grace of God seemed to be at work, drawing them toward a deeper and more intense spiritual life. As Rector of the American College in Rome, I proposed and taught it to the seminarians as an excellent means of acquiring the holiness of their priestly ideal. It was with my encouragement that there was formed among them a "Blessed De Montfort Society." The Legion of Mary, which we have heartily encouraged in our diocese with such happy results, derives from the spiritual teachings of Montfort to such an extent that he is said to be the "tutor of the Legion" (Handbook, p. 51). Several confraternities of Mary, Queen of All Hearts, are at present propagating the Perfect Devotion in various centers throughout the United States.

The more we reflect, the more we realize that the mission of Christianity is to take possession of man in his entirety in order to transform him into a soul worthy of Heaven. Hence, Pius XI, in speaking of Christian Education, says that its "proper and immediate end is to cooperate with divine grace in forming the true and perfect Christian, that is, to form Christ Himself in those regenerated by Baptism." In this work of transformation, a definite part has been assigned by God to the Blessed Virgin Mary, that of leading souls to Jesus Christ, and of keeping them in His love.

Hence, the role of Mary, Mother of God and Mediatrix of All Grace, ought not to be overlooked. Indeed, the recognition of the high dignity granted her by God leads her clients toward a richer understanding of the mysteries of Christ and a fuller participation in the fruits of the Redemption.

Our Holy Mother the Church has recognized the merit of the *Treatise on the True Devotion to Mary* in conferring upon its author the honor of beatification. She has approved and enriched with numerous indulgences the Confraternity of Mary, Queen of All Hearts. It is our conviction that a wider diffusion of this work "of great unction and authority"—to use the words of His Holiness, Benedict XV—will draw souls from every walk of life to a greater interior perfection and a fuller development of Christian piety.

W. Card. O'Connell,
Abp. Boston

December 8, 1940

FATHER FABER'S PREFACE

It was in the year 1846 or 1847, at St. Wilfrid's, that I first studied the life and spirit of the Venerable Grignion De Montfort; and now, after more than fifteen years, it may be allowable to say that those who take him for their master will hardly be able to name a saint or ascetical writer to whose grace and spirit their mind will be more subject than to his. We may not yet call him saint; but the process of his beatification is so far and so favorably advanced that we may not have long to wait before he will be raised upon the altars of the Church.

There are few men in the eighteenth century who have more strongly upon them the marks of the man of Providence than this Elias-like missionary of the Holy Ghost and of Mary. His entire life was such an exhibition of the holy folly of the Cross that his biographers unite in always classing him with St. Simon Salo and St. Philip Neri. Clement XI made him a missionary apostolic in France, in order that he might spend his life in fighting against Jansenism, so far as it affected the salvation of souls. Since the Apostolical Epistles it would be hard to find words that burn so marvelously as the twelve pages of his prayer for the Missionaries of the Holy Ghost, to which I earnestly refer all those who find it hard to keep up under their numberless trials the first fires of the love of souls.

He was at once persecuted and venerated everywhere. His amount of work, like that of St. Anthony of Padua, is incredible, and indeed, inexplicable. He wrote some spiritual treatises which have already had a remarkable influence on the Church during the few years they have been known, and bid fair to have a much wider influence in years to come. His preaching, his writing and his conversation were all impregnated with prophecy and with anticipations of the later ages of the Church. He comes forward like another St. Vincent Ferrer, as if on the days bordering on the Last Judgment, and proclaims that he brings an authentic message from God about the greater honor and wider knowledge and more prominent love of His Blessed Mother, and her connection with the second advent of her Son. He founded two religious congregations—one of men and one of women—which have been quite extraordinarily successful; and yet he died at the age of forty-three in 1716, after only sixteen years of priesthood.

It was on the 12th of May, 1853, that the decree was pronounced at Rome declaring his writing to be exempt from all error which could be a bar to his canonization. In this very treatise on the veritable devotion to our Blessed Lady, he has recorded this prophecy: "I clearly foresee that raging brutes will come in fury to tear with their diabolical teeth this little writing and him whom the Holy Ghost has made use of to write it; or at least to envelop it in the silence of a coffer, in order that it may not appear." Nevertheless, he prophesies both its appearance and its success. All this was fulfilled to the letter. The author died in 1716, and the treatise was found by accident by one of the priests of his congregation of St. Laurent-sur-Sèvre in 1842. The existing superior was able to attest the handwriting as being that of the venerable founder, and the autograph was sent to Rome to be examined in the process of canonization.

All those who are likely to read this book love God, and lament that they do not love Him more; all desire something for His glory—the spread of some good work, the success of some devotion, the coming of some good time. One man has been striving for years to overcome a particular fault, and has not succeeded. Another mourns, and almost wonders while he mourns, that so few of his relations and friends have been converted to the Faith. One grieves that he has not devotion enough; another that he has a cross to carry which is a peculiarly impossible cross to him; while a third has domestic troubles and family unhappinesses which feel almost incompatible with his salvation; and for all these things prayer appears to bring so little remedy.

But what is the remedy that is wanted? What is the remedy indicated by God Himself? If we may rely on the disclosures of the saints, it is an immense increase of devotion to our Blessed Lady; but, remember, nothing short of an immense one. Here in England, Mary is not half enough preached. Devotion to her is low and thin and poor. It is frightened out of its wits by the sneers of heresy. It is always invoking human respect and carnal prudence, wishing to make Mary so little of a Mary that Protestants may feel at ease about her. Its ignorance of theology makes it unsubstantial and unworthy. It is not the prominent characteristic of our religion which it ought to be. It has no faith in itself. Hence it is that Jesus is not loved, that heretics are not converted, that the Church is not exalted; that souls which might be saints wither and dwindle; that the Sacraments are not rightly frequented, or souls enthusiastically evangelized.

Jesus is obscured because Mary is kept in the background. Thousands of souls perish because Mary is withheld from them. It is the miserable, unworthy shadow which we call our devotion to the Blessed Virgin that is the cause of all these wants and blights, these evils and omissions and declines. Yet, if we are to believe the revelations of the saints, God is pressing for a greater, a wider, a stronger, quite another devotion to His Blessed Mother. I cannot think of a higher work or a broader vocation for anyone than the simple spreading of this peculiar devotion of the Venerable Grignion De Montfort. Let a man but try it for himself, and his surprise at the graces it brings with it, and the transformations it causes in his soul, will soon convince him of its otherwise almost incredible efficacy as a means for the salvation of men, and for the coming of the kingdom of Christ. Oh, if Mary were but known, there would be no coldness to Jesus then! Oh, if Mary were but known, how much more wonderful would be our faith, and how different would our Communions be! Oh, if Mary were but known, how much happier, how much holier, how much less worldly should we be, and how much more should we be living images of our sole Lord and Saviour, her dearest and most blessed Son!

I have translated the whole treatise myself, and have taken great pains with it, and have been scrupulously faithful. At the same time, I would venture to warn the reader that one perusal will be very far from making him master of it. If I may dare to say so, there is a growing feeling of something inspired and supernatural about it, as we go on studying it; and with that we cannot help experiencing, after repeated readings of it, that its novelty never seems to wear off, nor its fullness to be diminished, nor the fresh fragrance and sensible fire of its unction ever to abate. May the Holy Ghost, the Divine Zealot of Jesus and Mary, deign to give a new blessing to this work in England; and may He please to console us quickly with the canonization of this new apostle and fiery missionary of His most dear and most Immaculate spouse, and still more with the speedy coming of that great age of the Church which is to be the Age of Mary!

F. W. Faber
Priest of the Oratory
Presentation of Our Blessed Lady
November 21, 1862

—PART ONE—

DEVOTION TO THE BLESSED VIRGIN MARY

Necessity

Fundamental Truths

Choice of True Devotion
to the Blessed Virgin

PRELIMINARY REMARKS

by St. Louis De Montfort

1. It was through the most holy Virgin Mary that Jesus came into the world, and it is also through her that He has to reign in the world.

2. Mary was singularly hidden during her life. It is on this account that the Holy Ghost and the Church call her *Alma Mater*—"Mother secret and hidden."[1] Her humility was so profound that she had no inclination on earth more powerful or more constant than that of hiding herself, from herself as well as from every other creature, so as to be known to God only.

3. He heard her prayers when she begged to be hidden, to be humbled and to be treated as in all respects poor and of no account. He took pleasure in hiding her from all human creatures, in her conception, in her birth, in her life, in her mysteries, and in her resurrection and Assumption. Even her parents did not know her, and the angels often asked one another: "Who is that?" (*Cant.* 3:6; 8:5) because the Most High either had hidden her from them, or if He did reveal anything, it was nothing compared to what He kept undisclosed.

4. God the Father consented that she should work no miracle, at least no public one, during her life, although He had given her the power to do so. God the Son consented that she should hardly ever speak, though He had communicated His wisdom to her. God the

Holy Ghost, though she was His faithful spouse, consented that His Apostles and Evangelists should speak very little of her, and no more than was necessary to make Jesus Christ known.

5. Mary is the excellent masterpiece of the Most High, the knowledge and possession of which He has reserved to Himself. Mary is the admirable Mother of the Son, who took pleasure in humbling and concealing her during her life in order to favor her humility, calling her by the name of "woman" (*Jn.* 2:4; 19:26), as if she were a stranger, although in His heart He esteemed and loved her above all angels and all men. Mary is the "sealed fountain" (*Cant.* 4:12), the faithful spouse of the Holy Ghost, to whom He alone has entrance. Mary is the sanctuary and the repose of the Holy Trinity, where God dwells more magnificently and more divinely than in any other place in the universe, not excepting His dwelling between the Cherubim and Seraphim. Nor is any creature, no matter how pure, allowed to enter into that sanctuary except by a great and special privilege.

6. I say with the Saints, the divine[2] Mary is the terrestrial paradise of the New Adam, where He was made flesh by the operation of the Holy Ghost, in order to work there incomprehensible marvels. She is the grand and divine world of God, where there are beauties and treasures unspeakable. She is the magnificence of the Most High, where He hid, as in her bosom, His only Son, and in Him all that is most excellent and most precious. Oh, what grand and hidden things that mighty God has wrought in this admirable creature, as she herself had to acknowledge, in spite of her profound humility: "He that is mighty hath done great things to me." (*Lk.* 1:49). The world knows them not, because it is both incapable and unworthy of such knowledge.

7. The saints have said admirable things of this holy city of God; and, as they themselves avow, they were never more eloquent and more content than when they spoke of her. Yet, after all they have said, they cry out that the height of her merits, which she has raised up to the throne of the Divinity, cannot be fully seen; that the breadth of her charity, which is broader than the earth, is in truth immeasurable; that

the length of her power, which she exercises even over God Himself, is incomprehensible; and finally, that the depth of her humility, and of all her virtues and graces, is an abyss which never can be sounded. O height incomprehensible! O breadth unspeakable! O length immeasurable! O abyss impenetrable!

8. Every day, from one end of the earth to the other, in the highest heights of the heavens and in the profoundest depths of the abysses, everything preaches, everything publishes, the admirable Mary! The nine choirs of Angels, men of all ages, sexes, conditions and religions, the good and the bad, nay, even the devils themselves, willingly or unwillingly, are compelled by the force of truth to call her "Blessed." St. Bonaventure tells us that all the Angels in Heaven cry out incessantly to her: "Holy, holy, holy Mary, Mother of God and Virgin";[3] and that they offer to her, millions and millions of times a day, the Angelical Salutation, *Ave Maria*, prostrating themselves before her, and begging of her in her graciousness to honor them with some of her commands. Even St. Michael, as St. Augustine says, although the prince of the heavenly court, is the most zealous in honoring her and causing her to be honored, and is always anxiously awaiting the honor of going at her bidding to render service to some one of her servants.[4]

9. The whole earth is full of her glory, especially among Christians, by whom she is taken as the protectress of many kingdoms, provinces, dioceses and cities. Many cathedrals are consecrated to God under her name. There is not a church without an altar in her honor, not a country nor a canton where there are not some miraculous images where all sorts of evils are cured and all sorts of good gifts obtained. Who can count the confraternities and congregations in her honor? How many religious orders have been founded in her name and under her protection? How many members in these confraternities, and how many religious men and women in all these orders, who publish her praises and confess her mercies! There is not a little child who, as it lisps the Hail Mary, does not praise her. There is scarcely a sinner who, even in his obduracy, has not some spark of confidence in her. Nay, the very

devils in Hell respect her while they fear her.

10. After that, we must cry out with the saints: *"De Maria numquam satis"*—"Of Mary there is never enough." We have not yet praised, exalted, honored, loved and served Mary as we ought. She deserves still more praise, still more respect, still more love, and still more service.

11. After that, we must say with the Holy Ghost: "All the glory of the King's daughter is within." (*Ps.* 44:14). The outward glory which Heaven and earth rival each other in laying at her feet is as nothing in comparison with that which she receives within from the Creator and which is not known by creatures, who in their littleness are unable to penetrate the secret of secrets of the King.

12. After that, we must cry out with the Apostle, "Eye has not seen, nor ear heard, nor man's heart comprehended" (*1 Cor.* 2:9) the beauties, the grandeurs, the excellences of Mary—the miracle of the miracles[5] of grace, of nature and of glory. "If you wish to comprehend the Mother," says a saint,[6] "comprehend the Son; for she is the worthy Mother of God." "Here let every tongue be mute."

13. It is with a particular joy that my heart has dictated what I have just written, in order to show that the divine Mary has been up to this time unknown,[7] and that this is one of the reasons that Jesus Christ is not known as He ought to be. If then, as is certain, the knowledge and the kingdom of Jesus Christ are to come into the world, they will be but a necessary consequence of the knowledge and the kingdom of the most holy Virgin Mary, who brought Him into the world for the first time, and will make His second advent full of splendor.

NOTES

1. Antiphon to the Blessed Virgin for Advent; also the hymn, *Ave Maris Stella.*
2. ". . . the word 'divine' may be used without attributing the nature of divinity to the person or thing thus qualified. We speak of our own prayers, whether addressed to God or to His saints, as a 'divine service.' The Psalmist speaks of us all as being gods and sons of the Most High; and yet no one takes offense, because the sense given to the words uttered is understood. Mary may be called 'divine' because divinely chosen for the divine office

of Mother" of a divine Person, Jesus Christ. (Cardinal Vaughan, Preface to the English edition of *True Devotion*).

3. St. Bonaventure, *Psalt. majus B. V., Hymn. instar Ambrosiani.*
4. Quoted by St. Bonaventure, *Speculum B. V.*, lect. III, no. 5.
5. St. John Damascene, *Oratio Ia de Nativ. B. V.*
6. St. Eucherius.
7. Meaning insufficiently known, as the immediate context shows: "Jesus Christ is not known as He ought to be."

CHAPTER ONE

Necessity of the Blessed Virgin And of Devotion to Her

———— • ————

14. I avow, with all the Church, that Mary, being a mere creature that has come from the hands of the Most High, is in comparison with His Infinite Majesty less than an atom; or rather, she is nothing at all, because only He is "He who is" (*Exod.* 3:14); consequently that grand Lord, always independent and sufficient to Himself, never had, and has not now, any absolute need of the holy Virgin for the accomplishment of His will and for the manifestation of His glory. He has but to will in order to do everything.

15. Nevertheless, I say that, things being as they are now—that is, God having willed to commence and to complete His greatest works by the most holy Virgin ever since He created her—we may well think He will not change His conduct in the eternal ages; for He is God, and He changes not, either in His sentiments or in His conduct.

—ARTICLE ONE—

Mary Was Necessary to God
in the Incarnation of the Word

16. It was only through Mary that God the Father gave His Only-begotten to the world. Whatever sighs the patriarchs may have sent forth, whatever prayers the prophets and the saints of the Old Law may have offered up to obtain this treasure for full four thousand years, it was only Mary who merited it and found grace before God (*Lk.* 1:30) by the force of her prayers and the eminence of her virtues. The world was unworthy, says St. Augustine, to receive the Son of God directly from the Father's hands. He gave Him to Mary in order that the world might receive Him through her.

The Son of God became man for our salvation; but it was in Mary and by Mary. God the Holy Ghost formed Jesus Christ in Mary; but it was only after having asked her consent by one of the first ministers of His court.

17. God the Father communicated to Mary His fruitfulness, inasmuch as a mere creature was capable of it, in order that He might give her the power to produce His Son and all the members of His Mystical Body.

18. God the Son descended into her virginal womb as the New Adam into His terrestrial paradise, to take His pleasure there, and to work in secret marvels of grace.

God made Man found His liberty in seeing Himself imprisoned in her womb. He made His omnipotence shine forth in letting Himself be carried by that humble maiden. He found His glory and His Father's in hiding His splendors from all creatures here below, and revealing them to Mary only. He glorified His independence and His majesty in depending on that sweet Virgin in His conception, in His birth, in His presentation in the temple, in His hidden life of thirty years, and even in His death, where she was to be present in order that He might make with her but one same sacrifice and be immolated to the Eternal Father by her consent, just as Isaac of old was offered by Abraham's consent to the will of God. It is she who nourished Him, supported Him, brought Him up and then sacrificed Him for us.

Oh, admirable and incomprehensible dependence of God, which the Holy Ghost could not pass over in silence in the Gospel, although He has hidden from us nearly all the admirable things which the Incarnate Wisdom did in His hidden life—as if He would enable us, by His revelation of that at least, to understand something of its excellence and infinite glory! Jesus Christ gave more glory to God the Father by submission to His Mother during those thirty years than He would have given Him in converting the whole world by the working of the most stupendous miracles. Oh, how highly we glorify God when, to please Him, we submit ourselves to Mary, after the example of Jesus Christ, our sole Exemplar!

19. If we examine closely the rest of our Blessed Lord's life, we shall see that it was His will to begin His miracles by Mary. He sanctified St. John in the womb of his mother, St. Elizabeth, but it was by Mary's word. No sooner had she spoken than John was sanctified; and this was His first miracle of grace.

At the marriage of Cana He changed the water into wine, but it was at Mary's humble prayer; and this was His first miracle of nature. He began and continued His miracles by Mary, and He will continue them to the end of ages by Mary.

20. God the Holy Ghost, being barren in God—that is to say, not producing another Divine Person—is become fruitful by Mary, whom He has espoused. It was with her, in her, and of her that He produced His Masterpiece, which is God made Man, and that He goes on producing daily, to the end of the world, the predestinate and the members of the Body of that adorable Head. This is the reason why He, the Holy Ghost, the more He finds Mary, His dear and inseparable spouse,[1] in any soul, the more active and mighty He becomes in producing Jesus Christ in that soul, and that soul in Jesus Christ.

21. It is not that we mean that our Blessed Lady gives the Holy

Ghost His fruitfulness, as if He had it not Himself. For inasmuch as He is God, He has the same fruitfulness or capacity of producing as the Father and the Son; only He does not bring it into action, as He does not produce another Divine Person. But what we mean is that the Holy Ghost chose to make use of our Blessed Lady, though He had no absolute need of her, to bring His fruitfulness into action, by producing in her and by her Jesus Christ and His members—a mystery of grace unknown to even the wisest and most spiritual among Christians.

—ARTICLE TWO—
Mary Is Necessary to God
in the Sanctification of Souls

22. The conduct which the Three Persons of the Most Holy Trinity have deigned to pursue in the Incarnation and the first coming of Jesus Christ, They still pursue daily, in an invisible manner, throughout the whole Church; and They will still pursue it even to the consummation of ages in the last coming of Jesus Christ.

23. God the Father made an assemblage of all the waters and He named it the sea (*mare*). He made an assemblage of all His graces and he called it Mary (*Maria*).[2] This great God has a most rich treasury in which He has laid up all that He has of beauty and splendor, of rarity and preciousness, including even His own Son: and this immense treasury is none other than Mary, whom the saints have named the Treasure of the Lord,[3] out of whose plenitude all men are made rich.

24. God the Son has communicated to His Mother all that He acquired by His life and His death, His infinite merits and His admirable virtues; and He has made her the treasurer of all that His Father gave Him for His inheritance. It is by her that He applies His merits to His members, and that He communicates His virtues, and distributes His graces. She is His mysterious canal; she is His aqueduct, through which He makes His mercies flow gently and abundantly.

25. To Mary, His faithful spouse, God the Holy Ghost has

communicated His unspeakable gifts; and He has chosen her to be the dispenser of all He possesses, in such wise that she distributes to whom she wills, as much as she wills, as she wills and when she wills, all His gifts and graces. The Holy Ghost gives no heavenly gift to men which He does not have pass through her virginal hands. Such has been the will of God, who has willed that we should have everything through Mary; so that she who, impoverished, humbled, and who hid herself even unto the abyss of nothingness by her profound humility her whole life long, should now be enriched and exalted and honored by the Most High. Such are the sentiments of the Church and the holy Fathers.[4]

26. If I were speaking to the freethinkers of these times, I would prove what I have said so simply here, drawing it out more at length, and confirming it by the Holy Scriptures and the Fathers, quoting the original passages, and adducing various solid reasons, which may be seen at length in the book of Father Poiré, *La Triple Couronne de la Ste. Vierge*. But as I speak particularly to the poor and simple, who being of good will, and having more faith than the common run of scholars, believe more simply and more meritoriously, I content myself with stating the truth quite plainly, without stopping to quote the Latin passages, which they would not understand. Nevertheless, without making much research, I shall not fail to bring forward some of them from time to time. But now let us go on with our subject.

27. Inasmuch as grace perfects nature, and glory perfects grace, it is certain that Our Lord is still, in Heaven, as much the Son of Mary as He was on earth; and that, consequently, He has retained the obedience and submission of the most perfect Child toward the best of all mothers. But we must take great pains not to conceive this dependence as any abasement or imperfection in Jesus Christ. For Mary is infinitely below her Son, who is God, and therefore she does not command Him as a mother here below would command her child who is below her. Mary, being altogether transformed into God by grace and by the glory which transforms all the saints into Him, asks nothing, wishes nothing, does nothing contrary to the eternal and immutable will of God. When

we read then in the writings of Sts. Bernard, Bernardine, Bonaventure and others that in Heaven and on earth everything, even God Himself, is subject to the Blessed Virgin,[5] they mean that the authority which God has been well pleased to give her is so great that it seems as if she had the same power as God; and that her prayers and petitions are so powerful with God that they always pass for commandments with His Majesty, who never resists the prayer of His dear Mother, because she is always humble and conformed to His will.

If Moses, by the force of his prayer, stayed the anger of God against the Israelites in a manner so powerful that the most high and infinitely merciful Lord, being unable to resist him, told him to let Him alone that He might be angry with and punish that rebellious people, what must we not, with much greater reason, think of the prayer of the humble Mary, that worthy Mother of God, which is more powerful with His Majesty than the prayers and intercessions of all the Angels and Saints both in Heaven and on earth?[6]

28. In the Heavens Mary commands the Angels and the blessed. As a recompense for her profound humility, God has empowered her and commissioned her to fill with saints the empty thrones from which the apostate angels fell by pride.[7] The will of the Most High, who exalts the humble (*Lk.* 1:52), is that Heaven, earth and Hell bend, with good will or bad will, to the commandments of the humble Mary,[8] whom He has made sovereign of Heaven and earth, general of His armies, treasurer of His treasures, dispenser of His graces, worker of His greatest marvels, restorer of the human race, Mediatrix of men, the exterminator of the enemies of God, and the faithful companion of His grandeurs and triumphs.

29. God the Father wishes to have children by Mary till the consummation of the world; and He speaks to her these words: "Dwell in Jacob" (*Ecclus.* 24:13); that is to say: Make your dwelling and residence in My predestined children, prefigured by Jacob, and not in the reprobate children of the devil, prefigured by Esau.

30. Just as in the natural and corporal generation of children there

are a father and a mother, so in the supernatural and spiritual generation there are a Father, who is God, and a Mother, who is Mary. All
the true children of God, the predestinate, have God for their Father
and Mary for their Mother. He who has not Mary for his Mother has
not God for his Father. This is the reason why the reprobate, such as
heretics, schismatics and others, who hate our Blessed Lady or regard
her with contempt and indifference, have not God for their Father,
however much they boast of it, simply because they have not Mary for
their Mother. For if they had her for their Mother, they would love and
honor her as a true child naturally loves and honors the mother who
has given him life.

The most infallible and indubitable sign by which we may distinguish a heretic, a man of bad doctrine, a reprobate, from one of the
predestinate, is that the heretic and the reprobate have nothing but
contempt and indifference for Our Lady, endeavoring by their words
and examples to diminish the worship and love of her, openly or hiddenly, and sometimes by misrepresentation. Alas! God the Father has
not told Mary to dwell in them, for they are Esaus.

31. God the Son wishes to form Himself, and, so to speak, to incarnate Himself in His members every day, by His dear Mother, and He
says to her: "Take Israel for your inheritance." (*Ecclus.* 24:13). It is
as if He had said: God the Father has given Me for an inheritance
all the nations of the earth, all men, good and bad, predestinate and
reprobate. The ones I will lead with a rod of gold, and the others with
a rod of iron. Of the ones, I will be the Father and the Advocate; of
the others, the Just Punisher; and of all, the Judge. But as for you, My
dear Mother, you shall have for your heritage and possession only the
predestinate, prefigured by Israel; and as their Mother, you shall bring
them forth and take care of them; and as their sovereign, you shall conduct them, govern them and defend them.

32. "This man and that man is born in her" (*Ps.* 86:5), says the
Holy Ghost through the Royal Psalmist. According to the explanation of some of the Fathers,[9] the first man that is born in Mary is the

Man-God, Jesus Christ; the second is a mere man, the child of God and Mary by adoption. If Jesus Christ, the Head of men, is born in her, then the predestinate, who are the members of that Head, ought also to be born in her, by a necessary consequence. One and the same mother does not bring forth into the world the head without the members, or the members without the head; for this would be a monster of nature. So in like manner, in the order of grace, the head and the members are born of one and the same Mother; and if a member of the Mystical Body of Jesus Christ—that is to say, one of the predestinate—were born of any other mother than Mary, who has produced the Head, he would not be one of the predestinate, nor a member of Jesus Christ, but simply a monster in the order of grace.

33. Besides this, Jesus being at present as much as ever the fruit of Mary—as Heaven and earth repeat thousands and thousands of times a day, "and blessed is the fruit of thy womb, Jesus"—it is certain that Jesus Christ is, for each man in particular who possesses Him, as truly the fruit and the work of Mary as He is for the whole world in general; so that if any one of the faithful has Jesus Christ formed in his heart, he can say boldly, "All thanks be to Mary! What I possess is her effect and her fruit, and without her I should never have had it." We can apply to her more than St. Paul applied to himself the words: "I am in labor again with all the children of God, until Jesus Christ my Son be formed in them in the fullness of His age." (Cf. *Gal.* 4:19).

St. Augustine, surpassing himself, and going beyond all I have yet said, affirms that all the predestinate, in order to be conformed to the image of the Son of God, are in this world hidden in the womb of the most holy Virgin, where they are guarded, nourished, brought up and made to grow by that good Mother until she has brought them forth to glory after death, which is properly the day of their birth, as the Church calls the death of the just. O mystery of grace, unknown to the reprobate, and but little known even to the predestinate!

34. God the Holy Ghost wishes to form elect for Himself in her and by her, and He says to her: "Strike the roots," My Well-beloved

and My Spouse, "of all your virtues in My elect" (*Ecclus.* 24:13), in order that they may grow from virtue to virtue and from grace to grace. I took so much complacence in you when you lived on earth in the practice of the most sublime virtues, that I desire still to find you on earth, without your ceasing to be in Heaven. For this end, reproduce yourself in My elect, that I may behold in them with complacence the roots of your invincible faith, of your profound humility, of your universal mortification, of your sublime prayer, of your ardent charity, of your firm hope and of all your virtues. You are always My spouse, as faithful, as pure and as fruitful as ever. Let your faith give Me My faithful, your purity, My virgins, and your fertility, My temples and My elect.

35. When Mary has struck her roots in a soul, she produces there marvels of grace, which she alone can produce, because she alone is the fruitful Virgin who never has had, and never will have, her equal in purity and in fruitfulness.

Mary has produced, together with the Holy Ghost, the greatest thing which has been or ever will be—a God-Man; and she will consequently produce the greatest saints that there will be in the end of time. The formation and the education of the great saints who shall come at the end of the world are reserved for her. For it is only that singular and miraculous Virgin who can produce, in union with the Holy Ghost, singular and extraordinary things.

36. When the Holy Ghost, her Spouse, has found Mary in a soul, He flies there. He enters there in His fullness; He communicates Himself to that soul abundantly, and to the full extent to which it makes room for His spouse. Nay, one of the greatest reasons why the Holy Ghost does not now do startling wonders in our souls is because He does not find there a sufficiently great union with His faithful and inseparable spouse. I say "inseparable" spouse, because since that Substantial Love of the Father and the Son has espoused Mary, in order to produce Jesus Christ, the Head of the elect, and Jesus Christ in the elect, He has never repudiated her, because she has always been fruitful and faithful.

Consequences

I. Mary Is Queen of All Hearts

37. We may evidently conclude, then, from what I have said, first of all, that Mary has received from God a great domination over the souls of the elect; for she cannot make her residence in them as God the Father ordered her to do, and, as their mother, form, nourish and bring them forth to eternal life, and have them as her inheritance and portion, and form them in Jesus Christ and Jesus Christ in them, and strike the roots of her virtues in their hearts and be the inseparable companion of the Holy Ghost in all His works of grace—she cannot, I say, do all these things unless she has a right and a domination over their souls by a singular grace of the Most High, who, having given her power over His only and natural Son, has given it also to her over His adopted children, not only as to their bodies, which would be but a small matter, but also as to their souls.

38. Mary is the Queen of Heaven and earth by grace, as Jesus is the King of them by nature and by conquest. Now, as the kingdom of Jesus Christ consists principally in the heart or the interior of man—according to the words, "The kingdom of God is within you" (*Lk.* 17:21)—in like manner the kingdom of our Blessed Lady is principally in the interior of man; that is to say, his soul. And it is principally in souls that she is more glorified with her Son than in all visible creatures, and so we can call her, as the saints do, the Queen of All Hearts.

II. Mary Is Necessary to Men

39. In the second place we must conclude that, the most holy Virgin being necessary to God by a necessity which we call "hypothetical," in consequence of His will, she is far more necessary to men, in order that they may attain their last end. We must not confuse devotion to the Blessed Virgin with devotions to the other saints, as if devotion to her

were not far more necessary than devotion to them, and as if devotion to her were a matter of supererogation.

1. Necessary to all men to attain salvation.

40. The learned and pious Jesuit, Suarez, the erudite and devout Justus Lipsius, doctor of Louvain, and many others have proved invincibly, from the sentiments of the Fathers (among others, St. Augustine, St. Ephrem, deacon of Edessa, St. Cyril of Jerusalem, St. Germanus of Constantinople, St. John Damascene, St. Anselm, St. Bernard, St. Bernardine, St. Thomas and St. Bonaventure), that devotion to our Blessed Lady is necessary to salvation, and that (even in the opinion of Oecolampadius and some other heretics) it is an infallible mark of reprobation to have no esteem and love for the holy Virgin; while on the other hand, it is an infallible mark of predestination to be entirely and truly devoted to her.[10]

41. The figures and words of the Old and New Testaments prove this. The sentiments and the examples of the saints confirm it. Reason and experience teach and demonstrate it. Even the devil and his crew, constrained by the force of truth, have often been obliged to avow it in spite of themselves. Among all the passages of the holy Fathers and Doctors, of which I have made an ample collection in order to prove this truth, I shall for brevity's sake quote but one: "To be devout to you, O holy Virgin," says St. John Damascene, "is an arm of salvation which God gives to those whom He wishes to save."

42. I could bring forward here many anecdotes which prove the same thing, and among others one which is related in the chronicles of St. Francis. This same saint saw in ecstasy a great ladder ascending into Heaven, at the top of which stood the Blessed Virgin and by which it was shown him he must ascend to reach Heaven. There is another related in the chronicles of St. Dominic. There was an unfortunate heretic near Carcassonne, where St. Dominic was preaching the Rosary, who was possessed by a legion of fifteen thousand devils. These

evil spirits were compelled, to their confusion, by the command of our Blessed Lady, to avow many great and consoling truths touching devotion to the Blessed Virgin; and they did this with so much force and so much clearness that it is impossible to read this authentic account and the eulogy which the devil made, in spite of himself, of devotion to the most holy Virgin Mary, without shedding tears of joy, however lukewarm we may be in our devotion to her.

2. Still more necessary to those called to a special perfection.

43. If devotion to the most holy Virgin Mary is necessary to all men simply for working out their salvation, it is still more so for those who are called to any special perfection; and I do not think anyone can acquire an intimate union with Our Lord and a perfect fidelity to the Holy Ghost without a very great union with the most holy Virgin, and a great dependence on her assistance.

44. It is Mary alone who has found grace before God (*Lk.* 1:30) without the aid of any other mere creature; it is only through her that all those who have since found grace before God have found it at all; and it is only through her that all those who shall come afterward shall find it. She was full of grace when she was greeted by the Archangel Gabriel (*Lk.* 1:28), and she was superabundantly filled with grace by the Holy Ghost when He covered her with His unspeakable shadow (*Lk.* 1:35); and she has so augmented this double plenitude from day to day and from moment to moment that she has reached a point of grace immense and inconceivable—in such wise that the Most High has made her the sole treasurer of His treasures and the sole dispenser of His graces to ennoble, to exalt and to enrich whom she wishes; to give entry to whom she wills into the narrow way of Heaven; to bring whom she wills, and in spite of all obstacles, through the narrow gate of life; and to give the throne, the scepter and the crown of king to whom she wills. Jesus is everywhere and always the Fruit and the Son of Mary;

and Mary is everywhere the veritable tree who bears the Fruit of life, and the true Mother who produces it.[11]

45. It is Mary alone to whom God has given the keys of the cellars (*Cant.* 1:3) of divine love and the power to enter into the most sublime and secret ways of perfection, and the power likewise to make others enter in there also. It is Mary alone who has given to the miserable children of Eve, the faithless, entry into the terrestrial paradise; that they may walk there agreeably with God, hide there securely against their enemies, feed themselves there deliciously, without further fear of death, on the fruit of the trees of life and of the knowledge of good and evil, and drink in long draughts the heavenly waters of that fair fountain which gushes forth there with abundance; or rather, since she is herself that terrestrial paradise, that virgin and blessed earth from which Adam and Eve, the sinners, have been driven, she gives no entry there except to those whom it is her pleasure to make saints.

46. All the rich among the people, to make use of an expression of the Holy Ghost (*Ps.* 44:13) according to the explanation of St. Bernard—all the rich among the people shall supplicate her face from age to age, and particularly at the end of the world; that is to say, the greatest saints, the souls richest in graces and virtues, shall be the most assiduous in praying to our Blessed Lady, and in having her always present as their perfect model for imitation and their powerful aid for help.

3. Especially necessary to the great saints of the latter times.

47. I have said that this would come to pass, particularly at the end of the world and indeed presently,[12] because the Most High with His holy Mother has to form for Himself great saints who shall surpass most of the other saints in sanctity as much as the cedars of Lebanon outgrow the little shrubs, as has been revealed to a holy soul whose life has been written by M. de Renty.

48. These great souls, full of grace and zeal, shall be chosen to match themselves against the enemies of God, who shall rage on all sides; and they shall be singularly devout to our Blessed Lady, illuminated by her light, strengthened with her nourishment, led by her spirit, supported by her arm and sheltered under her protection, so that they shall fight with one hand and build with the other. With the one hand they shall fight, overthrow and crush the heretics with their heresies, the schismatics with their schisms, the idolaters with their idolatries and the sinners with their impieties. With the other hand they shall build (*Esd.* 4:7) the temple of the true Solomon[13] and the mystical city of God,[14] that is to say, the most holy Virgin, called by the Fathers the "Temple of Solomon" and the "City of God." By their words and their examples they shall draw the whole world to true devotion to Mary. This shall bring upon them many enemies, but shall also bring many victories and much glory for God alone. This is what God revealed to St. Vincent Ferrer, the great apostle of his age, as he has sufficiently noted in one of his works.

This is what the Holy Ghost seems to have prophesied in the Fifty-eighth Psalm: "And they shall know that God will rule Jacob and all the ends of the earth; they shall return at evening and shall suffer hunger like dogs and shall go round about the city." (*Ps.* 58:14-15). This city which men shall find at the end of the world to convert themselves in, and to satisfy the hunger they have for justice, is the most holy Virgin, who is called by the Holy Ghost the "City of God." (*Ps.* 86:3).

—ARTICLE THREE—

Providential Function of Mary in the Latter Times

49. It was through Mary that the salvation of the world was begun, and it is through Mary that it must be consummated. Mary hardly appeared at all in the first coming of Jesus Christ, in order that men, as yet but little instructed and enlightened on the Person of her Son, should not remove themselves from Him in attaching themselves too strongly and too grossly to her. This would have apparently taken place if she had been known, because of the admirable charms which the Most High had bestowed even upon her exterior. This is so true that St. Denis the Areopagite tells us in his writings that when he saw our Blessed Lady he would have taken her for a divinity, because of her secret charms and incomparable beauty, had not the Faith in which he was well established taught him the contrary.[15] But in the second coming of Jesus Christ, Mary has to be made known and revealed by the Holy Ghost in order that, through her, Jesus Christ may be known, loved and served. The reasons which moved the Holy Ghost to hide His spouse during her life, and to reveal her but very little since the preaching of the Gospel, subsist no longer.

I. Existence of This Function and Reasons for It

50. God, then, wishes to reveal and make known Mary, the masterpiece of His hands, in these latter times:

§ 1. Because she hid herself in this world and put herself lower than the dust by her profound humility, having obtained from God and from His Apostles and Evangelists that she should not be made manifest.

§ 2. Because, as she is the masterpiece of the hands of God, as well here below by grace as in Heaven by glory, He wishes to be glorified and praised in her by those who are living upon the earth.

§ 3. As she is the dawn which precedes and reveals the Sun of Justice, who is Jesus Christ, she must be seen and recognized in order that Jesus Christ may also be.

§ 4. Being the way by which Jesus came to us the first time, she will also be the way by which He will come the second time, though not in the same manner.

§ 5. Being the sure means and the straight and immaculate way to go to Jesus Christ and to find Him perfectly, it is by her that the souls who are to shine forth especially in sanctity have to find Our Lord. He who shall find Mary shall find life (*Prov.* 8:35), that is, Jesus Christ, who is the Way, the Truth and the Life. (*Jn.* 14:6). But no one can find Mary who does not seek her; and no one can seek her who does not know her; for we cannot seek or desire an unknown object. It is necessary, then, for the greater knowledge and glory of the Most Holy Trinity, that Mary should be more than ever known.

§ 6. Mary must shine forth more than ever in mercy, in might and in grace, in these latter times: in mercy, to bring back and lovingly receive the poor strayed sinners who shall be converted and shall return to the Catholic Church; in might, against the enemies of God, idolaters, schismatics, Mahometans, Jews and souls hardened in impiety, who shall rise in terrible revolt against God to seduce all those who shall oppose them and to make them fall by promises and threats; and finally, she must shine forth in grace, in order to animate and sustain the valiant soldiers and faithful servants of Jesus Christ, who shall battle for His interests.

§ 7. And lastly, Mary must be terrible to the devil and his crew, as an army ranged in battle, principally in these latter times,[16] because the devil, knowing that he has but little time, and now less than ever, to destroy souls, will every day redouble his efforts and his combats. He will presently raise up cruel persecutions and will put terrible snares before the faithful servants and true children of Mary, whom it gives him more trouble to conquer than it does to conquer others.

II. Exercise of This Function

1. In the struggle against Satan.

51. It is principally of these last and cruel persecutions of the devil, which shall go on increasing daily till the reign of Antichrist, that we ought to understand that first and celebrated prediction and curse of God pronounced in the terrestrial paradise against the serpent. It is to our purpose to explain this here for the glory of the most holy Virgin, for the salvation of her children and for the confusion of the devil: "I will put enmities between thee and the woman and thy seed and her seed; she shall crush thy head, and thou shalt lie in wait for her heel." (*Gen.* 3:15).

52. God has never made and formed but one enmity; but it is an irreconcilable one, which shall endure and grow even to the end. It is between Mary, His worthy Mother, and the devil—between the children and the servants of the Blessed Virgin, and the children and tools of Lucifer. The most terrible of all the enemies which God has set up against the devil is His holy Mother Mary. He has inspired her, even since the days of the earthly paradise—though she existed then only in His idea—with so much hatred against that cursed enemy of God, with so much ingenuity in unveiling the malice of that ancient serpent, with so much power to conquer, to overthrow and to crush that proud, impious rebel, that he fears her not only more than all angels and men, but in a sense more than God Himself. Not that the anger, the hatred and the power of God are not infinitely greater than those of the Blessed Virgin, for the perfections of Mary are limited; but first, because Satan, being proud, suffers infinitely more from being beaten and punished by a little and humble handmaid of God, and her humility humbles him more than the divine power; and secondly, because God has given Mary such great power against the devils that— as they have often been obliged to confess, in spite of themselves, by the mouths of the possessed—they fear one of her sighs for a soul more

than the prayers of all the saints, and one of her threats against them more than all other torments.

53. What Lucifer has lost by pride, Mary has gained by humility. What Eve has damned and lost by disobedience, Mary has saved by obedience. Eve, in obeying the serpent, has destroyed all her children together with herself, and has delivered them to him; Mary, in being perfectly faithful to God, has saved all her children and servants together with herself, and has consecrated them to His Majesty.

54. God has not only set an enmity, but enmities, not simply between Mary and the devil, but between the race of the holy Virgin and the race of the devil; that is to say, God has set enmities, antipathies and secret hatreds between the true children and servants of Mary and the children and slaves of the devil. They have no love for each other. They have no sympathy for each other. The children of Belial, the slaves of Satan, the friends of the world (for it is the same thing) have always up to this time persecuted those who belong to our Blessed Lady, and will in the future persecute them more than ever; just as Cain, of old, persecuted his brother Abel, and Esau his brother Jacob, who are the figures of the reprobate and the predestinate. But the humble Mary will always have the victory over that proud spirit, and so great a victory that she will go so far as to crush his head, where his pride dwells. She will always discover the malice of the serpent. She will always lay bare his infernal plots and dissipate his diabolical councils, and even to the end of time will guard her faithful servants from his cruel claw.

But the power of Mary over all the devils will especially shine forth in the latter times, when Satan will lay his snares against her heel: that is to say, her humble slaves and her poor children, whom she will raise up to make war against him. They shall be little and poor in the world's esteem, and abased before all like the heel, trodden underfoot and persecuted as the heel is by the other members of the body. But in return for this they shall be rich in the grace of God, which Mary shall distribute to them abundantly. They shall be great and exalted before God in sanctity, superior to all other creatures by their lively zeal, and so well sustained with God's assistance that, with the humility of their heel, in union with Mary, they shall crush the head of the devil and cause Jesus Christ to triumph.

2. In the formation of the apostles
of the latter times.

55. In a word, God wishes that His holy Mother should be at present more known, more loved, more honored than she has ever been. This, no doubt, will take place if the predestinate enter, with the grace and light of the Holy Ghost, into the interior and perfect practice which I will disclose to them shortly. Then they will see clearly, as far as faith allows, that beautiful Star of the Sea. They will arrive happily in harbor, following its guidance, in spite of the tempests and the pirates. They will know the grandeurs of that Queen, and will consecrate themselves entirely to her service as subjects and slaves of love. They will experience her sweetness and her maternal goodness, and they will love her tenderly like well-beloved children. They will know the mercies of which she is full, and the need they have of her help; and they will have recourse to her in all things, as to their dear advocate and Mediatrix with Jesus Christ. They will know what is the surest, the easiest, the shortest and the most perfect means of going to Jesus Christ; and they will give themselves to Mary, body and soul, without reserve, that they may thus belong entirely to Jesus Christ.

56. But who shall those servants, slaves and children of Mary be?

They shall be the ministers of the Lord who, like a burning fire, shall kindle the fire of divine love everywhere.

They shall be "like sharp arrows in the hand of the powerful" Mary to pierce her enemies. (*Ps.* 126:4).

They shall be the sons of Levi, well purified by the fire of great tribulation, and closely adhering to God (*1 Cor.* 6:17), who shall carry the gold of love in their heart, the incense of prayer in their spirit, and the myrrh of mortification in their body. They shall be everywhere the good odor of Jesus Christ to the poor and to the little, while at the same time, they shall be an odor of death to the great, to the rich and to the proud worldlings.

57. They shall be clouds thundering and flying through the air at the least breath of the Holy Ghost; who, detaching themselves from everything and troubling themselves about nothing, shall shower forth the rain of the Word of God and of life eternal. They shall thunder against sin; they shall storm against the world; they shall strike the devil and his crew; and they shall pierce through and through, for life or for death, with their two-edged sword of the Word of God (*Eph.* 6:17), all those to whom they shall be sent on the part of the Most High.

58. They shall be the true apostles of the latter times, to whom the Lord of Hosts shall give the word and the might to work marvels and to carry off with glory the spoils of His enemies. They shall sleep without gold or silver, and, what is more, without care, in the midst of the other priests, ecclesiastics, and clerics (*Ps.* 67:14); and yet they shall have the silvered wings of the dove to go, with the pure intention of the glory of God and the salvation of souls, wheresoever the Holy Ghost shall call them. Nor shall they leave behind them, in the places where they have preached, anything but the gold of charity, which is the fulfillment of the whole law. (*Rom.* 13:10).

59. In a word, we know that they shall be true disciples of Jesus Christ, walking in the footsteps of His poverty, humility, contempt of the world, charity; teaching the narrow way of God in pure truth, according to the holy Gospel, and not according to the maxims of the world; troubling themselves about nothing; not accepting persons; sparing, fearing and listening to no mortal, however influential he may be. They shall have in their mouths the two-edged sword of the Word of God. They shall carry on their shoulders the bloody standard of the Cross, the Crucifix in their right hand and the Rosary in their left, the sacred Names of Jesus and Mary in their hearts, and the modesty and mortification of Jesus Christ in their own behaviour.[17]

These are the great men who are to come; but Mary is the one who, by order of the Most High, shall fashion them for the purpose of extending His empire over that of the impious, the idolaters and the Mahometans. But when and how shall this be? God alone knows.[18]

As for us, we have but to hold our tongues, to pray, to sigh and to wait: "With expectation I have waited." (*Ps.* 39:2).

NOTES

1. *"Sponsa Spiritus Sancti"* (St. Ildephonsus, *Liber de Corona Virginis,* caput III); *"Sponsus ejus Spiritus veritatis"* (Bellarmin., *Concio 2 super Missus est*).
2. St. Antoninus, *Summa,* p. IV, Tit. 15, cap. 4, no. 5.
3. *Idiota (In contemplatione B.M. V.).*
4. Cf., among others, St. Bernard and St. Bernardine of Siena, whom St. Louis De Montfort quotes further on. (No. 141 and 142).
5. For their exact words cf. no. 76.
6. St. Augustine, *Sermo 208, in Assumptione,* no. 12 *(inter opera Sti. Aug.).*
7. St. Bonaventure, *Speculum B. V.,* lect. XI, no. 6.
8. St. Bonaventure, *Psalt. majus B. V., Cant. instar, can. Trium puerorum.*
9. For instance, Origen and St. Bonaventure; cf. no. 141.
10. In his classic work entitled *The Glories of Mary,* the great Doctor of the Church, St. Alphonsus Liguori (1696-1787) states that "the intercession of Mary is even necessary to salvation; we say necessary—not absolutely, but morally. This necessity proceeds from the will itself of God, that all graces that He dispenses should pass by the hands of Mary, according to the opinion of St. Bernard, and which we may now with safety call the general opinion of theologians and learned men." (p. 129, TAN edition). St. Alphonsus quotes St. Bernardine of Siena's words to the Blessed Virgin Mary: "O Lady, since thou art the dispenser of all graces, and since the grace of salvation can only come through thy hands, our salvation depends on thee." (p. 144).
11. Cf. no. 33.
12. St. Louis De Montfort may have believed, as many people of his time did, that the end of the world was at hand; perhaps, however, all he meant was that this would take place particularly at the end of the world, but would begin soon or presently. As a matter of fact, the century following the one in which he lived was one of increased Marian study and devotion.
13. *Idiota, De B. V.,* pars XVI, contempl. 7. (*S.A.,* X, 367). (The abbreviation *S.A.* refers to the *Summa Aurea*).
14. St. Augustine, *Enarratio in Ps.* 142, no. 3 (*S.A.,* IX, 1012).
15. *S.A.,* 842 (*Epistola ad Paulum*). Unauthentic.
16. It is worthy of note that today the increased efforts of the forces of evil are being countered by a corresponding increase of devotion to the Blessed Virgin, as evidenced by the remarkable growth of the Legion of Mary and the renewed interest in the Sodality of the Blessed Virgin.

17. Cf. prayer of St. Louis De Montfort asking God for missionaries for his Company of Mary (Montfort Fathers).
18. These words show that St. Louis De Montfort himself did not know all the circumstances of his own prophecy concerning the latter times.

CHAPTER TWO

Fundamental Truths of Devotion to the Blessed Virgin

———•———

60. Having spoken thus far of the necessity of devotion to the most holy Virgin, I must now show in what this devotion consists. This I will do, with God's help, after I shall have first laid down some fundamental truths which shall throw light on that grand and solid devotion which I desire to disclose.

—FIRST TRUTH—
Jesus Christ Is the Last End of Devotion to Mary

61. Jesus Christ our Saviour, true God and true Man, ought to be the last end of all our other devotions, else they are false and delusive. Jesus Christ is the Alpha and the Omega,[1] the beginning and the end, of all things. We labor not, as the Apostle says, except to render every man perfect in Jesus Christ; because it is in Him alone that the whole plenitude of the Divinity dwells together with all the other plenitudes of graces, virtues and perfections. It is in Him alone that we have been blessed with all spiritual benediction; and He is our only Master, who has to teach us; our only Lord on whom we ought to depend; our only Head to whom we must be united; our only Model to whom we

should conform ourselves; our only Physician who can heal us; our only Shepherd who can feed us; our only Way who can lead us; our only Truth whom we must believe; our only Life who can animate us; and our only All in all things who can satisfy us. There has been no other name given under Heaven, except the name of Jesus, by which we can be saved. God has laid no other foundation of our salvation, our perfection or our glory, than Jesus Christ. Every building which is not built on that firm rock is founded upon the moving sand, and sooner or later infallibly will fall. Every one of the faithful who is not united to Him, as a branch to the stock of the vine, shall fall, shall wither, and shall be fit only to be cast into the fire. Outside of Him there exists nothing but error, falsehood, iniquity, futility, death and damnation. But if we are in Jesus Christ and Jesus Christ is in us, we have no condemnation to fear. Neither the Angels of Heaven nor the men of earth nor the devils of Hell nor any other creature can injure us; because they cannot separate us from the love of God, which is in Jesus Christ. By Jesus Christ, with Jesus Christ, in Jesus Christ, we can do all things; we can render all honor and glory to the Father in the unity of the Holy Ghost;[2] we can become perfect ourselves, and be to our neighbor a good odor of eternal life. (*2 Cor.* 2:15-16).

62. If, then, we establish solid devotion to our Blessed Lady, it is only to establish more perfectly devotion to Jesus Christ, and to provide an easy and secure means for finding Jesus Christ. If devotion to Our Lady removed us from Jesus Christ, we should have to reject it as an illusion of the devil; but so far from this being the case, devotion to Our Lady is, on the contrary, necessary for us—as I have already shown, and will show still further hereafter—as a means of finding Jesus Christ perfectly, of loving Him tenderly, of serving Him faithfully.

63. I here turn for one moment to Thee, O sweet Jesus, to complain lovingly to Thy Divine Majesty that the greater part of Christians, even the most learned, do not know the necessary union there is between Thee and Thy holy Mother. Thou, Lord, art always with Mary, and Mary is always with Thee, and she cannot be without Thee, else

she would cease to be what she is. She is so transformed into Thee by grace that she lives no more, she is as though she were not. It is Thou only, my Jesus, who livest and reignest in her more perfectly than in all the angels and the blessed. Ah! If we knew the glory and the love which Thou receivest in this admirable creature, we should have very different thoughts both of Thee and her from what we have now. She is so intimately united with Thee that it were easier to separate the light from the sun, the heat from the fire; nay, it were easier to separate from Thee all the angels and the saints than the divine Mary, because she loves Thee more ardently and glorifies Thee more perfectly than all the other creatures put together.

64. After that, my sweet Master, is it not an astonishingly pitiable thing to see the ignorance and the darkness of all men here below in regard to Thy holy Mother? I speak not so much of idolaters and pagans, who, knowing Thee not, care not to know her. I speak not even of heretics and schismatics, who care not to be devout to Thy holy Mother, being separated as they are from Thee and Thy holy Church; but I speak of Catholic Christians, and even of doctors among Catholics,[3] who make profession of teaching truths to others, and yet know not Thee nor Thy holy Mother, except in a speculative, dry, barren and indifferent manner. These gentlemen speak but rarely of Thy holy Mother and of the devotion we ought to have to her, because they fear, so they say, lest we should abuse it, and do some injury to Thee in honoring Thy holy Mother too much. If they hear or see anyone devout to our Blessed Lady, speaking often of his devotion to that good Mother in a tender, strong and persuasive way, and as a secure means without delusion, as a short road without danger, as an immaculate way without imperfection, and as a wonderful secret for finding and loving Thee perfectly, they cry out against him, and give him a thousand false reasons by way of proving to him that he ought not to talk so much of our Blessed Lady; that there are great abuses in that devotion; and that we must direct our energies to destroy these abuses, and to speak of

Thee, rather than to incline the people to devotion to our Blessed Lady, whom they already love sufficiently.

We hear them sometimes speak of devotion to our Blessed Lady, not for the purpose of establishing it and persuading men to embrace it, but to destroy the abuses which are made of it; and all the while these teachers are without piety or tender devotion toward Thyself, simply because they have none for Mary. They regard the Rosary and the Scapular as devotions proper for weak and ignorant minds, without which men can save themselves; and if there falls into their hands any poor client of Our Lady who says his Rosary, or has any other practice of devotion toward her, they soon change his spirit and his heart. Instead of the Rosary, they counsel him the seven Penitential Psalms. Instead of devotion to the holy Virgin, they counsel him devotion to Jesus Christ.

O my sweet Jesus, do these people have Thy spirit? Do they please Thee in acting thus? Does it please Thee when, for fear of displeasing Thee, we neglect doing our utmost to please Thy Mother? Does devotion to Thy holy Mother hinder devotion to Thyself? Does she attribute to herself the honor we pay her? Does she head a faction of her own? Is she a stranger who has no connection with Thee? Does it displease Thee that we should try to please her? Do we separate or alienate ourselves from Thy love by giving ourselves to her and honoring her?

65. Yet, my sweet Master, the greater part of the learned could not discourage devotion to Thy holy Mother more, and could not show more indifference to it, even if all that I have just said were true. Thus have they been punished for their pride! Keep me, Lord, keep me from their sentiments and their practices, and give me some share of the sentiments of gratitude, esteem, respect and love which Thou hast in regard to Thy holy Mother, so that the more I imitate and follow her, the more I may love and glorify Thee.

66. So, as if up to this point I had still said nothing in honor of Thy holy Mother, "give me now the grace to praise Thee worthily," in spite of all her enemies, who are Thine as well; and grant me to say loudly

with the saints, "Let not that man presume to look for the mercy of God who offends His holy Mother."

67. Make me love Thee ardently, so that I may obtain of Thy mercy a true devotion to Thy holy Mother, and inspire the whole earth with it; and for that end, receive the burning prayer which I offer to Thee with St. Augustine[4] and Thy other true friends:

"Thou art Christ, my holy Father, my tender God, my great King, my good Shepherd, my one Master, my best Helper, my most Beautiful and my Beloved, my living Bread, my Priest forever, my Leader to my country, my true Light, my holy Sweetness, my straight Way, my excellent Wisdom, my pure Simplicity, my pacific Harmony, my whole Guard, my good Portion, my everlasting Salvation.

"Christ Jesus, my sweet Lord, why have I ever loved, why in my whole life have I ever desired anything except Thee, Jesus my God? Where was I when I was not in Thy mind with Thee? Now, from this time forth, do ye, all my desires, grow hot, and flow out upon the Lord Jesus; run, ye have been tardy thus far; hasten whither ye are going; seek whom ye are seeking. O Jesus, may he who loves Thee not, be anathema; may he who loves Thee not, be filled with bitterness!

"O sweet Jesus, may every good feeling that is fitted for Thy praise, love Thee, delight in Thee, admire Thee. God of my heart and my Portion, Christ Jesus, may my heart faint away in spirit and mayest Thou be my life within me! May the live coal of Thy love grow hot within my spirit, and break forth into a perfect fire; may it burn incessantly on the altar of my heart; may it glow in my innermost being; may it blaze in hidden recesses of my soul; and in the day of my consummation, may I be found consummated with Thee. Amen."

—Second Truth—
We belong to Jesus and Mary as Their Slaves

68. We must conclude, from what Jesus Christ is with regard to us, that, as the Apostle says (*1 Cor.* 6:19-20), we do not belong to ourselves but are entirely His, as His members and His slaves, whom He has bought at an infinitely dear price, the price of all His Blood. Before Baptism we belonged to the devil, as his slaves; but Baptism has made us true slaves of Jesus Christ, who have no right to live, to work or to die, except to bring forth fruit for that God-Man (*Rom.* 7:4); to glorify Him in our bodies and to let Him reign in our souls, because we are His conquest, His acquired people and His inheritance. It is for the same reason that the Holy Ghost compares us: (1) to trees planted along the waters of grace, in the field of the Church, who ought to bring forth their fruit in their seasons; (2) to the branches of a vine of which Jesus Christ is the stock, and which must yield good grapes; (3) to a flock of which Jesus Christ is the Shepherd, and which is to multiply and give milk; (4) to a good land of which God is the Husbandman, in which the seed multiplies itself and brings forth thirtyfold, sixtyfold and a hundredfold. (*Ps.* 1:3; *Jn.* 15:2; 10:11; *Matt.* 13:8). Jesus Christ cursed the unfruitful fig tree (*Matt.* 21:19), and pronounced sentence against the useless servant who had not made any profit on his talent. (*Matt.* 25:24-30). All this proves to us that Jesus Christ wishes to receive some fruits from our wretched selves, namely our good works, because those works belong to Him alone: "Created in good works, in Christ Jesus" (*Eph.* 2:10)—which words of the Holy Ghost show that Jesus Christ is the sole beginning, and ought to be the sole end, of all our good works, and also that we ought to serve Him, not as servants for wages, but as slaves of love. I will explain what I mean.

69. Here on earth there are two ways of belonging to another and of depending on his authority: namely, simple service and slavery, whence we derive the words "servant" and "slave."

34

By common service among Christians a man engages himself to serve another during a certain time, at a certain rate of wages or of recompense.

By slavery a man is entirely dependent on another during his whole life, and must serve his master without claiming any wages or reward, just as one of his beasts, over which he has the right of life and death.

70. There are three sorts of slavery:[5] a slavery of nature, a slavery of constraint and a slavery of will. All creatures are slaves of God in the first sense: "The earth is the Lord's and the fullness thereof" (*Ps.* 23:1); the demons and the damned are slaves in the second sense; the just and the saints in the third. Because by slavery of the will we make choice of God and His service above all things, even though nature did not oblige us to do so, slavery of the will is the most perfect and most glorious to God, who beholds the heart (*1 Kg.* 16:7), claims the heart (*Prov.* 23:26), and calls Himself the God of the heart (*Ps.* 72:26), that is, of the loving will.

71. There is an entire difference between a servant and a slave:

§ 1. A servant does not give all he is, all he has and all he can acquire, by himself or by another, to his master; but the slave gives himself whole and entire to his master, all he has and all he can acquire, without any exception.

§ 2. The servant demands wages for the services which he performs for his master; but the slave can demand nothing, whatever assiduity, whatever industry, whatever energy he may have at his work.

§ 3. The servant can leave his master when he pleases, or at least when the time of his service expires; but the slave has no right to quit his master at will.

§ 4. The master of the servant has no right of life and death over him, so that if he should kill him like one of his beasts of burden, he would commit an unjust homicide; but the master of the slave has by law a right of life and death over him,[6] so that he may sell him to anybody he likes, or kill him as if he stood on the same level as one of his horses.

§ 5. Lastly, the servant is only for a time in his master's service; the slave, always.

72. There is nothing among men which makes us belong to another more than slavery. There is nothing among Christians which makes us more absolutely belong to Jesus Christ and His holy Mother than the slavery of the will, according to the example of Jesus Christ Himself, who took on Himself the form of a slave for love of us (*Phil.* 2:7); and also according to the example of the holy Virgin, who called herself the servant and slave of the Lord. (*Lk.* 1:38). The Apostle calls himself, as by a title of honor, "the slave of Christ."[7] Christians are often so called in the Holy Scriptures; and the word for the designation, "*servus,*" as a great man has truly remarked,[8] signified in olden times a slave in the completest sense, because there were no servants then like those of the present day. Masters were served only by slaves or freedmen. This is what the Catechism of the holy Council of Trent, in order to leave no doubt about our being slaves of Jesus Christ, expresses by an unequivocal term, in calling us *mancipia Christi*, "slaves of Jesus Christ."[9]

73. Now that I have given these explanations, I say that we ought to belong to Jesus Christ, and to serve Him not only as mercenary servants, but as loving slaves who, as a result of their great love, give themselves up to serve Him in the quality of slaves simply for the honor of belonging to Him. Before Baptism we were the slaves of the devil. Baptism has made us the slaves of Jesus Christ: Christians must needs be either the slaves of the devil or the slaves of Jesus Christ.

74. What I say absolutely of Jesus Christ, I say relatively of Our Lady. Since Jesus Christ chose her for the inseparable companion of His life, of His death, of His glory and of His power in Heaven and upon earth, He gave her by grace, relatively to His Majesty, all the same rights and privileges which He possesses by nature. "All that is fitting to God by nature is fitting to Mary by grace," say the saints; so that, according to them, Mary and Jesus, having but the same will and the same power, have also the same subjects, servants and slaves.[10]

75. We may, therefore, following the sentiments of the saints and of many great men, call ourselves and make ourselves the loving slaves of the most holy Virgin, in order to be, by that very means, the more perfectly the slaves of Jesus Christ. Our Blessed Lady is the means Our Lord made use of to come to us. She is also the means which we must make use of to go to Him.[11] For she is not like all other creatures who, if we should attach ourselves to them, might rather draw us away from God than draw us near Him. The strongest inclination of Mary is to unite us to Jesus Christ, her Son; and the strongest inclination of the Son is that we should come to Him through His holy Mother. It is to honor and to please Him, just as it would be to do honor and pleasure to a king to become more perfectly his subject and his slave by making ourselves the slaves of the queen. It is on this account that the holy Fathers, and St. Bonaventure after them, say that Our Lady is the way to go to Our Lord: "The way of coming to Christ is to draw near to her."[12]

76. Moreover, if, as I have said,[13] the holy Virgin is the Queen and Sovereign of Heaven and earth, has she not then as many subjects and slaves as there are creatures?[14] St. Anselm, St. Bernard, St. Bernardine, St. Bonaventure say: "All things, the Virgin included, are subject to the empire of God: Behold, all things, and God included, are subject to the empire of the Virgin." Is it not reasonable that among so many slaves of constraint there should be some of love, who of their own good will, in the quality of slaves, should choose Mary for their Mistress? What! Are men and devils to have their voluntary slaves, and Mary to have none? What! Shall a king hold it to be for his honor that the queen, his companion, should have slaves over whom she has the right of life and death,[15] because the honor and power of the one is the honor and power of the other; and yet are we to think that Our Lord, who as the best of all sons has divided His entire power with His holy Mother, shall take it ill that she too has her slaves? Has He less respect and love for His Mother than Ahasuerus had for Esther, or than Solomon had for Bethsebee? Who shall dare say so, or even think so?

77. But whither is my pen hurrying me? Why am I stopping here to prove a thing so plain? If we do not wish to call ourselves slaves of the Blessed Virgin, what matter? Let us make ourselves, and call ourselves, slaves of Jesus Christ; for that is being the slave of the holy Virgin, inasmuch as Jesus is the fruit and the glory of Mary; and it is this very thing which we do perfectly by the devotion of which we are hereafter to speak.[16]

—THIRD TRUTH—
We Need Mary in Order to Die to Ourselves

78. Our best actions are ordinarily stained and corrupted by our corrupt nature. When we put clean, clear water into a vessel which has a foul and evil smell, or wine into a cask the inside of which has been tainted by another wine which has been in it, the clear water and the good wine are spoilt, and readily take on the bad odor. In like manner, when God puts into the vessel of our soul, spoilt by original and actual sin, His graces and heavenly dews, or the delicious wine of His love, His gifts are ordinarily spoilt and corrupted by the bad leaven and the evil which sin has left within us. Our actions, even the most sublime and virtuous, feel the effects of it. It is therefore of great importance in the acquiring of perfection—which, it must be remembered, is only acquired by union with Jesus Christ—to rid ourselves of everything that is bad within us; otherwise Our Lord, who is infinitely pure and hates infinitely the least stain upon our souls, will not unite Himself to us, and will cast us out from His presence.

79. To rid ourselves of self we must:

§ 1. Thoroughly recognize, by the light of the Holy Ghost, our inward corruption, our incapacity for every good thing useful for salvation, our weakness in all things, our inconstancy at all times, our unworthiness of every grace, and our iniquity in every position. The sin of our first father has spoilt us all, soured us, puffed us up and corrupted us, as the leaven sours, puffs up and corrupts the dough into which it is put. The actual sins which we have committed, whether mortal or venial, pardoned though they may be, have nevertheless increased our concupiscence, our weakness, our inconstancy and our corruption, and have left evil remains in our souls.

Our bodies are so corrupted that they are called by the Holy Ghost bodies of sin (*Rom.* 6:6), conceived in sin (*Ps.* 50:7), nourished in sin, and capable of all sin—bodies subject to thousands of maladies, which go on corrupting from day to day, and which engender nothing but disease, vermin and corruption.

Our soul, united to our body, has become so carnal that it is called flesh: "All flesh having corrupted its way." (*Gen.* 6:12). We have nothing for our portion but pride and blindness of spirit, hardness of heart, weakness and inconstancy of soul, concupiscence, revolted passions, and sicknesses in the body. We are naturally prouder than peacocks, more groveling than toads, more vile than unclean animals, more envious than serpents, more gluttonous than hogs, more furious than tigers, lazier than tortoises, weaker than reeds, and more capricious than weathercocks. We have within ourselves nothing but nothingness and sin, and we deserve nothing but the anger of God and everlasting Hell.[17]

80. After this, ought we to be astonished if Our Lord has said that whoever wishes to follow Him must renounce himself and hate his own life, and that whosoever shall love his own life shall lose it, and whosoever shall hate it, shall save it? (*Jn.* 12:25). He who is infinite Wisdom does not give commandments without reason, and He has commanded us to hate ourselves only because we so richly deserve to be hated. Nothing is worthier of love than God, and nothing is worthier of hatred than ourselves.

81. § 2. In order to rid ourselves of self, we must die to ourselves daily. That is to say, we must renounce the operations of the powers of our soul and of the senses of our body. We must see as if we saw not, understand as if we understood not, and make use of the things of this

world as if we made no use of them at all. (*1 Cor.* 7:29-31). This is what St. Paul calls dying daily. (*1 Cor.* 15:31). "Unless the grain of wheat falling into the ground die, itself remaineth alone," and bringeth forth no good fruit. (*Jn.* 12:24-25). If we do not die to ourselves, and if our holiest devotions do not incline us to this necessary and useful death, we shall bring forth no fruit worth anything, and our devotions will become useless. All our good works will be stained by self-love and our own will; and this will cause God to hold in abomination the greatest sacrifices we can make and the best actions we can do; so that at our death we shall find our hands empty of virtues and of merits and we shall not have one spark of pure love, which is only communicated to souls dead to themselves, souls whose life is hidden with Jesus Christ in God. (*Col.* 3:3).

82. § 3. We must choose, therefore, among all the devotions to the Blessed Virgin, the one which draws us most toward this death to ourselves, inasmuch as it will be the best and the most sanctifying. For we must not think that all that shines is gold, that all that tastes sweet is honey, or that all that is easy to do and is done by the greatest number is the most sanctifying. As there are secrets of nature by which natural operations are performed more easily, in a short time and at little cost, so also are there secrets in the order of grace by which supernatural operations, such as ridding ourselves of self, filling ourselves with God, and becoming perfect, are performed more easily.

The practice which I am about to disclose is one of these secrets of grace, unknown to the greater number of Christians, known even to few of the devout, and practiced and relished by a lesser number still. But by way of beginning the explanation of this practice, let us consider a fourth truth which is a consequence of the third.

—Fourth Truth—
We Need Mary as Our Mediatrix with Our Mediator, Jesus Christ

83. It is more perfect, because it is more humble, not to approach God of ourselves without taking a mediator. Our nature, as I have just shown, is so corrupted that if we rely on our own works, efforts and preparations in order to reach God and please Him, it is certain that our good works will be defiled or be of little weight before God in inducing Him to unite Himself to us and to hear us. It is not without reason that God has given us mediators with His Majesty. He has seen our unworthiness and our incapacity; He has had pity on us; and in order to give us access to His mercies, He has provided us with powerful intercessors with His Grandeur, so that to neglect these mediators, and to draw near to His Holiness directly, and without any recommendation, is to fail in humility. It is to fail in respect toward God, so high and so holy. It is to make less account of that King of Kings than we should make of a king or prince of this earth, whom we would not willingly approach without some friend to speak for us.

84. Our Lord is our advocate and Mediator of redemption with God the Father. It is through Him that we ought to pray, in union with the whole Church, Triumphant and Militant. It is through Him that we have access to the Majesty of the Father, before whom we ought never to appear except sustained and clothed with the merits of His Son, just as the young Jacob came before his father Isaac in the skins of the kids to receive his blessing.

85. But have we not need of a mediator with the Mediator Himself? Is our purity great enough to unite us directly to Him, and by ourselves? Is He not God, in all things equal to His Father, and consequently the Holy of Holies, as worthy of respect as His Father? If through His infinite charity He has made Himself our bail and our Mediator with God His Father, in order to appease Him and to pay Him what we owed

Him, are we, on that account, to have less respect and less fear for His Majesty and His Sanctity?

Let us say boldly with St. Bernard[18] that we have need of a mediator with the Mediator Himself, and that it is the divine Mary who is the most capable of filling that charitable office. It was through her that Jesus Christ came to us, and it is through her that we must go to Him. If we fear to go directly to Jesus Christ, our God, whether because of His infinite greatness or because of our vileness or because of our sins, let us boldly implore the aid and intercession of Mary, our Mother. She is good, she is tender, she has nothing in her austere and forbidding, nothing too sublime and too brilliant. In seeing her, we see our pure nature. She is not the sun, which by the brightness of its rays blinds us because of our weakness; but she is fair and gentle as the moon (*Cant.* 6:9), which receives the light of the sun, and tempers it to make it more suitable to our capacity. She is so charitable that she repels none of those who ask her intercession, no matter how great sinners they have been; for, as the saints say, never has it been heard since the world was the world that anyone has confidently and perseveringly had recourse to our Blessed Lady and yet has been repelled.[19] She is so powerful that none of her petitions has ever been refused. She has but to show herself before her Son to pray to Him, and straightaway He grants her desires, straightaway He receives her prayers. He is always lovingly vanquished by the prayers of His dearest Mother, who bore Him and nourished Him.[20]

86. All this is taken from St. Bernard and St. Bonaventure, so that according to them, we have three steps to mount to go to God: the first, which is nearest to us and the most suited to our capacity, is Mary; the second is Jesus Christ; and the third is God the Father. To go to Jesus, we must go to Mary; she is our mediatrix of intercession. To go to God the Father, we must go to Jesus; for He is our Mediator of redemption. Now the devotion that I am about to bring forward observes this order perfectly.

—Fifth Truth—

*We Need Mary in Order to Preserve the Graces
and Treasures We Have Received from God*

87. It is very difficult, considering our weakness and frailty, to preserve in ourselves the graces and treasures which we have received from God:

§ 1. Because we have this treasure, which is worth more than Heaven and earth put together, in frail vessels, i.e., in a corruptible body and in a weak and inconstant soul, which a mere nothing disturbs and dejects: "We have this treasure in earthen vessels." (*2 Cor.* 4:7).

88. § 2. Because the devils, who are skillful thieves, wish to surprise us unawares, and to strip us. They watch day and night for the favorable moment. For that end they go round about us incessantly to devour us and to snatch from us in one moment, by a sin, all the graces and merits we have gained for many years. Their malice, their experience, their stratagems and their number ought to make us fear this misfortune immensely, especially when we see how many persons fuller of grace than we are, richer in virtues, better founded in experience and far higher exalted in sanctity, have been surprised, robbed and unhappily pillaged. Ah! How many cedars of Lebanon, how many stars of the firmament, have we not seen fall miserably, and in the twinkling of an eye lose all their height and their brightness! Whence comes that sad and curious change? It was not for want of grace, which is wanting to no man; but it was for want of humility. They thought themselves capable of guarding their own treasures. They trusted in themselves, relied upon themselves. They thought their house secure enough, and their coffers strong enough, to keep the precious treasure of grace. It is because of that scarcely perceptible reliance upon themselves, though all the while it seemed to them that they were relying only on the grace of God, that the most just Lord permitted them to be robbed by leaving them to themselves. Alas! If they had but known the admirable devotion which I will unfold presently, they would have confided their

treasure to a Virgin powerful and faithful, who would have kept it for them as if it had been her own possession; nay, who would have even taken it as an obligation of justice on herself to preserve it for them.

89. § 3. It is difficult to persevere in justice because of the strange corruption of the world. The world is now so corrupt it seems inevitable that religious hearts should be soiled, if not by its mud, at least by its dust; so that it has become a kind of miracle for anyone to remain in the midst of that impetuous torrent without being drawn in by it, in the midst of that stormy sea without being drowned in it or stripped by the pirates and the corsairs, in the midst of that pestilent air without being infected by it. It is the Virgin, alone faithful, in whom the serpent has never had part, who works this miracle for those who serve her in that sweet way which I have shortly to unfold.

NOTES

1. The following is taken almost entirely from Holy Scripture; cf. *Apoc.* 1:8; *Eph.* 4:13; *Col.* 2:9; *Matt.* 23:8-10; *Jn.* 13:13; *1 Cor.* 8:6; *Col.* 1:18; *Jn.* 13:15; 10:16; *Acts* 4:12; *1 Cor.* 3:11, etc.
2. Canon of the Mass.
3. We should remember that St. Louis De Montfort wrote this at a time when Jansenism, which opposed devotion to the Blessed Virgin, was flourishing throughout Europe. Even eminent authors were deceived by this heretical sect.
4. *Meditationum* lib. I, cap. XVIII, no. 2 (inter opera Sancti Augustini).
5. St. Thomas, *Summa Theol.*, III, Q. 48, a. 4., corp. et ad 1.
6. By law, i.e., by the ancient civil law of some of those countries where slavery existed; not by the law of God, nor the law of Moses, nor our modern civil codes, which all condemn such an action. St. Louis De Montfort merely states a fact as it once existed. He prescinds entirely from the question of morality and *wishes only to give an example of the complete dependence of which he is speaking.*
7. *Rom.* 1:1; *Gal.* 1:10; *Phil.* 1:1; *Tit.* 1:1; also cf. *1 Cor.* 7:22; *2 Tim.* 2:24. The insistence of Sts. Paul, Peter, James and Jude on calling themselves slaves of Jesus Christ, shows that there is no opposition between this appellation and the words of Jesus: "I will not call you now servants [slaves] . . . but I have called you friends."
8. Henri Marie Boudon, archdeacon of Evreux, in his book, *Le Saint Esclavage de l'admirable Mère de Dieu*, chapter II.
9. *Catechismus Roman.*, Pars Ia, Caput III, De secundo Symboli articulo (in fine).
10. St. John Damascene, *Sermo 2 in Dormitione B. Mariae.*
11. St. Augustine, *Sermo 113 in Nativit. Domini* (inter opera Sti. Augustini).
12. Psalt. majus B.V.Ps. 117.
13. Cf. no. 38.

14. *Speculum B.M.V.*, lect. III, no. 5.
15. Cf. no. 71, note 6.
16. For a further explanation of this second truth, cf. *La Vie Spirituelle à l'école de St. Louis Marie de Montfort*, by A. Lhoumeau, S.M.M., 1 Partie, ch. IV.
17. St. Louis De Montfort speaks here of our nothingness and impotence in the supernatural order, without the help of grace. Thus he says further on, in no. 83: "Our nature is so corrupted that if we rely on our own works . . . *to reach God. . . .*"
18. *Sermo in Dom. infra octav. Assumptionis*, no. 2.
19. St. Bernard, *Sermo in Dom. infra. oct. Assumptionis*, no. 2.
20. St. Bonaventure, *Speculum B.M.V.*, lectio XI.

CHAPTER THREE

Choice of True Devotion to the Blessed Virgin

———————•———————

90. Having laid down these five truths, let us continue. Today, more than ever, we must take pains in choosing true devotion to our Blessed Lady, because, more than ever before, there are false devotions to our Blessed Lady which are easily mistaken for true ones. The devil, like a false coiner and a subtle and experienced sharper, has already deceived and destroyed so many souls by a false devotion to the Blessed Virgin that he makes a daily use of his diabolical experience to plunge many others by this same way into everlasting perdition; amusing them, lulling them to sleep in sin, under the pretext of some prayers badly said or of some outward practices which he inspires. As a false coiner does not ordinarily counterfeit anything but gold or silver, and very rarely other metals, because they are not worth the trouble, so the evil spirit does not for the most part counterfeit other devotions, but only those to Jesus and Mary—devotion to Holy Communion and to our Blessed Lady—because they are among other devotions what gold and silver are among other metals.

91. It is then very important to recognize, first of all, false devotions to our Blessed Lady, in order to avoid them, and true devotion, in order to embrace it; secondly, which of the many practices of true devotion to our Blessed Lady is the most perfect, the most agreeable to

her, the most glorious to God, and the most sanctifying for ourselves, so that we may adopt that one.

—ARTICLE ONE—

False Devotions to the Blessed Virgin and False Devotees

92. I find seven kinds of false devotees and false devotions to Our Lady, namely: 1. the critical devotees; 2. the scrupulous devotees; 3. the external devotees; 4. the presumptuous devotees; 5. the inconstant devotees; 6. the hypocritical devotees; 7. the interested devotees.

I. Critical Devotees

93. The critical devotees are, for the most part, proud scholars, rash and self-sufficient spirits, who have at heart some devotion to the holy Virgin, but who criticize nearly all the practices of devotion which simple people pay simply and holily to their good Mother, because these practices do not fall in with their own humor and fancy. They call in doubt all the miracles and pious stories recorded by authors worthy of faith, or drawn from the chronicles of religious orders: narratives which testify to us the mercies and the power of the most holy Virgin. They cannot see, without uneasiness, simple and humble people on their knees before an altar or an image of Our Lady, sometimes at the corner of a street, in order to pray to God there; and they even accuse them of idolatry, as if they adored the wood or the stone. They say that, for their part, they are not fond of these external devotions, and that they are not so credulous as to believe so many tales and stories that are told about Our Lady. When they are told how admirably the Fathers of the Church praised the Blessed Virgin, they either reply that the Fathers spoke as professional orators, with exaggeration; or they misinterpret their words.[1]

These kinds of false devotees and of proud and worldly people are greatly to be feared. They do an infinite wrong to devotion to Our Lady; and they are but too successful in alienating people from it, under the pretext of destroying its abuses.

II. Scrupulous Devotees

94. The scrupulous devotees are those who fear to dishonor the Son by honoring the Mother, to abase the one in elevating the other. They cannot bear that we should attribute to Our Lady the most just praise which the holy Fathers have given her. It is all they can do to endure that there should be more people before the altar of the Blessed Virgin than before the Blessed Sacrament—as if the one were contrary to the other, as if those who prayed to our Blessed Lady did not pray to Jesus Christ through her. They are unwilling that we should speak so often of Our Lady and address her so frequently.

Here are some of their favorite sayings: "Why so many Rosaries, so many confraternities and so many external devotions to the Blessed Virgin? There is much ignorance in all this. It makes a mummery of our religion. Speak to us of those who are devout to Jesus Christ." (Yet they often name Him without raising their hats—I say this by way of parenthesis.) "We must have recourse to Jesus Christ; He is our only Mediator. We must preach Jesus Christ; this is the solid devotion." What they say is in a certain sense true, but in the application they make of it, namely, to hinder devotion to our Blessed Lady, very dangerous; and it is, under pretext of a greater good, a subtle snare of the evil one. For the more we honor the Blessed Virgin, the more we honor Jesus Christ, because we honor Mary only that we may the more perfectly honor Jesus, since we go to her only as the way by which we are to find the end we are seeking, which is Jesus.

95. The Church, with the Holy Ghost, blesses Our Lady first, and Our Lord second: "Blessed art thou among women, and blessed is the fruit of thy womb, Jesus." It is not that Mary is more than Jesus or

even equal to Him—that would be intolerable heresy; but it is that, in order to bless Jesus more perfectly, we must begin by blessing Mary. Let us then say, with all the true clients of Our Lady, in opposition to these false, scrupulous devotees, "O Mary, thou art blessed among all women, and blessed is the fruit of thy womb, Jesus."

III. External Devotees

96. External devotees are persons who make all devotion to our Blessed Lady consist in outward practices. They have no taste except for the exterior of this devotion, because they have no interior spirit of their own. They will say quantities of Rosaries with the greatest precipitation; they will hear many Masses distractedly; they will go, without devotion, to processions; they will enroll themselves in all her confraternities—without amending their lives, without doing any violence to their passions, or without imitating the virtues of that most holy Virgin. They have no love but for the sensible[2] part of devotion, without having any relish for its solidity. If they have not sensible sweetness in their practices, they think they are doing nothing; they get all out of joint, throw everything up, or do everything at random. The world is full of these exterior devotees, and there are no people who are more critical than they of men of prayer, who foster an interior spirit as the essential thing, without, however, disregarding that outward modesty which always accompanies true devotion.

IV. Presumptuous Devotees

97. Presumptuous devotees are sinners abandoned to their passions, or lovers of the world, who under the fair name of Christians and clients of our Blessed Lady conceal pride, avarice, impurity, drunkenness, anger, swearing, detraction, injustice or some other sin. They sleep in peace in the midst of their bad habits, without doing any violence to themselves to correct their faults, under the pretext that they are devout

to the Blessed Virgin. They promise themselves that God will pardon them; that they will not be allowed to die without confession; and that they will not be lost eternally because they say the Rosary, because they fast on Saturdays, because they belong to the Confraternity of the Holy Rosary, or wear the Scapular, or are enrolled in other congregations, or they wear the little habit or little chain of Our Lady.

They will not believe us when we tell them that their devotion is only an illusion of the devil and a pernicious presumption likely to destroy their souls. They say that God is good and merciful; that He has not made us to condemn us everlastingly; that no man is without sin; that they shall not die without confession; that one good act of contrition at the hour of death is enough; that they are devout to Our Lady, wear the Scapular, say daily, without fail and without vanity, seven Our Fathers and seven Hail Marys in her honor; and that they sometimes say the Rosary and the Office of Our Lady, besides fasting and other things. To give authority to all this, and to blind themselves still further, they quote certain stories which they have heard or read— it does not matter to them whether they be true or false—relating how people have died in mortal sin without confession, and then, because in their lifetime they sometimes said some prayers or went through some practices of devotion to Our Lady, how they have been raised to life again in order to go to confession; or their soul has been miraculously retained in their bodies till confession; or through the clemency of the Blessed Virgin they have obtained from God, at the moment of death, contrition and pardon of their sins, and so have been saved; and that they themselves expect similar favors.

98. Nothing in Christianity is more detestable than this diabolical presumption. For how can we truly say that we love and honor our Blessed Lady when by our sins we are pitilessly piercing, wounding, crucifying and outraging Jesus Christ, her Son? If Mary laid down a law to herself, to save by her mercy this sort of people, she would be authorizing crime and helping crucify and outrage her Son. Who would ever dare think of such a thing?

99. I say that to thus abuse devotion to Our Lady, which, after devotion to Our Lord in the Blessed Sacrament, is the holiest and solidest of all devotions, is to be guilty of a horrible sacrilege, which, after the sacrilege of an unworthy Communion, is the greatest and least pardonable of all sacrileges.

I confess that, in order to be truly devout to our Blessed Lady, it is not absolutely necessary to be so holy as to avoid every sin, though this were desirable; but this much at least is necessary, and I beg you to lay it well to heart: (1) to have a sincere resolution to avoid at least all mortal sin, which outrages the Mother as well as the Son; (2) to do violence to ourselves to avoid sin; (3) to enroll ourselves in confraternities, to say the Rosary or other prayers, to fast on Saturdays and the like.

100. These good works are likewise wonderfully useful for the conversion of a sinner, however hardened he may be. If my reader be such a one, even though he have one foot in the abyss, I would advise him to practice them, but only on condition that he do so with the intention of obtaining from God, through the intercession of the Blessed Virgin, the grace of contrition and pardon of his sins and the grace to conquer his evil habits, and not to remain quietly in the state of sin, contrary to his remorse of conscience, the example of Jesus Christ and the saints and the maxims of the holy Gospel.

V. Inconstant Devotees

101. The inconstant devotees are those who are devout to our Blessed Lady by fits and starts. Sometimes they are fervent and sometimes lukewarm. Sometimes they seem ready to do anything for her, and then a little afterward, they are not like the same people. They begin by taking up all the devotions to her, and enrolling themselves in the confraternities; and then they do not practice the rules with fidelity. They change like the moon;[3] and Mary puts them under her feet with the crescent, because they are changeable and unworthy to be reckoned among the servants of that faithful Virgin who have for their special

graces fidelity and constancy. It were better for such persons not to burden themselves with so many prayers and practices but to choose a few and fulfill them with faithfulness and love, in spite of the world, the devil and the flesh.

VI. Hypocritical Devotees

102. We have still to mention the false devotees to our Blessed Lady who are the hypocritical devotees, who cloak their sins and sinful habits with her mantle, in order to be taken by men for what they are not.

VII. Interested Devotees

103. There are also the interested devotees, who have recourse to Our Lady only to gain some lawsuit, or to avoid some danger, or to be cured of some illness, or for some other similar necessity, without which they would forget her altogether. All these are false devotees, pleasing neither to God nor to His holy Mother.

104. Let us then take great care not to be of the number of the critical devotees, who believe nothing and criticize everything; nor of the scrupulous devotees, who are afraid of being too devout to Our Lady, out of respect to Our Lord; nor of the exterior devotees, who make all their devotion consist in outward practices; nor of the presumptuous devotees, who, under the pretext of their false devotion to the Blessed Virgin, wallow in their sins; nor of the inconstant devotees, who from levity change their practices of devotion, or give them up altogether, at the least temptation; nor of the hypocritical devotees, who join confraternities and wear the liveries of the Blessed Virgin in order to pass for good people; nor, finally, of the interested devotees, who have recourse to Our Lady only to be delivered from bodily evils, or to obtain temporal goods.

—Article Two—
True Devotion to the Blessed Virgin

I. Characteristics

105. After having laid bare and condemned the false devotions to the most holy Virgin, we must, in a few words, give the characteristics of true devotion. It must be: 1. interior, 2. tender, 3. holy, 4. constant, and 5. disinterested.

1. Interior.

106. True devotion to Our Lady is interior; that is, it comes from the mind and the heart. It flows from the esteem we have for her, the high idea we have formed of her greatness, and the love which we have for her.

2. Tender.

107. It is tender; that is, full of confidence in her, like a child's confidence in his loving mother. This confidence makes the soul have recourse to her in all its bodily and mental necessities, with much simplicity, trust and tenderness. It implores the aid of its good Mother at all times, in all places and above all things: in its doubts, that it may be enlightened; in its wanderings, that it may be brought into the right path; in its temptations, that it may be supported; in its weaknesses, that it may be strengthened; in its falls, that it may be lifted up; in its discouragements, that it may be cheered; in its scruples, that they may be taken away; in the crosses, toils and disappointments of life, that it may be consoled under them. In a word, in all the evils of body and mind, the soul ordinarily has recourse to Mary, without fear of annoying her or displeasing Jesus Christ.

3. Holy.

108. True devotion to Our Lady is holy; that is to say, it leads the soul to avoid sin and to imitate the virtues of the Blessed Virgin, particularly her profound humility, her lively faith, her blind obedience, her continual prayer, her universal mortification, her divine purity, her ardent charity, her heroic patience, her angelic sweetness and her divine wisdom. These are the ten principal virtues of the most holy Virgin.

4. Constant.

109. True devotion to Our Lady is constant. It confirms the soul in good, and does not let it easily abandon its spiritual exercises. It makes it courageous in opposing the world in its fashions and maxims, the flesh in its wearinesses and passions, and the devil in his temptations; so that a person truly devout to our Blessed Lady is neither changeable, irritable, scrupulous nor timid. It is not that such a person does not fall, or change sometimes in the sensible feeling of devotion. But when he falls, he rises again by stretching out his hand to his good Mother. When he loses the taste and relish of devotion, he does not become disturbed because of that; for the just and faithful client of Mary lives by the faith (*Heb.* 10:38) of Jesus and Mary, and not by natural sentiment.

5. Disinterested.

110. Lastly, true devotion to Our Lady is disinterested; that is to say, it inspires the soul not to seek itself but only God, and God in His holy Mother. A true client of Mary does not serve that august Queen from a spirit of lucre and interest, nor for his own good, whether temporal or eternal, corporal or spiritual, but exclusively because she deserves to be served, and God alone in her. He does not love Mary just because she obtains favors for him, or because he hopes she will, but

solely because she is so worthy of love. It is on this account that he loves and serves her as faithfully in his disgusts and drynesses as in his sweetnesses and sensible fervors. He loves her as much on Calvary as at the marriage of Cana.

Oh, how agreeable and precious in the eyes of God and of His holy Mother is such a client of our Blessed Lady, who has no self-seeking in his service of her! But in these days how rare is such a sight! It is that it may be less rare that I have taken my pen in hand to put on paper what I have taught with good results, in public and in private, during my missions for many years.

111. I have now said many things about the most holy Virgin; but I have many more to say, and there are infinitely more which I shall omit, either from ignorance, inability or want of time, in unfolding the plan for forming a true client of Mary and a true disciple of Jesus Christ.

112. Oh, but my labor will have been well expended if this little writing, falling into the hands of a soul of good dispositions—a soul well-born of God and of Mary, and not of blood, nor of the will of the flesh, nor of the will of man (*Jn.* 1: 13)—should unfold to him, and should by the grace of the Holy Ghost inspire him with the excellence and the value of that true and solid devotion to our Blessed Lady which I am going presently to describe. If I knew that my guilty blood could serve in engraving upon anyone's heart the truths which I am writing in honor of my true Mother and Sovereign Mistress, of whose children and slaves I am the least, I would use my blood instead of ink to form the letters, in the hope of finding some good souls who, by their fidelity to the practice which I teach, should compensate my dear Mother and Mistress for the losses which she has suffered through my ingratitude and infidelities.

113. I feel myself more than ever encouraged to believe and to hope for the fulfillment of all that I have deeply engraven upon my heart and have asked of God these many years, namely, that sooner or later the Blessed Virgin shall have more children, servants and slaves of love than

ever;[4] and that by this means, Jesus Christ, my dear Master, shall reign in hearts more than ever.

114. I clearly foresee that raging beasts shall come in fury to tear with their diabolical teeth this little writing and him whom the Holy Ghost has made use of to write it—or at least to smother it in the darkness and silence of a coffer, that it may not appear. They shall even attack and persecute those who shall read it and carry it out in practice.[5] But what matter? On the contrary, so much the better! This very foresight encourages me, and makes me hope for great success, that is to say, for a great squadron of brave and valiant soldiers of Jesus and Mary, of both sexes, to combat the world, the devil and corrupted nature, in those more-than-ever perilous times which are about to come. "He who reads, let him understand." (*Matt.* 24:15). "He who can receive it, let him receive it." (*Matt.* 19:12).

II. Practices

1. Common practices, both interior and exterior.

115. There are several interior practices of true devotion to the Blessed Virgin. Here are the principal ones, stated compendiously: (1) to honor her as the worthy Mother of God, with the worship of hyperdulia; that is to say, to esteem her and honor her above all the other saints, as the masterpiece of grace, and the first after Jesus Christ, true God and true Man; (2) to meditate on her virtues, her privileges and her actions; (3) to contemplate her grandeurs; (4) to make acts of love, of praise, of gratitude to her; (5) to invoke her cordially; (6) to offer ourselves to her and unite ourselves with her; (7) to do all our actions with the view of pleasing her; (8) to begin, to continue and to finish all our actions by her, in her, with her and for her, in order that we may do them by Jesus Christ, in Jesus Christ, with Jesus Christ and for Jesus Christ, our Last End. We will presently explain this last practice.[6]

116. True devotion to Our Lady also has several exterior practices, of which the following are the principal ones: (1) to enroll ourselves in her confraternities and enter her congregations; (2) to join the religious orders instituted in her honor; (3) to proclaim her praises; (4) to give alms, to fast and to undergo outward and inward mortifications in her honor; (5) to wear her liveries, such as the Rosary, the Scapular or the little chain; (6) to recite with attention, devotion and modesty the holy Rosary, composed of fifteen decades of Hail Marys in honor of the fifteen principal mysteries of Jesus Christ; or five decades, which is one third of the Rosary, either in honor of the five Joyful Mysteries, which are the Annunciation, the Visitation, the Nativity of Jesus Christ, the Purification, and the Finding of Our Lord in the Temple; or in honor of the five Sorrowful Mysteries, which are the Agony of Our Lord in the Garden of Olives, His Scourging, His Crowning with Thorns, His Carrying of the Cross, and His Crucifixion; or in honor of the five Glorious Mysteries, which are the Resurrection, the Ascension, the Descent of the Holy Ghost at Pentecost, the Assumption of our Blessed Lady, body and soul, into Heaven, and her Coronation by the Three Persons of the Most Holy Trinity. We may also say a chaplet of six or seven decades in honor of the years which we believe Our Lady lived on earth; or the Little Crown of the Blessed Virgin, composed of three Our Fathers and twelve Hail Marys, in honor of her crown of twelve stars or privileges; or the Office of Our Lady, so universally received and recited in the Church; or the little Psalter of the holy Virgin, which St. Bonaventure composed in her honor, and which is so tender and so devout that one cannot say it without being moved by it; or fourteen Our Fathers and Hail Marys in honor of her fourteen joys; or some other prayers, hymns and canticles of the Church, such as the *Salve Regina*, the *Alma*, the *Ave Regina Coelorum*, or the *Regina Coeli*, according to the different seasons; or the *Ave Maris Stella*, the *O Gloriosa Domina*, the *Magnificat*, or some other practices of devotion, of which books are full; (7) to sing, or have sung, spiritual canticles in her honor; (8) to make a number of genuflections or reverences, while saying, for

example, every morning, sixty or a hundred times, *Ave Maria, Virgo Fidelis* ("Hail Mary, Faithful Virgin"), to obtain from God through her the grace to be faithful to the graces of God during the day; and then again in the evening, *Ave Maria, Mater Misericordiae* ("Hail Mary, Mother of Mercy") to ask pardon of God through her for the sins that we have committed during the day; (9) to take care of her confraternities, to adorn her altars, to crown and ornament her images; (10) to carry her images, or to have them carried, in procession, and to carry a picture or an image of her about our own persons, as a mighty arm against the evil spirit; (11) to have copies of her name or picture made and placed in churches, or in houses, or on the gates and entrances into cities, churches and houses; (12) to consecrate ourselves to her in a special and solemn manner.

117. There are numerous other practices of true devotion toward the Blessed Virgin which the Holy Ghost has inspired in saintly souls and which are very sanctifying; they can be read at length in the *Paradise Opened to Philagius* of Father Barry, the Jesuit, in which he has collected a great number of devotions which the saints have practiced in honor of Our Lady—devotions which serve marvelously to sanctify our souls, provided they are performed as they ought to be, that is to say, (1) with a good and pure intention to please God only, to unite ourselves to Jesus Christ as to our Last End, and to edify our neighbor; (2) with attention and without voluntary distraction; (3) with devotion, equally avoiding precipitation and negligence; (4) with modesty, and a respectful and edifying posture of the body.

2. Its *perfect* practice.

118. But after all, I loudly protest that, having read nearly all the books which profess to treat of devotion to Our Lady, and having conversed familiarly with the best and wisest of men of these latter times, I have never known nor heard of any practice of devotion toward her at all equal to the one which I now wish to unfold; demanding from

the soul, as it does, more sacrifices for God, ridding the soul more of itself and of its self-love, keeping it more faithfully in grace and grace more faithfully in it, uniting it more perfectly and more easily to Jesus Christ; and finally, being more glorious to God, more sanctifying to the soul and more useful to our neighbor than any other of the devotions to her.

119. As the essential of this devotion consists in the interior which it ought to form, it will not be equally understood by everybody. Some will stop at what is exterior in it, and will go no further, and these will be the greatest number. Some, in small number, will enter into its inward spirit; but they will only mount one step. Who will mount to the second step? Who will get as far as the third? Lastly, who will so advance as to make this devotion his habitual state? He alone to whom the Spirit of Jesus Christ shall have revealed this secret, the faultlessly faithful soul whom He shall conduct there Himself, to advance from virtue to virtue, from grace to grace, from light to light, until he arrives at the transformation of himself into Jesus Christ, and to the plenitude of His age on earth and of His glory in Heaven.

NOTES

1. This description by St. Louis De Montfort is not exaggerated in the light of the activity of "critical devotees" at this period in spreading among the faithful such virulent writings as *Salutary Advice of the Blessed Virgin to Her Indiscreet Devotees*, by Widenfelt. Cf. Lhoumeau: *La vie Spirituelle à l'école de St. Louis Marie de Montfort*, p. 17; also Terrien, *La Mère de Dieu et la mère des hommes*, Vol. IV, p. 478.

2. In this context, "sensible" means "of the senses"; it refers to sweet feelings of religious fervor.

3. Because of its continual variations, the moon is often taken by ancient mystical writers as a symbol of the changing, inconstant soul. Cf. Eccles. 27:12; St. Bernard, *Sermo super signum magnum*, no. 3.

4. Notice the association of these two terms, "child" and "slave." Similar use of these terms was made by the *Catechism of the Council of Trent* (Part 1, Cap. 3, De secundo symboli articulo, in fine).

5. The prediction was fulfilled to the letter. Throughout the whole eighteenth century, the spiritual sons of St. Louis De Montfort were persecuted by the Jansenists for their zeal in spreading this devotion; and the precious manuscript of De Montfort remained hidden

during the troublous times of the French Revolution, and was brought to light only in the year 1842, when it was found in a chest of old books by a Montfort Father.

6.   See no. 257-265.

PART TWO

PERFECT DEVOTION TO THE BLESSED VIRGIN MARY

Nature

Motives

Wonderful Effects

Practices

CHAPTER ONE

Nature of Perfect Devotion to the Blessed Virgin
OR
Perfect Consecration to Jesus Christ

———•———

120. All our perfection consists in being conformed, united and consecrated to Jesus Christ; and therefore the most perfect of all devotions is, without any doubt, that which the most perfectly conforms, unites and consecrates us to Jesus Christ. Now, Mary being the most conformed of all creatures to Jesus Christ, it follows that, of all devotions, that which most consecrates and conforms the soul to Our Lord is devotion to His holy Mother, and that the more a soul is consecrated to Mary, the more it is consecrated to Jesus.

Hence it comes to pass that the most perfect consecration to Jesus Christ is nothing else but a perfect and entire consecration of ourselves to the Blessed Virgin, and this is the devotion which I teach; or, in other words, a perfect renewal of the vows and promises of holy Baptism.

—ARTICLE ONE—
A Perfect and Entire Consecration of Oneself to the Blessed Virgin

121. This devotion consists, then, in giving ourselves entirely to Our Lady, in order to belong entirely to Jesus through her.[1] We must give her (1) our body, with all its senses and its members; (2) our soul,

with all its powers; (3) our exterior goods of fortune, whether present or to come; (4) our interior and spiritual goods, which are our merits and our virtues, and our good works, past, present and future. In a word, we must give her all we have in the order of nature and in the order of grace, and all that may become ours in the future, in the orders of nature, grace and glory; and this we must do without the reserve of so much as one farthing, one hair, or one least good action; and we must do it also for all eternity; and we must do it, further, without pretending to, or hoping for, any other recompense for our offering and service except the honor of belonging to Jesus Christ through Mary and in Mary—as though that sweet Mistress were not (as she always *is*) the most generous and the most grateful of creatures.

122. Here we must note that there are two things in the good works we perform, namely, satisfaction and merit; in other words, their satisfactory or impetratory value, and their meritorious value. The satisfactory or impetratory value of a good action is that action inasmuch as it satisfies for the pain due to sin, or obtains some new grace; the meritorious value, or the merit, is the good action inasmuch as it merits grace now and eternal glory hereafter. Now, in this consecration of ourselves to Our Lady, we give her all the satisfactory, impetratory and meritorious value of our actions; in other words, the satisfactions and the merits of all our good works. We give her all our merits, graces and virtues—not to communicate them to others, for our merits, graces and virtues are, properly speaking, incommunicable, and it is only Jesus Christ who, in making Himself our surety with His Father, is able to communicate His merits—but we give her them to keep them, augment them and embellish them for us, as we shall explain by and by.[2] Our satisfactions, however, we give her to communicate to whom she likes, and for the greatest glory of God.

123. It follows from this that:

§ 1. By this devotion we give to Jesus Christ in the most perfect manner, inasmuch as it is by Mary's hands, all we can give Him, and far more than by any other devotions in which we give Him either a part of our time, or a part of our good works, or a part of our satisfactions and mortifications; because here everything is given and consecrated to Him, even the right of disposing of our interior goods and of the satisfactions which we gain by our good works day after day. This is more than we do even in a religious order. In religious orders we give God the goods of fortune by the vow of poverty, the goods of the body by the vow of chastity, our own will by the vow of obedience, and sometimes the liberty of the body by the vow of cloister. But we do not by these vows give Him the liberty or the right to dispose of the value of our good works; and we do not strip ourselves, as far as a Christian man can do so, of that which is dearest and most precious, namely, our merits and our satisfactions.

124. § 2. A person who is thus voluntarily consecrated and sacrificed to Jesus Christ through Mary can no longer dispose of the value of any of his good actions. All he suffers, all he thinks, all the good he says or does, belongs to Mary, in order that she may dispose of it according to the will of her Son and His greatest glory—without, however, that dependence interfering in any way with the obligations of the state we may be in at present or may be placed in for the future; for example, without interfering with the obligations of a priest who, by his office or otherwise, ought to apply the satisfactory and impetratory value of the Holy Mass to some private person. For we make the offering of this devotion only according to the order of God and the duties of our state.

125. § 3. We consecrate ourselves at one and the same time to the most holy Virgin and to Jesus Christ; to the most holy Virgin as to the perfect means which Jesus Christ has chosen whereby to unite Himself to us, and us to Him; and to Our Lord as to our Last End, to whom, as our Redeemer and our God, we owe all we are.

—Article Two—

A Perfect Renewal of the Vows of Holy Baptism

126. I have said[3] that this devotion may rightly be called a perfect renewal of the vows or promises of holy Baptism.

For every Christian, before his Baptism, was the slave of the devil, seeing that he belonged to him. He has in his Baptism, by his own mouth or by his sponsor's, solemnly renounced Satan, his pomps and his works; and he has taken Jesus Christ for his Master and Sovereign Lord, to depend upon Him in the quality of a slave of love. That is what we do by the present devotion. We renounce, as is expressed in the formula of consecration,[4] the devil, the world, sin and self; and we give ourselves entirely to Jesus Christ by the hands of Mary. Nay, we even do something more; for in Baptism, we ordinarily speak by the mouth of another, our godfather or godmother, and so we give ourselves to Jesus Christ not by ourselves but through another. But in this devotion we do it by ourselves, voluntarily, knowing what we are doing.

Moreover, in holy Baptism we do not give ourselves to Jesus by the hands of Mary, at least not in an explicit manner; and we do not give Him the value of our good actions. We remain entirely free after Baptism, either to apply them to whom we please or to keep them for ourselves. But by this devotion we give ourselves to Our Lord explicitly by the hands of Mary, and we consecrate to Him the value of all our actions.

127. Men, says St. Thomas, make a vow at their Baptism to re-nounce the devil and all his pomps.[5] This vow, says St. Augustine, is the greatest and most indispensable of all vows.[6] It is thus also that canonists speak: "The principal vow is the one we make at Baptism." Yet who has kept this great vow? Who is it that faithfully performs the promises of holy Baptism? Have not almost all Christians swerved from the loyalty which they promised Jesus in their Baptism? Whence can come this universal disobedience, except from our forgetfulness of the promises and obligations of holy Baptism, and from the fact that hardly

anyone ratifies, of himself, the contract he made with God by those who stood sponsors for him?

128. This is so true that the Council of Sens, convoked by order of Louis the Debonair to remedy the disorders of Christians, which were then so great, judged that the principal cause of that corruption of morals arose from the oblivion and the ignorance in which men lived of the obligations of holy Baptism; and it could think of no better means for remedying so great an evil than to persuade Christians to renew the vows and promises of Baptism.

129. The *Catechism of the Council of Trent,* the faithful interpreter of that holy Council, exhorts the parish priests to do the same thing, and to induce the people to remind themselves, and to believe, that they are bound and consecrated as slaves to Our Lord Jesus Christ, their Redeemer and their Lord. These are its words: "The parish priest shall exhort the faithful people so that they may know that it is most just . . . that we should devote and consecrate ourselves forever to our Redeemer and Lord as His very slaves."[7]

130. Now, if the Councils, the Fathers and even experience show us that the best means of remedying the irregularities of Christians is by making them call to mind the obligations of their Baptism, and persuading them to renew now the vows they made then, is it not only right that we should do it in a perfect manner, by this devotion and consecration of ourselves to Our Lord through His holy Mother? I say "in a perfect manner," because in thus consecrating ourselves to Him, we make use of the most perfect of all means, namely, the Blessed Virgin.

Objections and Answers

131. No one can object to this devotion as being either a new or an indifferent one. It is not new, because the Councils, the Fathers and many authors both ancient and modern speak of this consecration to Our Lord, or renewal of the vows and promises of Baptism, as of

a thing anciently practiced, and which they counsel to all Christians. Neither is it a matter of indifference, because the principal source of all disorders, and consequently of the eternal perdition of Christians, comes from their forgetfulness and indifference about this practice.

132. But some may object that this devotion, in making us give to Our Lord, by Our Lady's hands, the value of all our good works, prayers, mortifications and alms, puts us in a state of incapacity for assisting the souls of our parents, friends and benefactors.

I answer them as follows:

§ 1. That it is not credible that our parents, friends and benefactors should suffer from the fact of our being devoted and consecrated without exception to the service of Our Lord and His holy Mother. To think this would be to think unworthily of the goodness and power of Jesus and Mary, who know well how to assist our parents, friends and benefactors, out of our own little spiritual revenue or by other ways.

§ 2. This practice does not hinder us from praying for others, whether dead or living, although the application of our good works depends on the will of our Blessed Lady. On the contrary, it is this very thing which will lead us to pray with more confidence; just as a rich person who has given all his wealth to his prince in order to honor him the more, would beg the prince all the more confidently to give an alms to one of his friends who should ask for it. It would even be a source of pleasure to the prince to be given an occasion of proving his gratitude toward a person who had stripped himself to clothe him, and impoverished himself to honor him. We must say the same of our Blessed Lord and of Our Lady. They will never let themselves be outdone in gratitude.

133. Someone may perhaps say, "If I give to our Blessed Lady all the value of my actions to apply to whom she wills, I may have to suffer a long time in Purgatory."

This objection, which comes from self-love and ignorance of the generosity of God and His holy Mother, refutes itself. A fervent and generous soul who gives God all he has, without reserve, so that he can do nothing more; who lives only for the glory and reign of Jesus Christ, through His holy Mother, and who makes an entire sacrifice of himself to bring it about—will this generous and liberal soul, I say, be more punished in the other world because it has been more liberal and more disinterested than others? Far, indeed, will that be from the truth! Rather, it is toward that soul, as we shall see by what follows, that Our Lord and His holy Mother are the most liberal in this world and in the other, in the orders of nature, grace and glory.

134. But we must now, as briefly as we can, run over the motives which ought to recommend this devotion to us, the marvelous effects it produces in the souls of the faithful, and its practices.

NOTES

1. St. John Damascene: *"Mentem, animam, corpus, nos ipsosque totos tibi consecramus."* (Sermo I in Dormitione B. V.).
2. Cf no. 146 and following.
3. Cf. no. 120.
4. The consecration is to be found on page 196.
5. *Summa Theologica*, IIa IIae, Q. 88, art. 2, ad 1.
6. *Epistola 59 ad Paulinum.*
7. *Catech. Conc. Trid.* (Parte Ia, caput 3, art. 2, no. 15, De secundo Symboli articulo, in fine).

CHAPTER TWO

Motives of This Perfect Devotion

———●———

—First Motive—
It Devotes Us Entirely to the Service of God

135. *The first motive, which shows us the excellence of this consecration of ourselves to Jesus Christ by the hands of Mary.*

If we can conceive on earth no employment more lofty than the service of God—if the least servant of God is richer, more powerful and more noble than all the kings and emperors of this earth, unless they also are the servants of God—what must be the riches, the power and the dignity of the faithful and perfect servant of God, who is devoted to His service entirely and without reserve, to the utmost extent possible? Such is the faithful and loving slave of Jesus in Mary who has given himself up entirely to the service of that King of Kings, by the hands of His holy Mother, and has reserved nothing for himself. Not all the gold of earth nor all the beauties of the heavens can repay him.

136. The other congregations, associations and confraternities erected in honor of Our Lord and His holy Mother, which do such immense good in Christendom, do not make us give everything without reserve. They prescribe to their members only certain practices and actions to satisfy their obligations. They leave them free for all other

actions and moments and occupations. But this devotion makes us give to Jesus and Mary, without reserve, all our thoughts, words, actions and sufferings, every moment of our life, in such wise that whether we wake or sleep, whether we eat or drink, whether we do great actions or very little ones, it is always true to say that whatever we do, even without thinking of it, is, by virtue of our offering—at least if it has not been intentionally retracted—done for Jesus and Mary. What a consolation this is!

137. Moreover, as I have already said,[1] there is no other practice equal to this for enabling us to rid ourselves easily of a certain proprietorship which imperceptibly creeps into our best actions. Our good Jesus gives us this great grace in recompense for the heroic and disinterested action of giving over to Him, by the hands of His holy Mother, all the value of our good works. If He gives a hundredfold even in this world to those who, for His love, quit outward and temporal and perishable goods (*Matt.* 19:29), what will that hundredfold be which He will give to the man who sacrifices for Him even his inward and spiritual goods!

138. Jesus, our great Friend, has given Himself to us without reserve, body and soul, virtues, graces and merits. "He has bought the whole of me with the whole of Himself," says St. Bernard. Is it not then a simple matter of justice and of gratitude that we should give Him all that we can give Him? He has been the first to be liberal toward us; let us, at least, be the second; and then, in life and death and throughout all eternity, we shall find Him still more liberal. "With the liberal He will be liberal."

—Second Motive—

It Makes Us Imitate the Example of Jesus Christ and of the Holy Trinity and Practice Humility

139. *The second motive, which shows us how just it is in itself, and how advantageous to Christians, to consecrate themselves entirely to the Blessed Virgin by this practice, in order to belong more perfectly to Jesus Christ.*

This good Master did not disdain to shut Himself up in the womb of the Blessed Virgin, as a captive and as a loving slave, and later to be subject and obedient to her for thirty years. It is here, I repeat, that the human mind loses itself, when it seriously reflects on the conduct of the Incarnate Wisdom who willed to give Himself to men—not directly, though He might have done so, but through the Blessed Virgin. He did not will to come into the world at the age of a perfect man, independent of others, but like a poor little babe, dependent on the care and support of this holy Mother. He is that Infinite Wisdom who had a boundless desire to glorify God His Father and to save men; and yet He found no more perfect means, no shorter way to do it, than to submit Himself in all things to the Blessed Virgin, not only during the first eight, ten or fifteen years of His life, like other children, but for thirty years! He gave more glory to God His Father during all that time of submission to and dependence on our Blessed Lady than He would have given Him if He had employed those thirty years in working miracles, in preaching to the whole world and in converting all men—all of which He would have done, could He have thereby contributed more to God's glory. Oh, how highly we glorify God when, after the example of Jesus, we submit ourselves to Mary!

Having, then, before our eyes an example so plain and so well known to the whole world, are we so senseless as to imagine that we can find a more perfect or a shorter means of glorifying God than that of submitting ourselves to Mary, after the example of her Son?

140. Let us recall here, as a proof of the dependence we ought to have on our Blessed Lady, what I have said above[2] in bringing forward

the example which the Father, the Son and the Holy Ghost give of this dependence. The Father has not given, and does not give, His Son, except by her; He has no children but by her, and communicates no graces but through her. The Son has not been formed for the whole world in general, except by her; and He is not daily formed and engendered except by her, in union with the Holy Ghost; neither does He communicate His merits and His virtues except through her. The Holy Ghost has not formed Jesus Christ except by her; neither does He form the members of Our Lord's Mystical Body, except by her; and through her alone does He dispense His favors and His gifts. After so many and such pressing examples of the Most Holy Trinity, can we without extreme blindness dispense with Mary, can we fail to consecrate ourselves to her and depend on her for the purpose of going to God and sacrificing ourselves to God?

141. Here are some passages of the Fathers which I have chosen to prove what has just been said:

"Mary has two sons, a God-Man and a pure man; she is Mother of the first corporally, of the second spiritually."[3]

"This is the will of God, who wished us to have all things through Mary; if, therefore, there is in us any hope, any grace, any salutary gift, we know it comes to us through her."[4]

"All the gifts, virtues and graces of the Holy Ghost are distributed by Mary, to whom she wishes, when she wishes, the way she wishes and as much as she wishes."[5]

"Since you were unworthy to receive the divine graces, they were given to Mary, so that whatever you would have, you would receive through her."[6]

142. God, says St. Bernard, seeing that we are unworthy to receive His graces immediately from His own hand, gives them to Mary, in order that we may have through her whatever He wills to give us; and He also finds His glory in receiving, through the hands of Mary, the gratitude, respect and love which we owe Him for His benefits. It is most just, then, that we imitate this conduct of God, in order, as the

same St. Bernard says,[7] that grace return to its Author by the same channel through which it came: "That grace should return to the Giver by the same channel through which it came."

This is precisely what our devotion does. We offer and consecrate all we are and all we have to the Blessed Virgin in order that Our Lord may receive through her mediation the glory and the gratitude which we owe Him. We acknowledge ourselves unworthy and unfit to approach His Infinite Majesty by ourselves; and it is on this account that we avail ourselves of the intercession of the most holy Virgin.

143. Moreover, this devotion is a practice of great humility, which God loves above all the other virtues. A soul which exalts itself abases God; a soul which abases itself exalts God. God resists the proud and gives His grace to the humble.[8] If you abase yourself, thinking yourself unworthy to appear before Him and to draw nigh to Him, He descends and lowers Himself to come to you, to take pleasure in you and to exalt you in spite of yourself. On the contrary, when you are bold enough to approach God without a mediator, God flies from you and you cannot reach Him. Oh, how He loves humility of heart! It is to this humility that this devotion induces us, because it teaches us never to draw nigh, of ourselves, to Our Lord, however sweet and merciful He may be, but always to avail ourselves of the intercession of our Blessed Lady, whether it be to appear before God, or to speak to Him, or to draw near to Him, or to offer Him anything, or to unite and consecrate ourselves to Him.

—THIRD MOTIVE—

It Obtains for Us the Good Offices of the Blessed Virgin

I. Mary Gives Herself to Her Slave of Love

144. The most holy Virgin, who is a Mother of sweetness and mercy, and who never lets herself be outdone in love and liberality, seeing that we give ourselves entirely to her, to honor and to serve her, and for

that end strip ourselves of all that is dearest to us, in order to adorn her, meets us in the same spirit. She also gives her whole self, and gives it in an unspeakable manner, to him who gives all to her. She causes him to be engulfed in the abyss of her graces. She adorns him with her merits; she supports him with her power; she illuminates him with her light; she inflames him with her love; she communicates to him her virtues: her humility, her faith, her purity and the rest. She makes herself his bail, his supplement, and his dear all toward Jesus. In a word, as that consecrated person is all Mary's, so Mary is all his, after such a fashion that we can say of that perfect servant and child[9] of Mary what St. John the Evangelist said of himself, that he took the holy Virgin for his own: "The disciple took her for his own." (*Jn.* 19:27).

145. It is this which produces in the soul, if it is faithful, a great distrust, contempt and hatred of self, and a great confidence in and self-abandonment to the Blessed Virgin, its good Mistress. A man no longer, as before, relies on his own dispositions, intentions, merits, virtues and good works; because, having made an entire sacrifice of them to Jesus Christ by that good Mother, he has but one treasure now, where all his goods are laid up, and that is no longer in himself, for his treasure is Mary.

This is what makes him approach Our Lord without servile or scrupulous fear, and pray to Him with great confidence. This is what makes him share the sentiments of the devout and learned Abbot Rupert, who, alluding to the victory that Jacob gained over the angel (*Gen.* 32:24), said to our Blessed Lady these beautiful words: "O Mary, my Princess, Immaculate Mother of the God-Man, Jesus Christ, I desire to wrestle with that Man, namely, the Divine Word, not armed with my own merits but with yours."[10]

Oh, how strong and mighty we are with Jesus Christ when we are armed with the merits and intercession of the worthy Mother of God, who, as St. Augustine says, has lovingly vanquished the Most High.

II. Mary Purifies Our Good Works, Embellishes Them and Makes Them Acceptable to Her Son

146. As by this practice we give to Our Lord, by His Mother's hands, all our good works, that good Mother purifies them, embellishes them and makes them acceptable to her Son.

§ 1. She purifies them of all the stain of self-love, and of that imperceptible attachment to created things which slips unnoticed into our best actions. As soon as they are in her most pure and fruitful hands, those same hands, which have never been sullied or idle and which purify whatever they touch, take away from the present which we give her all that was spoiled or imperfect about it.

147. § 2. She embellishes our works, adorning them with her own merits and virtues. It is as if a peasant, wishing to gain the friendship and benevolence of the king, went to the queen and presented her with a fruit which was his whole revenue, in order that she might present it to the king. The queen, having accepted the poor little offering from the peasant, would place the fruit on a large and beautiful dish of gold, and so, on the peasant's behalf, would present it to the king. Then the fruit, however unworthy in itself to be a king's present, would become worthy of his majesty because of the dish of gold on which it rested and the person who presented it.

148. § 3. She presents these good works to Jesus Christ; for she keeps nothing of what is given her for herself, as if she were our last end. She faithfully passes it all on to Jesus. If we give to her, we give necessarily to Jesus. If we praise her or glorify her, she immediately praises and glorifies Jesus. As of old when St. Elizabeth praised her, so now when we praise her and bless her, she sings: "My soul doth magnify the Lord." (*Lk.* 1:46).

149. She persuades Jesus to accept these good works, however little and poor the present may be for that Saint of Saints and that King of Kings. When we present anything to Jesus by ourselves, and relying on our own efforts and dispositions, Jesus examines the offering, and

often rejects it because of the stains it has contracted through self-love, just as of old He rejected the sacrifices of the Jews when they were full of their own will. But when we present Him anything by the pure and virginal hands of His well-beloved, we take Him by His weak side, if it is allowable to use such a term. He does not consider so much the thing that is given Him as the Mother who presents it. He does not consider so much whence the offering comes, as by whom it comes. Thus Mary, who is never repelled but always well received by her Son, makes everything she presents to Him, great or small, acceptable to His Majesty. Mary has but to present it for Jesus to accept it and be pleased with it. St. Bernard used to give to those whom he conducted to perfection this great counsel: "When you want to offer anything to God, take care to offer it by the most agreeable and worthy hands of Mary, unless you wish to have it rejected."[11]

150. Is not this what nature itself suggests to the little with regard to the great, as we have already seen?[12] Why should not grace lead us to do the same thing with regard to God, who is infinitely exalted above us and before whom we are less than atoms—especially since we have an advocate so powerful that she is never refused; so ingenious that she knows all the secret ways of winning the heart of God; and so good and charitable that she repels no one, however little and wretched he may be.

I shall speak further on[13] of the true figure of these truths in the story of Jacob and Rebecca.

—Fourth Motive—

It Is an Excellent Means of Procuring God's Greater Glory

151. This devotion, faithfully practiced, is an excellent means of making sure that the value of all our good works shall be employed for the greater glory of God. Scarcely anyone acts for that noble end, although we are all under an obligation to do so. Either we do not know

where the greater glory of God is to be found, or we do not wish to find it. But our Blessed Lady, to whom we cede the value and merit of our good works, knows most perfectly where the greater glory of God is to be found; and inasmuch as she never does anything except for the greater glory of God, a perfect servant of that good Mistress, who is wholly consecrated to her, may say with the hardiest assurance that the value of all his actions, thoughts and words is employed for the greater glory of God, unless he purposely revokes his offering. Is there any consolation equal to this for a soul who loves God with a pure and disinterested love, and who prizes the glory and interest of God far beyond his own?

—Fifth Motive—
It Leads Us to Union with Our Lord

152. This devotion is an *easy*, *short*, *perfect* and *secure* way of attaining union with Our Lord, in which union the perfection of a Christian consists.

I. It Is an Easy Way

It is an easy way. It is the way which Jesus Christ Himself trod in coming to us, and in which there is no obstacle in reaching Him. It is true that we can attain divine union by other roads; but it is by many more crosses and strange deaths, and with many more difficulties, which we shall find it hard to overcome. We must pass through obscure nights, through combats, through strange agonies, over craggy mountains, through cruel thorns and over frightful deserts. But by the path of Mary we pass more gently and more tranquilly.

We do find, it is true, great battles to fight, and great hardships to master; but that good Mother makes herself so present and so near to her faithful servants, to enlighten them in their darknesses and their doubts, to strengthen them in their fears, and to sustain them in their struggles and their difficulties, that in truth this virginal path to find Jesus Christ is a path of roses and honey compared with the other paths. There have been some Saints, but they have been in small numbers, who have walked upon this sweet path to go to Jesus, because the Holy Ghost, faithful Spouse of Mary, by a singular grace disclosed it to them. Such were St. Ephrem, St. John Damascene, St. Bernard, St. Bernardine, St. Bonaventure, St. Francis de Sales, and others. But the rest of the saints, who are the greater number, although they have all had devotion to our Blessed Lady, nevertheless have either not at all, or at least very little, entered upon this way. That is why they have had to pass through ruder and more dangerous trials.

153. How is it, then, some of the faithful servants of Mary will say to me, that the faithful servants of this good Mother have so many occasions of suffering, nay, even more than others who are not so devout to her? They are contradicted, they are persecuted, they are calumniated, the world cannot endure them;[14] or again, they walk in interior darkness and in deserts where there is not the least drop of the dew of Heaven. If this devotion to our Blessed Lady makes the road to Jesus easier, how is it that they who follow it are the most despised of men?

154. I reply that it is quite true that the most faithful servants of the Blessed Virgin, being also her greatest favorites, receive from her the greatest graces and favors of Heaven, which are crosses. But I maintain that it is also the servants of Mary who carry these crosses with more ease, more merit and more glory. That which would stay the progress of another a thousand times over, or perhaps would make him fall, does not once stop their steps, but rather enables them to advance; because that good Mother, all full of grace and of the unction of the Holy Ghost, prepares her servants' crosses with so much maternal sweetness and pure love as to make them gladly acceptable, no matter how bitter they may be in themselves; and I believe that a person who wishes to be devout, and to live piously in Jesus Christ, and consequently to suffer persecutions and carry his cross daily, either will never carry

great crosses, or will not carry them joyously or perseveringly, without a tender devotion to Our Lady, which is the sweetmeat and confection of crosses; just as a person would not be able to eat unripe fruits without a great effort which he could hardly keep up, unless they had been preserved in sugar.

II. It Is a Short Way

155. This devotion to our Blessed Lady is a short road[15] to find Jesus Christ, both because it is a road from which we do not stray, and because, as I have just said, it is a road we tread with joy and facility, and consequently with promptitude. We make more progress in a brief period of submission to and dependence on Mary than in whole years of following our own will and of relying upon ourselves. A man obedient and submissive to Mary shall sing the signal victories which he shall gain over his enemies. (*Prov.* 21:28). They will try to hinder his advancing, or to make him retrace his steps or fall; this is true. But with the support, the aid and the guidance of Mary, he shall advance with giant strides toward Jesus, without falling, without drawing back one step, without even slackening his pace, along the same path by which he knows (*Ps.* 18:6) that Jesus also came to us with giant strides and in the briefest space of time.

156. Why do you think that Jesus lived so few years on earth, and of those few years, spent nearly all of them in subjection and obedience to His Mother? The truth is that, being perfected in a short time (*Wis.* 4:13), He lived a long time—longer than Adam, whose fall He had come to repair, although the patriarch lived above nine hundred years. Jesus Christ lived a long time because He lived in complete subjection to His holy Mother, and closely united with her, in order that He might thus obey His Father. For (1) the Holy Ghost says that a man who honors his mother is like a man who layeth up a treasure; that is to say, he who honors Mary, his Mother, to the extent of subjecting himself to her and obeying her in all things, will soon become exceed-

ingly rich, because he is every day amassing treasures by the secret of that touchstone: "He who honors his mother is as one who lays up a treasure" (*Ecclus*. 3:5); (2) because, according to a mystical interpretation of the inspired text, "My old age is to be found in the mercy of the bosom" (*Ps.* 91:11), it is in the bosom of Mary, which has surrounded and engendered a perfect man (*Jer*. 31:22), and has had the capacity of containing Him whom the whole universe could neither contain nor comprehend[16]—it is, I say, in the bosom of Mary that they who are youthful become elders in light, in holiness, in experience and in wisdom, and that we arrive in a few years at the fullness of the age of Jesus Christ.

III. It Is a Perfect Way

157. This practice of devotion to our Blessed Lady is also a perfect path by which to go and unite ourselves to Jesus; because the divine Mary is the most perfect and the most holy of creatures, and because Jesus, who has come to us most perfectly, took no other road for His great and admirable journey. The Most High, the Incomprehensible, the Inaccessible, He Who is, has willed to come to us, little worms of earth who are nothing. How has He done this? The Most High has come down to us perfectly and divinely, by the humble Mary, without losing anything of His divinity and sanctity. So it is by Mary that the very little ones are to ascend perfectly and divinely, without any fear, to the Most High. The Incomprehensible has allowed Himself to be comprehended and perfectly contained by the little Mary, without losing anything of His immensity. So also it is by the little Mary that we must let ourselves be contained and guided perfectly without any reserve. The Inaccessible has drawn near to us and has united Himself closely, perfectly and even personally to our humanity, by Mary, without losing anything of His majesty. So also it is by Mary that we must draw near to God and unite ourselves perfectly and closely to His Majesty without fear of being repulsed. In a word, He who is has willed to come

to that which is not, and to make that which is not, become He who is; and He has done this perfectly in giving Himself and subjecting Himself entirely to the young Virgin Mary, without ceasing to be in time He who is from all eternity. In like manner, it is by Mary that we, who are nothing, can become like to God by grace and glory, by giving ourselves to her so perfectly and entirely as to be nothing in ourselves, but everything in her, without fear of delusion.

158. Make for me, if you will, a new road to go to Jesus, and pave it with all the merits of the blessed, adorn it with all their heroic virtues, illuminate and embellish it with all the lights and beauties of the angels, and let all the angels and saints be there themselves, to escort, defend and sustain those who are ready to walk there; and yet in truth, in simple truth, I say boldly, and I repeat that I say truly, I would prefer to this new, perfect path the immaculate way of Mary. "He made my way blameless." (Ps. 17:33). It is the way without stain or spot, without original or actual sin, without shadow or darkness. When my sweet Jesus comes a second time on earth in His glory, as it is most certain He will do, to reign there, He will choose no other way for His journey than the divine Mary, by whom He came the first time so surely and so perfectly. But there will be a difference between His first and His last coming. The first time He came secretly and hiddenly; the second time He will come gloriously and resplendently. But both times He will have come perfectly, because both times He will have come by Mary. Alas! Here is a mystery which is not understood. "Here let all tongues be mute."

IV. It Is a Secure Way

159. This devotion to our Blessed Lady is also a secure way to go to Jesus and to acquire perfection by uniting ourselves to Him.

§ 1. It is a secure way, because the practice which I am teaching is not new. Father Boudon,[17] who died a short time ago in the odor of sanctity, says in a book which he composed on this devotion that it is so ancient that we cannot fix precisely the date of its beginning. It is, however, certain that for more than seven hundred years we find traces of it in the Church.[18]

St. Odilon, the Abbot of Cluny, who lived about the year 1040, was one of the first who publicly practiced it in France, as is told in his life.

Peter Cardinal Damian[19] relates that in the year 1016 Blessed Marino, his brother, made himself a slave of the Blessed Virgin in the presence of his director in a most edifying manner. He put a rope around his neck, took the discipline, and laid on the altar a sum of money, as a token of his devotedness and consecration to Our Lady; and he continued this devotion so faithfully during his whole life that he deserved to be visited and consoled at his death by his good Mistress, and to receive from her mouth the promise of paradise in recompense for his services.[20]

Caesarius Bollandus[21] mentions an illustrious knight, Vautier de Birbac, a near relative of the Duke of Louvain, who about the year 1300 consecrated himself to the Blessed Virgin.[22]

This devotion was also practiced by several private individuals up to the seventeenth century, when it became public.

160. Father Simon de Roias, of the Order of the Most Holy Trinity, known as the Order of Redemption of Captives, and preacher of Philip III, made this devotion popular in Spain[23] and Germany;[24] and at the request of Philip III, obtained of Gregory XV ample indulgences for those who practiced it.

Father de Los Rios, the Augustinian, devoted himself, with his intimate friend, Father de Roias, to spreading this devotion throughout Spain and Germany both by preaching and by writing.[25] He composed a thick volume called *Hierarchia Mariana*,[26] in which he treats with as much piety as learning of the antiquity, excellence and solidity of this devotion.[27]

161. In the seventeenth century the Theatine Fathers established this devotion in Italy, Sicily and Savoy.

Father Stanislaus Phalacius, the Jesuit, furthered this devotion wonderfully in Poland.[28]

Father de Los Rios, in his work just cited, quotes the names of princes, princesses, bishops and cardinals of different kingdoms, who embraced this devotion.

Cornelius à Lapide, as praiseworthy for his piety as for his profound erudition, having been commissioned by several bishops and theologians to examine this devotion, did so with great thoroughness and deliberation, and praised it in a manner which we might have expected from his well-known piety; and many other distinguished persons have followed his example.

The Jesuit Fathers, always zealous in the service of our Blessed Lady, in the name of the Sodalists of Cologne presented a little treatise[29] on this devotion to Duke Ferdinand of Bavaria, who was then Archbishop of Cologne. He approved it, granted permission for its printing, and exhorted all the parish priests and religious of his diocese to promote this solid devotion as much as they could.

162. Cardinal de Berulle, whose memory is held in veneration throughout all France, was one of the most zealous in spreading this devotion in that country, in spite of all the calumnies and persecutions which he suffered from critics and freethinkers. They accused him of novelty and superstition. They wrote and published a libel against him, in order to defame him; and they, or rather the devil by their ministry, made use of a thousand artifices to hinder his spreading the devotion in France. But that great and holy man only answered their calumnies by his patience; and he met the objections contained in their libel by a short treatise in which he most convincingly refuted them. He showed them that the devotion was founded on the example of Jesus Christ, on the obligations which we have toward Him, and on the vows which we have made in holy Baptism. It was chiefly by means of this last reason that he shut his adversaries' mouths, making them see that this consecration to the holy Virgin, and to Jesus Christ by her hands, is nothing else than a perfect renewal of the vows and promises of Baptism. He

has said many beautiful things about this practice, which can be read in his works.

163. We may also see in Father Boudon's book[30] the different Popes who have approved this devotion, the theologians who have examined it, the persecutions it has undergone and has overcome, and the thousands of persons who have embraced it, without any Pope ever having condemned it. Indeed, we cannot see how it could be condemned without overturning the foundations of Christianity.

It is clear, then, that this devotion is not new; and that if it is not common, that is because it is too precious to be relished and practiced by everyone.[31]

164. § 2. This devotion is a secure means of going to Jesus Christ, because it is the very characteristic of our Blessed Lady to conduct us surely to Jesus, just as it is the very characteristic of Jesus to conduct us surely to the Eternal Father. Spiritual persons, therefore, must not fall into the false belief that Mary can be a hindrance to them in attaining divine union; for is it possible that she who has found grace before God for the whole world in general and for each one in particular, should be a hindrance to a soul in finding the great grace of union with Him? Can it be possible that she who has been full and superabounding with graces, so united and transformed into God that it has been a kind of necessity that He should be incarnate in her, should be a stumbling-block in the way of a soul's perfect union with God?

It is quite true that the view of other creatures, however holy, may perhaps at certain times retard divine union. But this cannot be said of Mary, as I have remarked before and shall never weary of repeating. One reason why so few souls come to the fullness of the age of Jesus Christ is that Mary, who is as much as ever the Mother of the Son, and as much as ever the fruitful spouse of the Holy Ghost, is not sufficiently formed in their hearts. He who wishes to have the fruit well ripened and well formed must have the tree that produces it; he who wishes to have the fruit of life, Jesus Christ, must have the tree of life, which is Mary; he who wishes to have in himself the operation of the Holy

Ghost must have His faithful and inseparable spouse, the divine Mary, who makes Him fertile and fruitbearing, as we have said elsewhere.[32]

165. Be persuaded, then, that the more you look at Mary in your prayers, contemplations, actions and sufferings, if not with a distinct and definite view, at least with a general and imperceptible one, the more perfectly will you find Jesus Christ, who is always, with Mary, great, powerful, active and incomprehensible—more than in Heaven or in any other creature. Thus, so far from the divine Mary, all absorbed in God, being an obstacle to the perfect in attaining union with God, there has never been up to this time, and there never will be, any creature who will aid us more efficaciously in this great work; either by the graces she will communicate to us for this purpose—for, as a saint has said, "No one can be filled with the thought of God except by her"[33]—or by the protection she will afford us against the illusions and trickeries of the evil spirit.

166. Where Mary is, there the evil spirit is not. One of the most infallible marks we can have of our being conducted by the good spirit is our being very devout to Mary, thinking often of her and speaking often of her. This last is the thought of a saint,[34] who adds that as respiration is a certain sign the body is not dead, the frequent thought and loving invocation of Mary is a certain sign the soul is not dead by sin.

167. As it is Mary alone, says the Church (and the Holy Ghost who guides the Church), who makes all heresies come to naught—"Thou alone hast destroyed all heresies in the whole world"[35]—we may be sure that, however critics may grumble, no faithful client of Mary will ever fall into heresy or illusions, at least formal ones. He may very well err materially, take falsehood for truth, and the evil spirit for the good; and yet he will do even this less readily than others. But sooner or later he will acknowledge his material fault and error; and when he knows it, he will not be in any way self-opinionated by continuing to believe and maintain what he had once thought true.

168. Whoever, then, wishes to put aside the fear of illusion, which is the besetting timidity of men of prayer, and to advance in the way

of perfection and surely and perfectly find Jesus Christ, let him embrace with great-heartedness— "with a great heart and willing mind" (*2 Mach.* 1:3)—this devotion to our Blessed Lady which perhaps he has not known before; let him enter into this excellent way which was unknown to him and which I now point out: "I show you a more excellent way." (*1 Cor.* 12:31). It is a path trodden by Jesus Christ, the Incarnate Wisdom, our sole Head. One of His members cannot make a mistake in passing by the same road.

It is an easy road, because of the fullness of the grace and unction of the Holy Ghost which fills it to overflowing. No one wearies there; no one walking there ever has to retrace his steps. It is a short road which leads us to Jesus in a little time. It is a perfect road, where there is no mud, no dust, not the least spot of sin. Lastly, it is a secure road, which conducts us to Jesus Christ and life eternal in a straight and secure manner, without turning to the right hand or to the left. Let us, then, set forth upon that road and walk there day and night, until we come to the fullness of the age of Jesus Christ. (*Eph.* 4:13).

—SIXTH MOTIVE—
It Gives Us Great Interior Liberty

169. This practice of devotion gives to those who make use of it faithfully a great interior liberty, which is the liberty of the children of God. (*Rom.* 8:21). Since, by this devotion, we make ourselves slaves of Jesus Christ and consecrate ourselves entirely to Him in this capacity, our good Master, in recompense for the loving captivity in which we put ourselves, (1) takes from the soul all scruple and servile fear, which are capable only of cramping, imprisoning or confusing it; (2) He enlarges the heart with firm confidence in God, making it look upon Him as a Father; and (3) He inspires us with a tender and filial love.

170. Without stopping to prove these truths with arguments, I shall be content to relate here what I have read in the life of Mother Agnes

of Jesus, a Dominican nun of the convent of Langeac, in Auvergne, who died there in the odor of sanctity in the year 1634. When she was only seven years old, and was suffering from great spiritual anguish, she heard a voice which told her that if she wished to be delivered from her anguish, and to be protected against all her enemies, she was as quickly as possible to make herself the slave of Jesus and His most holy Mother. She had no sooner returned to the house than she gave herself up entirely to Jesus and His Mother in this capacity, although up to that time she did not so much as know what the devotion meant. Taking an iron chain, she put it around her body and wore it until her death. After this, all her anguish and scruples ceased, and she experienced great peace and dilation of heart. This is what brought her to teach the devotion to many persons who made great progress in it—among others, Father Olier, the founder of St. Sulpice, as well as many priests and ecclesiastics of the same seminary. One day Our Lady appeared to her and put around her neck a chain of gold, to show her the joy she had at Mother Agnes' having made herself her Son's slave and her own; and St. Cecilia, who accompanied Our Lady in that apparition, said to the religious: "Happy are the faithful slaves of the Queen of Heaven: for they shall enjoy true liberty."

"To serve thee is liberty."

—Seventh Motive—
It Procures Great Blessings for Our Neighbor

171. Another consideration which may bring us to embrace this practice is the great good which our neighbor receives from it. For by this practice we exercise charity toward him in an eminent manner, seeing that we give him by Mary's hands all that is most precious to ourselves—namely, the satisfactory and impetratory value of all our good works, without excepting the least good thought or the least little suffering. We agree that all the satisfactions we may have acquired, or

may acquire up to the moment of our death, should be employed at Our Lady's will either for the conversion of sinners or for the deliverance of souls from Purgatory.

Is this not loving our neighbor perfectly? Is this not being a true disciple of Jesus Christ, who is always to be recognized by his charity? (*Jn.* 13:35). Is this not the way to convert sinners, without any fear of vanity; and to deliver souls from Purgatory, with scarcely doing anything but what we are obliged to do by our state of life?

172. To understand the excellence of this motive, we must understand also how great a good it is to convert a sinner or to deliver a soul from Purgatory. It is an infinite good, greater than creating Heaven and earth;[36] because we give to a soul the possession of God. If by this practice we deliver but one soul in our life from Purgatory, or convert but one sinner, would not that be enough to induce a truly charitable man to embrace it?

But we must remark that, inasmuch as our good works pass through the hands of Mary, they receive an augmentation of purity, and consequently of merit, and of satisfactory and impetratory value. On this account they become more capable of solacing the souls in Purgatory and of converting sinners than if they did not pass through the virginal and liberal hands of Mary. It may be little that we give by Our Lady; but, in truth, if it is given without self-will and with a disinterested charity, that little becomes very mighty to turn away the wrath of God and to draw down His mercy. It would be no wonder if, at the hour of death, it should be found that a person faithful to this practice should by means of it have delivered many souls from Purgatory and converted many sinners, though he should have done nothing more than the ordinary actions of his state of life. What joy at his judgment! What glory in his eternity!

—Eighth Motive—
It Is an Admirable Means of Perseverance

173. Lastly, that which in some sense most persuasively draws us to this devotion to Our Lady is that it is an admirable means of persevering and being faithful in virtue. Whence comes it that the majority of the conversions of sinners are not durable? Whence comes it that we relapse so easily into sin? Whence comes it that the greater part of the just, instead of advancing from virtue to virtue and acquiring new graces, often lose the little virtue and the little grace they have? This misfortune comes, as I have shown before,[37] from the fact that man is so corrupt, so feeble and so inconstant, and yet trusts in himself, relies on his own strength and believes himself capable of safeguarding the treasure of his graces, virtues and merits.

But by this devotion, we entrust all that we possess to the Blessed Virgin, who is faithful; we take her for the universal depositary of all our goods of nature and of grace. It is in her fidelity that we trust; it is on her power that we lean; it is on her mercy and charity that we build, in order that she may preserve and augment our virtues and merits, in spite of the devil, the world and the flesh, who put forth all their efforts to take them from us. We say to her as a good child to his mother, and a faithful servant to her mistress: "Keep that which is committed to your trust. (*1 Tim.* 6:20). My good Mother and Mistress, I acknowledge that up to this time I have, through your intercession, received more graces from God than I deserve; and my sad experience teaches me that I carry this treasure in a very frail vessel, and that I am too weak and too miserable to keep it safely of myself: 'I am very young and despised' (*Ps.* 118:141); I beseech you, therefore, receive in trust all that I possess, and keep it for me by your fidelity and power. If you keep it for me, I shall lose nothing; if you hold me up, I shall not fall; if you protect me, I shall be sheltered from my enemies."

174. Listen to what St. Bernard says in order to encourage us to adopt this practice: "When Mary holds you up, you do not fall; when

she protects you, you need not fear; when she leads you, you do not tire; when she is favorable to you, you arrive at the harbor of safety."[38] St. Bonaventure seems to say the same thing still more clearly. "The Blessed Virgin," he says, "is not only retained in the plenitude of the saints, but she also retains and keeps the saints in their plenitude, so that it may not diminish. She prevents their virtues from being dissipated, their merits from perishing, their graces from being lost, the devil from harming them, and even Our Lord from punishing them when they sin."[39]

175. Our Blessed Lady is the faithful Virgin who by her fidelity to God repairs the losses which the faithless Eve has caused by her infidelity. It is she who obtains for those who attach themselves to her the graces of fidelity to God and perseverance. It is for this reason that a saint compares her to a firm anchor which holds her servants fast and hinders them from being shipwrecked in the agitated sea of this world, where so many persons perish simply through not being fastened to that anchor. "We fasten our souls," says he, "to thy hope, as to an abiding anchor."[40] It is to her that the saints who have saved themselves have been the most attached and have done their best to attach others, in order to persevere in virtue. Happy, then, a thousand times happy, are the Christians who are now fastened faithfully and entirely to her, as to a firm anchor! The violence of the storms of this world will not make them founder, nor sink their heavenly treasures! Happy those who enter into Mary, as into the ark of Noe! The waters of the deluge of sin, which drown so great a portion of the world, shall do no harm to them; for "They who work in me shall not sin," says Mary, together with the Divine Wisdom. (*Ecclus.* 24:30). Blessed are the faithless children of the unhappy Eve, if only they attach themselves to the faithful Mother and Virgin who "remains always faithful and never belies herself."[41] "She always loves those who love her" (*Prov.* 8:17)—not only with an affective love, but with an effectual and efficacious one, by hindering them, through a great abundance of graces, from drawing

back in the pursuit of virtue, from falling in the road, and from losing the grace of her Son.

176. This good Mother, out of pure charity, always receives whatever we deposit with her—and what she has once received as depositary, she is obliged in justice, by virtue of the contract of trusteeship, to keep safe for us; just as a person with whom I had left a thousand dollars in trust would be under the obligation of keeping them safe for me, so that if, by his negligence, they were lost, he would in justice be responsible to me for them. But the faithful Mary cannot let anything which has been entrusted to her be lost through her negligence. Heaven and earth could pass away sooner than that she could be negligent and faithless to those who trust in her.

177. Poor children of Mary, your weakness is extreme, your inconstancy is great, your inward nature is very much corrupted. You are drawn (I grant it) from the same corrupt mass as all the children of Adam and Eve. Yet do not be discouraged because of that. Console yourselves and exult in having the secret which I teach you—a secret unknown to almost all Christians, even the most devout.

Leave not your gold and silver in your coffers, which have already been broken open by the evil spirits who have robbed you. These coffers are too little, too weak, too old, to hold a treasure so precious and so great. Put not the pure and clear water of the fountain into your vessels, all spoilt and infected by sin. If the sin is there no longer, at least the odor of it is, and so the water will be spoilt. Put not your exquisite wines into your old casks, which have had bad wine in them; else even these wines will be spoilt and perhaps break the casks, and be spilled on the ground.

178. Though you, predestinate souls, understand me well enough, I will speak yet more openly. Trust not the gold of your charity, the silver of your purity, the waters of your heavenly graces, nor the wines of your merits and virtues, to a torn sack, an old and broken coffer, a spoilt and corrupted vessel, like yourselves, else you will be stripped by the robbers—that is to say, the demons—who are seeking and watching night

and day for the right time to do it; and you will infect by your own bad odor of self-love, self-confidence and self-will, every most pure thing which God has given you.

Pour, pour into the bosom and the heart of Mary all your treasures, all your graces, all your virtues. She is a spiritual vessel, she is a vessel of honor, she is a singular vessel of devotion.[42] Since God Himself has been shut up in person, with all His perfections, in that vessel, it has become altogether spiritual, and the spiritual abode of the most spiritual souls. It has become honorable and the throne of honor for the grandest princes of eternity. It has become wonderful in devotion, and a dwelling the most illustrious for sweetness, for graces and for virtues. It has become rich as a house of gold, strong as a tower of David, and pure as a tower of ivory.

179. Oh, how happy is the man who has given everything to Mary, and has entrusted himself to Mary, and lost himself in her, in everything and for everything! He belongs all to Mary, and Mary belongs all to him. He can say boldly with David: "Mary is made for me" (Cf. *Ps.* 118:56); or with the beloved disciple: "I have taken her for my own" (*Jn.* 19:27); or with Jesus Christ: "All that I have is thine, and all that thou hast is Mine." (*Jn.* 17:10).

180. If any critic who reads this shall take it into his head that I speak here exaggeratedly, and with an extravagance of devotion, alas! He does not understand me—either because he is a carnal man who has no relish for spiritual things; or because he is a worldling who cannot receive the Holy Ghost; or because he is proud and critical, condemning and despising whatever he does not understand himself. But the souls which are not born of blood, nor of flesh, nor of the will of man (*Jn.* 1:13), but of God and Mary, understand me and relish me—and it is for these that I also write.

181. Nevertheless, I say now, both for the former and for the latter, in returning from this digression, that the divine Mary, being the most gracious and liberal of all pure creatures, never lets herself be outdone in love and liberality. As a holy man said of her, for an egg she gives an

ox; that is to say, for a little that is given to her, she gives much of what she has received from God. Hence, if a soul gives itself to her without reserve, she gives herself to that soul without reserve, if only we put our confidence in her without presumption, and on our side labor to acquire virtues and to bridle our passions.

182. Then let the faithful servants of the Blessed Virgin say boldly with St. John Damascene, "Having confidence in you, O Mother of God, I shall be saved; being under your protection, I shall fear nothing; with your help I shall give battle to my enemies and put them to flight; for devotion to you is an arm of salvation which God gives to those whom it is His will to save."

183. Of all the truths which I have been explaining with regard to our Blessed Lady and her children and servants, the Holy Ghost gives us an admirable figure in the Scriptures. (*Gen.* 27). It is in the story of Jacob, who received the blessing of his father Isaac through the skill and pains of his mother Rebecca.

This is the story as the Holy Ghost relates it. I will afterward add the explanation of it.

—ARTICLE ONE—
Rebecca and Jacob

I. The Biblical Narrative

184. Esau having sold Jacob his birthright, Rebecca, the mother of the two brothers, who loved Jacob tenderly, secured this advantage of the birthright for him many years afterward by a stroke of skill most holy but most full of mystery. Isaac, feeling very old, and wishing to bless his children before he died, called his son Esau, who was his favorite, and commanded him to go out hunting and get him something to eat, in order that he might afterward bless him. Rebecca promptly informed Jacob of what had passed, and ordered him to go and take two kids from the flock. When he had given them to his mother, she

prepared for Isaac what she knew he liked. She clothed Jacob in the garments of Esau, which she kept, and covered his hands and his neck with the skin of the kids, so that his father, who was blind, even though he heard Jacob's voice, might think by touching the skin of his hands that it was Esau.

Isaac, having been surprised by the voice, which he thought was Jacob's voice, made him come near. Having touched the skins with which his hands were covered, he said that the voice truly was the voice of Jacob, but that the hands were the hands of Esau.

After he had eaten, and, in kissing Jacob, had smelt the odor of his perfumed garments, he blessed him and wished for him the dew of Heaven and the fruitfulness of earth. He made him lord over all his brethren, and finished his blessing with these words: "Cursed be he that curseth thee, and let him that blesseth thee be filled with blessings."

Isaac had hardly finished these words when Esau entered, bringing with him what he had captured while out hunting in order that his father might eat it, and then bless him. The holy patriarch was surprised with an incredible astonishment when he understood what had happened. But, far from retracting what he had done, on the contrary he confirmed it, for he saw plainly that the finger of God was in the matter. Esau then uttered great cries, as the Holy Scripture says, and loudly accusing the deceitfulness of his brother, he asked his father if he had but one blessing. In this conduct of his, as the holy Fathers remark, Esau was the image of those who are only too glad to ally God with the world and would fain enjoy both the consolations of Heaven and the consolations of earth. At last Isaac, touched with the cries of Esau, blessed him, but with a blessing of the earth, subjecting him to his brother. This made him conceive such an envenomed hatred for Jacob that he waited only for his father's death in order to attempt to kill him. Nor would Jacob have escaped death if his dear mother Rebecca had not saved him from it by her efforts and by the good counsels which she gave him, and which he followed.

II. Interpretation

185. Before explaining this beautiful story, we must observe that, according to the holy Fathers and the interpreters of Scripture, Jacob is the figure of Jesus Christ and the predestinate, and Esau that of the reprobate. We have but to examine the actions and conduct of each to be convinced of this.

1. Esau, figure of the reprobate.

(1) Esau, the elder, was strong and robust of body, adroit and skillful in drawing the bow and in taking much game in the chase. (2) He hardly ever stayed in the house; and putting no confidence in anything but his own strength and address, he worked only out of doors. (3) He took very few pains to please his mother Rebecca, and indeed did nothing for that end. (4) He was such a glutton and loved eating so much that he sold his birthright for a mess of pottage. (5) He was, like Cain, full of envy against his brother, and persecuted him beyond measure.

186. Now this is the daily conduct of the reprobate. They trust in their own strength and aptitude for temporal affairs. They are very strong, very able and very enlightened in earthly business; but very weak and very ignorant in heavenly things.

187. It is on this account that they are never at all, or at least very seldom, at their own homes—that is to say, in their own interior, which is the inward and essential house which God has given to every man, to live there, after His example; for God always dwells in Himself. The reprobate do not love retirement, nor spirituality, nor inward devotion; and they treat as little, or as bigots, or as savages, those who are interior or retired from the world, and who work more within than without.

188. The reprobate care next to nothing for devotion to our Blessed Lady, the Mother of the predestinate. It is true that they do not hate her formally. Indeed they sometimes praise her and say they love her, and even practice some devotion in her honor. Nevertheless, they

cannot bear that we should love her tenderly, because they have not the tenderness of Jacob for her. They find much to say against the practices of devotion her good children and servants faithfully perform in order to gain her affection, because they do not think that devotion necessary to salvation; and they consider that, provided that they do not hate Our Lady formally or openly despise her devotion, they do enough. Moreover, they imagine that they are already in her good graces, and that, in fine, they are her servants, inasmuch as they recite and mumble certain prayers in her honor, without tenderness for her or amendment in themselves.

189. The reprobate sell their birthright, that is to say, the pleasures of paradise. They sell it for a pottage of lentils, that is to say, for the pleasures of the earth. They laugh, they eat, they drink, they amuse themselves, they gamble, they dance, and take no more pains than Esau did to render themselves worthy of the blessing of their Father. In a word, they think only of earth and they love earth only; they speak and act only for earth and for its pleasures, selling for one moment of enjoyment, for one vain puff of honor, for a morsel of hard metal, yellow or white, their Baptismal grace, their robe of innocence and their heavenly inheritance.

190. Finally, the reprobate daily hate and persecute the predestinate, openly and secretly. They feel the predestinate are a burden to them, they despise them, they criticize them, they ridicule them, they abuse them, they rob them, they cheat them, they impoverish them, they drive them away, they bring them low into the dust; while they themselves are making fortunes, are taking their pleasures, getting themselves into good positions, enriching themselves, becoming greater and living at their ease.

2. Jacob, figure of the predestinate.

(a) Conduct of Jacob

191. As to Jacob, the younger son, he was of a feeble constitution, meek and peaceful. He lived for the most part at home, in order to gain the good graces of his mother Rebecca, whom he loved tenderly. If he went abroad, it was not of his own will, nor through any confidence in his own skill, but to obey his mother.

192. He loved and honored his mother. It was on this account that he kept at home. He was never so happy as when watching her. He avoided everything which could displease her, and did everything which he thought would please her; and this increased the love which Rebecca already had for him.

193. He was subject in all things to his dear mother. He obeyed her entirely in all matters—promptly, without delaying, and lovingly, without complaining. At the least indication of her will, the little Jacob ran and worked; and he believed, without questioning, everything she said to him. For example, when she told him to fetch two kids in order that she might prepare something for his father Isaac to eat, Jacob did not reply that one was enough to make a dish for a single man, but did without argument what she told him to do.

194. He had great confidence in his dear mother. As he did not rely in the least on his own ability, he depended exclusively on her care and protection. He appealed to her in all his necessities, and consulted her in all his doubts. For example, when he asked if, instead of a blessing, he should not receive a curse from his father, he believed her and trusted her when she said that she would take the curse upon herself.

195. Lastly, he imitated as far as he could the virtues he saw in his mother. It seems as if one of his reasons for leading such a sedentary life at home was to imitate his dear mother, who was virtuous, and kept away from bad companions who corrupt the morals. By this means he made himself worthy of receiving the double blessing of his beloved father.

(b) Conduct of the Predestinate

196. Such also is the conduct which the predestinate daily observe.

They are sedentary and homekeepers with their Mother. In other words, they love retirement and are interior. They give themselves to prayer; but it is after the example and in the company of their Mother, the holy Virgin, the whole of whose glory is within, and who during her entire life loved retirement and prayer so much. It is true that they sometimes appear without, in the world; but it is in obedience to the will of God and that of their dear Mother, to fulfill the duties of their state. However apparently important their outward works may be, they esteem still more highly those which they do within themselves, in their interior, in the company of the Blessed Virgin. For it is within that they accomplish the great work of their perfection, compared with which all their other works are but child's play. It is on this account that, while sometimes their brothers and sisters are working outwardly with much energy, success and skill, in the praise and with the approbation of the world, they on the contrary know by the light of the Holy Ghost that there is far more glory, more good and more joy in remaining hidden in retreat with Jesus Christ, their Model, in an entire and perfect subjection to their Mother, than to do of themselves wonders of nature and grace in the world, as so many Esaus and reprobates do. "Glory for God and riches for men are to be found in the house of Mary." (Cf. *Ps.* 111:3).

Lord Jesus, how sweet are Thy tabernacles! The sparrow has found a house to lodge in, and the turtledove a nest for her little ones. Oh, happy is the man who dwells in the house of Mary, where Thou wast the first to make Thy dwelling! It is in this house of the predestinate that he receives assistance from Thee alone, and that he has arranged in his heart the steps and ascents of all the virtues by which to raise himself to perfection in this vale of tears. "How lovely are Thy tabernacles." (*Ps.* 83:2).

197. The predestinate tenderly love and truly honor our Blessed Lady as their good Mother and Mistress. They love her not only in word but in truth. They honor her not only outwardly but in the depths of their hearts. They avoid, like Jacob, everything which can displease her; and they practice with fervor whatever they think will make them find favor with her. They bring to her and give her, not two kids, as did Jacob to Rebecca, but their body and their soul, with all that depends on them, symbolized by the two kids of Jacob. They bring them to her: (1) that she may receive them as things which belong to her; (2) that she may kill them, that is, make them die to sin and self, by stripping them of their own skin and their own self-love, so as by this means to please Jesus, her Son, who wills not to have any for His disciples and friends but those who are dead to themselves; (3) that she may prepare them for the taste of our heavenly Father, and for His greatest glory, which she knows better than any other creature; and (4) that by her care and intercession this body and soul, thoroughly purified from every stain, thoroughly dead, thoroughly stripped and prepared, may be a delicate meat, worthy of the mouth and the blessing of our heavenly Father. Is this not what the predestinate do, who by way of testifying to Jesus and Mary an effective and courageous love, relish and practice the perfect consecration to Jesus Christ by the hands of Mary which we are now teaching them?

The reprobate tell us loudly enough that they love Jesus, and that they love and honor Mary; but it is not with their substance (*Prov.* 3:9), it is not to the extent of sacrificing their body with its senses, their soul with its passions, as the predestinate do.

198. The predestinate are subject and obedient to our Blessed Lady as to their good Mother, after the example of Jesus Christ, who, of the three and thirty years He lived on earth, employed thirty to glorify God His Father by a perfect and entire subjection to His holy Mother. They obey Mary in following her counsels exactly as the little Jacob did those of Rebecca, who said to him: "My son, follow my counsels" (*Gen.* 27:8); or like the people at the marriage of Cana, to whom Our Lady

said: "Whatever my Son shall say to you, that do." (*Jn.* 2:5). Jacob, for having obeyed his mother, received the blessing as it were miraculously, although naturally he would not have had it. The people at the marriage of Cana, for having followed Our Lady's counsel, were honored with the first miracle of Our Lord, who there changed the water into wine at the prayer of His holy Mother. In like manner, all those who, to the end of time, shall receive the blessing of our heavenly Father, and shall be honored with the wonders of God, shall only receive their graces as a result of their perfect obedience to Mary. The Esaus, on the contrary, lose their blessing through their want of subjection to the Blessed Virgin.

199. The predestinate have also great confidence in the goodness and power of our Blessed Lady, their good Mother. They call incessantly for her help. They look upon her as their polar star, to lead them to a good port. They lay bare to her their troubles and their necessities with much openness of heart. They depend on her mercy and her gentleness, in order to obtain pardon of their sins through her intercession, or to taste her maternal sweetness in their troubles and weariness. They even throw themselves, hide themselves and lose themselves in an admirable manner in her loving and virginal bosom, that they may be enkindled there with the fire of pure love, that they may be cleansed there from their least stain, and fully find Jesus, who dwells there as on His most glorious throne. Oh, what happiness! "Think not," says Abbot Gueric, "that it is happier to dwell in Abraham's bosom than in Mary's; for it is in this last that Our Lord has placed His throne."[43]

The reprobate, on the contrary, put all their trust in themselves. They only eat, with the prodigal, what the swine eat. They eat earth like the toads, and, like the children of the world, they love only visible and external things. They have no relish for the sweetness of Mary's bosom. They have not that feeling of a certain resting-place and a sure confidence, which the predestinate feel in the holy Virgin, their good Mother. They are miserably attached to their outward hunger, as St.

Gregory says,[44] because they do not wish to taste the sweetness which is prepared within themselves, and within Jesus and Mary.

200. Lastly, the predestinate keep the ways of our Blessed Lady, their good Mother; that is to say, they imitate her. It is on this point that they are truly happy and truly devout, and bear the infallible mark of their predestination, according to the words this good Mother speaks to them: Blessed are they who practice my virtues (*Prov.* 8:32), and with the help of divine grace walk in the footsteps of my life. During life they are happy in this world through the abundance of grace and sweetness which I impart to them from my fullness, and more abundantly to them than to others who do not imitate me so closely. They are happy in their death, which is mild and tranquil, and at which I am ordinarily present myself, that I may conduct them to the joys of eternity; for never has any one of my good servants been lost who imitated my virtues during life.

The reprobate, on the contrary, are unhappy during their life, at their death and for eternity, because they do not imitate Our Lady in her virtues, but content themselves with sometimes being enrolled in her confraternities, reciting some prayers in her honor, or going through some other exterior devotion.

O holy Virgin, my good Mother, how happy are those (I repeat it with the transports of my heart), how happy are those who, not letting themselves be seduced by a false devotion toward you, faithfully keep your ways, your counsels and your orders! But how unhappy and accursed are those who abuse your devotion, and keep not the commandments of your Son: "Cursed are all who fall from Thy commandments!" (*Ps.* 118:21).

—ARTICLE TWO—

The Blessed Virgin and Her Slaves of Love

201. Let us now turn to look at the charitable duties which our Blessed Lady, as the best of all mothers, fulfills for the faithful servants who have given themselves to her after the manner I have described, and according to the figure of Jacob.

I. She Loves Them

She loves them: "I love those who love me." (*Prov.* 8:17). She loves them: (1) because she is their true Mother, and a mother always loves her child, the fruit of her womb; (2) out of gratitude, because they effectively love her as their good Mother; (3) because, as they are predestinate, God loves them: "Jacob I have loved, but Esau I have hated" (*Rom.* 9:13); (4) because they are entirely consecrated to her, and are her portion and her inheritance: "Let thy inheritance be in Israel." (*Ecclus.* 24:13).

202. She loves them tenderly, and more tenderly than all other mothers put together. Throw, if you can, all the natural love which all the mothers of the world have for their children into the heart of one mother for one only child. Surely that mother will love that child immensely. Nevertheless, it is true that Mary loves her children still more tenderly than that mother would love that child of hers.

She loves them not only with affection but with efficacy. Her love for them is active and effective, like that of Rebecca for Jacob, and far beyond it. See what this good Mother, of whom Rebecca was but the type, does to obtain for her children the blessing of our heavenly Father.

203. § 1. She is on the lookout, as Rebecca was, for favorable occasions to do them good, to advance and enrich them. She sees clearly all good and evil, all prosperous and adverse fortunes, the blessings and the cursings of God; and then she so disposes things from afar that she may

exempt her servants from all sorts of evils, and obtain for them all sorts of blessings; so that if there is a good fortune to make by the fidelity of a creature to any high employment, it is certain that Mary will procure that good fortune for some of her true children and servants, and will give them the grace to go through with it faithfully: "She herself takes care of our interests," says a certain saint.

204. § 2. She also gives them good counsels, as Rebecca did to Jacob: "My son, follow my counsels." (*Gen.* 27:8). Among other counsels, she inspires them to bring her the two kids, that is to say, their body and soul, and to consecrate them to her, so that she may make of them a dish agreeable to God; and she inspires them to do everything which Jesus Christ her Son has taught by His words and His examples. If it is not by herself that she gives these counsels, it is by the ministry of the angels, who have no greater honor or pleasure than to descend to earth to obey any of her commands, and to help any of her servants.

205. § 3. When they have brought to her and consecrated to her their body and soul, and all that depends on them, without excepting anything, what does that good Mother do? Just what Rebecca did of old with the two kids Jacob brought her: (1) She kills them, makes them die to the life of the old Adam. (2) She flays and strips them of their natural skin, their natural inclinations, their self-love, their own will and all attachment to creatures. (3) She cleanses them of their spots, their vilenesses and their sins. (4) She dresses them to the taste of God, and for His greatest glory; and as it is Mary alone who knows perfectly what the divine taste is, and what the greatest glory of the Most High is, it is Mary alone who, without making any mistake, can adapt and dress our body and soul for that taste infinitely exalted, and for that glory infinitely hidden.

206. § 4. This good Mother, having received the perfect offering which we make to her of ourselves and our merits and satisfactions, by the devotion I am describing, strips us of our old garments; she cleanses us and so makes us worthy to appear before our heavenly Father. (1) She clothes us in the clean, new, precious and perfumed garments of

Esau the elder—that is, of Jesus Christ her Son—which she keeps in her house, that is, which she has in her own power, inasmuch as she is the treasurer and universal dispenser of the merits and virtues of her Son, which she gives and communicates to whom she wills, when she wills, as she wills, and in such quantity as she wills; as we have seen before.[45] (2) She covers the neck and the hands of her servants with the skins of the kids she has killed; that is to say, she adorns them with the merits and value of their own actions. She kills and mortifies, it is true, all that is impure and imperfect in them, but she neither loses nor dissipates one atom of the good which grace has done there. On the contrary, she preserves and augments it, to make it the ornament and the strength of their neck and their hands; that is to say, to fortify them and help them carry the yoke of the Lord, which is worn upon the neck, and to work great things for the glory of God and the salvation of their poor brethren. (3) She bestows a new perfume and a new grace upon their garments and adornments in communicating to them her own garments, that is, her merits and virtues, which she bequeathed to them by her testament when she died; as said a holy religious of the last century, who died in the odor of sanctity, and learnt this by revelation. Thus all her domestics, faithful servants and slaves, are doubly clad in the garments of her Son and in her own: "All her domestics are clothed in double clothing." (*Prov.* 31:21). It is on this account that they have nothing to fear from the cold of Jesus Christ, who is white as snow—a cold which the reprobate, all naked and stripped of the merits of Jesus and Mary, cannot for one moment bear.

207. § 5. Finally, she enables them to obtain the blessing of our heavenly Father, though being but the youngest born and indeed only adopted children, they have no natural right to have it. With these garments all new, most precious and of most fragrant odor, and with their body and soul well prepared and dressed, they draw near with confidence to the Father's bed of repose. He understands and distinguishes their voice, which is the voice of the sinner; He touches their hands, covered with skins; He smells the good odor of their clothes; He eats

with joy of that which Mary their Mother has dressed for Him. He recognizes in them the merits and the good odor of His Son and of His holy Mother, and so: First, He gives them His double blessing, the blessing of the "dew of Heaven" (*Gen.* 27:28), that is to say, of divine grace, which is the seed of glory: "He hath blessed us with spiritual blessings in Christ" (*Eph.* 1:3); and then the blessing "of the fat of the earth" (*Gen.* 27:28); that is to say, the good Father gives them their daily bread, and a sufficient abundance of the goods of this world. Secondly, He makes them masters of their other brethren, the reprobate. But this primacy is not always apparent in this world, which passes in an instant (*1 Cor.* 7:31), and where the reprobate are often masters. "How long shall sinners glory? Shall they utter and speak iniquity?" (*Ps.* 93:3-4). "I have seen the wicked highly exalted and lifted up." (*Ps.* 36:35). But it is nevertheless a true primacy; and it will appear manifestly in the other world for all eternity, where the just, as the Holy Ghost says, "shall reign over the nations and command them." (*Wis.* 3:8). Thirdly, His Majesty, not content with blessing them in their person and their goods, blesses also those who shall bless them and curses those who shall curse and persecute them.

II. She Fosters and Nurtures Them

208. The second charitable duty which our Blessed Lady fulfills toward her faithful servants is that she furnishes them with everything, both for their body and for their soul. She gives them double clothing, as we have just seen. She gives them to eat of the most exquisite meats of the table of God; for she gives them to eat of the bread of life, which she herself has formed. (*Ecclus.* 24:26). My dear children, she says, under the name of Divine Wisdom, be filled with my generations; that is to say, with Jesus, the fruit of life, whom I have brought into the world for you. (*Prov.* 9:5). Come, she repeats to them in another place, eat my bread, which is Jesus, and drink the wine of His love, which I have mixed for you. (*Cant.* 5:1). As it is Mary who is the treasurer and

dispenser of the gifts and graces of the Most High, she gives a good portion, and indeed the best portion, to nourish and maintain her children and her servants. They are fattened on the Living Bread, they are inebriated with the wine which brings forth virgins. (*Zach.* 9:17). They are borne at the bosom of Mary. (*Is.* 66:12). They have such facility in carrying the yoke of Jesus Christ that they feel almost nothing of its weight; the oil of devotion has made it soften and decay: "And the yoke shall putrefy in the presence of the oil." (*Is.* 10:27).

III. *She Conducts and Directs Them*

209. The third good which Our Lady does for her servants is that she conducts and directs them according to the will of her Divine Son. Rebecca guided her little Jacob, and gave him good advice from time to time; either to draw upon him the blessing of his father, or to avert from him the hatred and persecutions of his brother Esau. Mary, who is the Star of the Sea, leads all her faithful servants into a safe harbor. She shows them the paths of eternal life. She makes them avoid the dangerous places. She conducts them by her hand along the paths of justice. She steadies them when they are about to fall; she lifts them up when they have fallen. She reproves them like a charitable mother when they fail; and sometimes she even lovingly chastises them. Can a child obedient to Mary, his foster-Mother and his enlightened guide, go astray in the paths of eternity? "If you follow her," says St. Bernard, "you cannot wander from the road." Fear not, therefore, that a true child of Mary can be deceived by the evil one, or fall into any formal heresy. There where the guidance of Mary is, neither the evil spirit with his illusions, nor the heretics with their subtleties, can ever come.[46]

IV. *She Defends and Protects Them*

210. The fourth good office which Our Lady renders to her children and faithful servants is to protect and defend them against their

enemies. Rebecca, by her cares and artifices, delivered Jacob from all the dangers in which he found himself, and particularly from the death which his brother Esau would have inflicted on him because of the envy and hatred which he bore him; as Cain did of old to his brother Abel. Mary, the good Mother of the predestinate, hides them under the wings of her protection, as a hen hides her chickens. She speaks, she stoops down to them, she condescends to all their weaknesses. To secure them from the hawk and vulture, she puts herself round about them, and accompanies them "like an army in battle array." (*Cant.* 6:3). Shall a man who has an army of a hundred thousand soldiers around him fear his enemies? A faithful servant of Mary, surrounded by her protection and her imperial power, has still less to fear. This good Mother and powerful Princess of the Heavens would rather dispatch battalions of millions of Angels to assist one of her servants than that it should ever be said that a faithful servant of Mary, who trusted in her, had had to succumb to the malice, the number and the vehemence of his enemies.

V. She Intercedes for Them

211. Lastly, the fifth and greatest good which Mary procures for her faithful clients is to intercede for them with her Son, to appease Him by her prayers, to unite them to Him in a most intimate union, and to keep them unshaken in that union.

Rebecca made Jacob draw near to his father's bed. The good man touched him, embraced him, and even kissed him with joy, being content and satisfied with the well-dressed viands which the boy had brought him; and having smelt with much contentment the exquisite perfume of his garments, he cried out: "Behold the odor of my son, which is like the odor of a full field that the Lord hath blessed." (*Gen.* 27:27). This odor of the full field which charms the heart of the Father is nothing else than the odor of the virtues and merits of Mary, who is a field full of grace where God the Father has sown His only Son, as a grain of the wheat of the elect.

Oh, how welcome to Jesus Christ, the Father of the world to come, is a child perfumed with the good odor of Mary! (*Is.* 9:6). Oh, how promptly and how perfectly is such a child united to his Lord! But we have shown this at length already.

212. Furthermore, after Mary has heaped her favors upon her children and faithful servants, and has obtained for them the blessing of the heavenly Father and union with Jesus Christ, she preserves them in Jesus and Jesus in them. She takes care of them, watches over them always, for fear they should lose the grace of God and fall into the snares of their enemies. "She retains the saints in their fullness,"[47] and makes them persevere to the end, as we have seen.

This is the interpretation of the story of Jacob and Esau, that great and ancient figure of predestination and reprobation, so unknown and so full of mysteries.[48]

NOTES

1. Cf. no. 110.
2. Cf. nos. 14-39.
3. Origen and St. Bonaventure, *Speculum B.V.*, lect. III, § 1, 2.
4. St. Bernard, *De Aquaeductu*, no. 6.
5. St. Bernardine of Siena, *Sermo in Nativ. B.V.*, Art. un., cap. 8.
6. St. Bernard, *Sermo III in Vigilia Nativitatis Domini*, no. 10.
7. *De Aquaeductu*, no. 18.
8. *James* 4:6. Cf. also St. Augustine, *Sermo 2 de Ascensione*, 175.
9. Cf. note on no. 113.
10. Rupert, *Prolog. in Cantic.*
11. St. Bernard, *De Aquaeductu.*
12. Cf. no. 146.
13. Cf. no. 183 and following.
14. St. Bonaventure, *Psalt. Majus B.V. Psalm* 118.
15. "*Tu es via compendiosa in caelo*" (*Laudes gloriosae Virg.*, S.A., VI. 939).
16. Cf. Gradual of the Mass of the Blessed Virgin (Pentecost to Advent), and first Responsory, first Nocturn, of her Office.
17. Father Boudon was Archdeacon of Evreux and author of the book, *Le Saint Esclavage de la Mère de Dieu.*

18. The pious King Dagobert II (seventh century) consecrated himself to the Blessed Virgin as her slave (Kronenburg in *Marias Heerlijkheid*, I, 98), as also did Pope John VII (701-707). Cf. S.A., X, 627.

19. Declared Doctor of the Church by Leo XII in 1828.

20. *S.A.*, X, 1310.

21. Caesarius d'Heisterbach.

22. Cf. *S.A.*, XI, 347.

23. In the year 1611.

24. The Emperor Ferdinand himself made this consecration, together with all his court, in 1640.

25. He established this devotion especially in Belgium, with Louvain, Mechlin and Brussels as principal centers.

26. Published at Anvers in 1641.

27. It was approved by the Bishops of Mechlin, Cambrai and Gand.

28. The King of Poland, Wladislaf IV, was enrolled in it at Louvain, and had the Jesuits preach it throughout his kingdom. (S.A., XI, 124. ss).

29. Entitled *Mancipium Virginis*, or *The Slavery of the Virgin*, Cologne, 1634. Cf. Kronenburg, VII, 316, 317.

30. Cf. no. 159, note 17.

31. "Boudon says in his *Saint Esclavage* that the English Catholics were remarkable for this devotion in the seventeenth century." (F. W. Faber).

32. Cf. nos. 20, 21.

33. St. Germanus of Constantinople, *Sermo secunda in Dormit.* (cit. S.A., VI, 37).

34. Idem, *Oratio in Encaenia venerandae aedis B.V.* (S.A., VI, 51).

35. Office of the Blessed Virgin, first Antiphon of third Nocturn.

36. St. Augustine, *Tract 72 in Joannem*, a medio.

37. Cf. nos. 87-89.

38. *Homilia 2ᵃ super Missus est*, no. 17.

39. *Speculum B.V.*, lect. VII, no. 6.

40. St. John Damascene, *Sermo Iᵃ in Dormitione B.V.*

41. Application to the Blessed Virgin of St. Paul's text, *2 Tim.* 2:13.

42. Litany of the Blessed Virgin.

43. *Sermo Iᵃ in Assumptione*, no. 4.

44. *Homilia 36, in Evangelium*. "Amamus foris miseri famem nostram."

45. Cf. nos. 25 and 141.

46. Words of St. Bernard. Cf. no. 174.

47. Words of St. Bonaventure. Cf. no. 174.

48. The preceding article (nos. 201-212) contains a beautiful exposition of the harmony existing between the childlike way of confidence in God on the one hand, and on the other, the way of filial piety toward the Blessed Virgin Mary such as is required by the holy slavery. No real opposition can be established between these different forms of devotion without danger of misunderstanding the nature of Christian life viewed as a whole. The holy slavery of love is indeed the complete expression of filial love toward our Mother Mary, whose great desire is that we be pleasing to God our Father. God is honored by the confidence we place in the Mother He has given us; trust in Mary is trust in God.

CHAPTER THREE

Wonderful Effects of This Devotion

———— • ————

213. My dear brother, be sure that if you are faithful to the interior and exterior practices of this devotion which I will point out,[1] the following effects will take place in your soul.

—First Effect—
Knowledge and Contempt of Self

By the light which the Holy Ghost will give you through His dear spouse, Mary, you will understand your own evil, your corruption and your incapacity for anything good. In consequence of this knowledge, you will despise yourself. You will think of yourself only with horror. You will regard yourself as a snail that spoils everything with its slime; or a toad that poisons everything with its venom; or as a spiteful serpent seeking only to deceive. In other words, the humble Mary will communicate to you a portion of her profound humility, which will make you despise yourself—despise nobody else, but love to be despised yourself.

—Second Effect—
Participation in Mary's Faith

214. Our Blessed Lady will give you also a portion of her faith, which was the greatest of all faiths that ever were on earth, greater than the faith of all the patriarchs, prophets, apostles and saints put together. Now that she is reigning in Heaven, she no longer exercises this faith, because she sees all things clearly in God by the light of glory. Nevertheless, with the consent of the Most High, in entering into glory she did not lose her faith. She kept it for her faithful servants in the Church Militant. The more, then, that you gain the favor of that august Princess and faithful Virgin, the more will you act by pure faith; a pure faith which will make you care hardly at all about sensible consolations and extraordinary favors; a lively faith animated by charity, which will enable you to perform all your actions from the motive of pure love; a faith firm and immovable as a rock, through which you will rest quiet and constant in the midst of storms and hurricanes; a faith active and piercing, which like a mysterious pass-key, will give you entrance into all the mysteries of Jesus, into the last ends of man, and into the Heart of God Himself; a courageous faith, which will enable you to undertake and carry out without hesitation great things for God and for the salvation of souls; lastly, a faith which will be your blazing torch, your divine life, your hidden treasure of divine wisdom and your omnipotent arm; which you will use to enlighten those who are in the darkness of the shadow of death, to inflame those who are lukewarm and who have need of the heated gold of charity, to give life to those who are dead in sin, to touch and overthrow, by your meek and powerful words, the hearts of marble and the cedars of Lebanon; and finally, to resist the devil and all the enemies of salvation.

— Third Effect—
Deliverance from Scruples, Cares and Fears

215. This Mother of fair love (*Ecclus.* 24:24) will take away from your heart all scruple and all disorder of servile fear. She will open and enlarge it to run the way of her Son's commandments (*Ps.* 118:32) with the holy liberty of the children of God. She will introduce into it pure love, of which she has the treasure,[2] So that you shall no longer be guided by fear, as hitherto, in your dealings with the God of charity, but by love alone. You will look on Him as your good Father, whom you will be incessantly trying to please, and with whom you will converse confidently, as a child with its tender father. If, unfortunately, you offend Him, you will at once humble yourself before Him. You will ask His pardon with great lowliness, but at the same time you will stretch your hand out to Him with simplicity, and you will raise yourself up lovingly, without trouble or disquietude, and go on your way to Him without discouragement.

—Fourth Effect—
Great Confidence in God and Mary

216. Our Blessed Lady will fill you with great confidence in God and in herself: (1) because you will not be approaching Jesus by yourself, but always by that good Mother; (2) because, as you have given her all your merits, graces and satisfactions to dispose of at her will, she will communicate to you her virtues and will clothe you in her merits, so that you will be able to say to God with confidence: "Behold Mary Thy handmaid; be it done unto me according to Thy word" (*Lk.* 1:38); (3) because, as you have given yourself entirely to her, body and soul, she, who is liberal with the liberal, and more liberal even than the liberal, will in return give herself to you in a marvelous but real manner, so that you may say to her with assurance: "I am thine, holy Virgin; save me" (Cf. *Ps.* 118:94); or as I have said before,[3] with the beloved

disciple: "I have taken thee, holy Mother, for my own." You may also say with St. Bonaventure: "My loving and redeeming Mistress, I will have confidence and will not fear, because you are my strength and my praise in the Lord . . . I am altogether yours, and all that I have belongs to you!"[4] And in another place: "O glorious Virgin, blessed above all created things! I will put you as a seal upon my heart, because your love is as strong as death."[5] "Lord, my heart and my eyes have no right to extol themselves, or to be proud, or to seek great and wonderful things. Yet even at that, I am not humble; but I have lifted up and encouraged my soul by confidence; I am like a child, weaned from the pleasures of earth and resting on its mother's lap; and it is on that lap that all good things come to me." (Cf. *Ps.* 130:1-2). What will still further increase your confidence in her is that you will have less confidence in yourself. You have given her in trust all you have of good about you, that she may have it and keep it; and so all the trust you once had in yourself has become an increase of confidence in her, who is your treasure. Oh, what confidence and what consolation is this for a soul who can say that the treasure of God, where He was pleased to put all He had most precious, is his own treasure also! It was a saint who said she is the treasure of the Lord.[6]

—Fifth Effect—
Communication of the Soul and Spirit of Mary

217. The soul of our Blessed Lady will communicate itself to you, to glorify the Lord. Her spirit will enter into the place of yours, to rejoice in God her salvation, provided only that you are faithful to the practices of this devotion. "Let the soul of Mary be in each of us to glorify the Lord: let the spirit of Mary be in each of us to rejoice in God."[7] Ah! When will the happy time come, said a holy man of our own days who was all absorbed in Mary—Ah! When will the happy time come when the divine Mary will be established Mistress and Queen of all hearts, in order that she may subject them fully to the

empire of her great and holy Jesus? When will souls breathe Mary as the body breathes air? When that time comes, wonderful things will happen in those lowly places where the Holy Ghost, finding His dear spouse, as it were, reproduced, in souls, shall come in with abundance, and fill them to overflowing with His gifts, and particularly with the gift of wisdom, to work miracles of grace. My dear brother, when will that happy time, that age of Mary, come, when many souls, chosen and procured from the Most High by Mary, shall lose themselves in the abyss of her interior, shall become living copies of Mary, to love and glorify Jesus? That time will not come until men shall know and practice this devotion which I am teaching. "That Thy reign may come, let the reign of Mary come."

—Sixth Effect—
Transformation of the Faithful Soul
by Mary into the Likeness of Jesus Christ

218. If Mary, who is the tree of life, is well cultivated in our soul by fidelity to the practices of this devotion, she will bear her fruit in her own time, and her fruit is none other than Jesus Christ. How many devout souls do I see who seek Jesus Christ, some by one way or by one practice, and others by other ways and other practices; and oftentimes, after they have toiled much throughout the night, they say, "We have toiled all night, and have taken nothing!" (*Lk.* 5:5). We may say to them: "You have labored much and gained little";[8] Jesus is yet feeble in you. But by that immaculate way of Mary and that divine practice which I am teaching, we toil during the day, we toil in a holy place, we toil but little. There is no night in Mary, because there is no sin nor even the slightest shade. Mary is a holy place, and the holy of holies where saints are formed and molded.

219. Take notice, if you please, that I say the saints are molded in Mary. There is a great difference between making a figure in relief by blows of hammer and chisel, and making a figure by throwing it into a

mold. Statuaries and sculptors labor much to make figures in the first manner; but to make them in the second manner, they work little and do their work quickly.

St. Augustine calls our Blessed Lady "the mold of God"[9]—the mold fit to cast and mold gods. He who is cast in this mold is presently formed and molded in Jesus Christ, and Jesus Christ in him. At a slight expense and in a short time he will become God,* because he has been cast in the same mold which has formed a God.

220. It seems to me that I can very aptly compare directors and devout persons, who wish to form Jesus Christ in themselves or others by practices different from this one, to sculptors who trust in their own professional skill, ingenuity or art, and so give an infinity of hammerings and chiselings to a hard stone or a piece of badly polished wood, to make an image of Jesus Christ out of it. Sometimes they do not succeed in giving anything like the natural expression of Jesus, either from having no knowledge or experience of the Person of Jesus, or from some blow awkwardly given, which has spoiled the work. But those who embrace the secret of grace which I am revealing to them I may rightly compare to founders and casters who have discovered the beautiful mold of Mary, where Jesus was naturally and divinely formed; and without trusting in their own skill, but only in the goodness of the mold, they cast themselves and lose themselves in Mary, to become the faithful portraits of Jesus Christ.

221. Oh, beautiful and true comparison! But who will comprehend it? I desire that you may, my dear brother. But remember that we cast in a mold only what is melted and liquid; that is to say, you must destroy and melt down in yourself the old Adam to become the new one in Mary.

---

* The French text shows this word in lower case, that is, *dieu*, in contrast to the word *Dieu* ("God") at the end of the sentence. This accords with the Catholic teaching that by Sanctifying Grace one receives "a created sharing in the Divine Nature."—*Publisher*, 1999.

—Seventh Effect—
The Greater Glory of God

222. By this practice, faithfully observed, you will give Jesus more glory in a month than by any other practice, however difficult, in many years; and I give the following reasons for it:

§ 1. Because, doing your actions by our Blessed Lady, as this practice teaches you, you abandon your own intentions and operations, although good and known, to lose yourself, so to speak, in the intentions of the Blessed Virgin, although they are unknown. Thus you enter by participation into the sublimity of her intentions, which are so pure that she gives more glory to God by the least of her actions—for example, in twirling her distaff or pointing her needle—than St. Lawrence by his cruel martyrdom on the gridiron, or even all the saints by all their heroic actions put together. It was thus that, during her sojourn here below, she acquired such an unspeakable aggregate of graces and merits that it were easier to count the stars of the firmament, the drops of water in the sea or the grains of sand upon its shore, than her merits and graces. Thus it was that she gave more glory to God than all the angels and saints have given Him or ever will give Him. O prodigy of a Mary! Thou canst not help but do prodigies of grace in souls that wish to lose themselves altogether in thee!

223. § 2. Because the soul in this practice counts as nothing whatever it thinks or does of itself, and puts its trust and takes its pleasures only in the dispositions of Mary, when it approaches Jesus or even speaks to Him. Thus it practices humility far more than the souls who act of themselves and trust, with however imperceptible a complacency, in their own dispositions. But if the soul acts more humbly, it therefore more highly glorifies God, who is perfectly glorified only by the humble and those that are little and lowly in heart.

224. § 3. Because our Blessed Lady, being pleased, out of great charity, to receive the present of our actions in her virginal hands, gives them an admirable beauty and splendor. Moreover, she offers them

herself to Jesus Christ, and it is evident that Our Lord is thus more glorified by them than if we offered them by our own criminal hands. 225. § 4. Lastly, because you never think of Mary without Mary's thinking of God for you. You never praise or honor Mary without Mary's praising and honoring God with you. Mary is altogether relative to God; and indeed, I might well call her the relation to God. She only exists with reference to God. She is the echo of God that says nothing, repeats nothing, but God. If you say "Mary," she says "God." St. Elizabeth praised Mary, and called her blessed, because she had believed. Mary, the faithful echo of God, at once intoned: "My soul doth magnify the Lord." (*Lk.* 1:46).

That which Mary did then, she does daily now. When we praise her, love her, honor her or give anything to her, it is God who is praised, God who is loved, God who is glorified, and it is to God that we give, through Mary and in Mary.

NOTES

1. Cf. no. 226.
2. Cf. no. 169.
3. Cf. no. 179.
4. *Psalterium majus B.M.V.*, Canticum instar Isaiae 12:2.
5. *Psalterium majus B.M.V.*, Canticum instar Ex. 15.
6. *Idiota*; *In contemplatione B.M.V.*
7. St. Ambrose, *Expositio in Luc.*, Lib. 11, no. 26.
8. *Ag.* 1:6. The exact text is: "*Seminastis multum.*"
9. *Sermo 208* (inter opera Sti. Augustini): "You are worthy to be called the mold of God."

CHAPTER FOUR

Particular Practices of This Devotion

———•———

—ARTICLE ONE—
Exterior Practices

226. Although what is essential in this devotion consists in the interior,[1] we must not fail to unite to the inward practice certain external observances. "We must do the one, yet not leave the other undone" (*Matt.* 23:23); because the outward practices, well performed, aid the inward ones; and because they remind man, who is always guided by his senses, of what he has done or ought to do; and also because they are suitable for edifying our neighbor, who sees them; these are things which inward practices cannot do. Let no worldling, then, or critic, intrude here to say that because true devotion is in the heart, we must avoid external devotion; or that devotion ought to be hidden, and that there may be vanity in showing it. I answer, with my Master, that men should see our good works, that they may glorify our Father who is in Heaven (*Matt.* 5:16); not, as St. Gregory says,[2] that we ought to perform our actions and exterior devotions to please men and get praise— that would be vanity; but that we should sometimes do them before men with the view of pleasing God, and glorifying Him thereby, without caring either for the contempt or the praise of men.

I will allude only briefly to some exterior practices, which I call "exterior" not because we do not perform them interiorly, but because they have something outward about them to distinguish them from those which are purely inward.

I. Preparatory Exercises and Consecration

227. Those who wish to enter into this particular devotion, which is not at present erected into a confraternity (though that were to be wished),[3] after having, as I said in the first part of this preparation for the reign of Jesus Christ,[4] employed twelve days at least in ridding themselves of the spirit of the world, which is contrary to the spirit of Jesus Christ, should employ three weeks in filling themselves with Jesus Christ by the holy Virgin. They can follow this order:

228. During the first week they should offer up all their prayers and pious actions to ask for a knowledge of themselves and contrition for their sins; and they should do this in a spirit of humility. For that end they can, if they choose, meditate on what I have said before of our inward corruption.[5] They can look upon themselves during the six days of this week as snails, crawling things, toads, swine, serpents and unclean animals; or they can reflect on these three considerations of St. Bernard: the vileness of our origin, the dishonors of our present state, and our ending as the food of worms. They should pray Our Lord and the Holy Ghost to enlighten them; and for that end they might use the ejaculations, "Lord, that I may see!" (*Lk.* 18:41); or "May I know myself!";[6] or "Come, Holy Ghost," together with the Litany of the Holy Ghost and the prayer which follows, as indicated in the first part of this work. They should have recourse to the Blessed Virgin and ask her to grant them this immense grace, which must be the foundation of all the others; for this end, they should say daily the *Ave Maris Stella* and the Litany of the Blessed Virgin.

229. During the second week they should apply themselves, in all their prayers and works each day, to know the Blessed Virgin. They

should ask this knowledge of the Holy Ghost; they should read and meditate on what we have said about it. For this intention they should recite, as in the first week, the Litany of the Holy Ghost and the *Ave Maris Stella*, and in addition a Rosary daily, or if not a whole Rosary, at least the beads.

230. They should apply themselves during the third week to know Jesus Christ. They can meditate upon what we have said about Him, and say the prayer of St. Augustine which they will find in the beginning of the second part of this treatise. They can, with the same saint, repeat a hundred times a day: "Lord, that I may know Thee!" or: "Lord, that I may see Who Thou art!" They should recite, as in the preceding weeks, the Litany of the Holy Ghost and the *Ave Maris Stella,* and should add daily the Litany of the Holy Name of Jesus.

231. At the end of the three weeks they should go to confession and Communion, with the intention of giving themselves to Jesus Christ in the quality of slaves of love, by the hands of Mary. After Communion, which they should try to make according to the method given further on,[7] they should recite the formula of their consecration, which they will also find further on. They ought to write it, or have it written, unless they have a printed copy of it; and they should sign it the same day on which they have made it.

232. It would be well also that on that day they should pay some tribute to Jesus Christ and our Blessed Lady, either as a penance for their past unfaithfulness to the vows of their Baptism, or as a testimony of their dependence on the dominion of Jesus and Mary. This tribute ought to be according to the devotion and ability of each one, such as a fast, a mortification, an alms or a candle. If they had but a pin to give in homage, and gave it with a good heart, it would be enough for Jesus, who looks only at the good will.

233. Once a year at least, and on the same day, they should renew the same consecration, observing the same practices during the three weeks.

They might also, once a month or even once a day, renew all they have done, in these few words: "I am all Thine and all that I have is Thine, O most loving Jesus, through Mary, Thy most holy Mother."

II. Recitation of the Little Crown of the Blessed Virgin

234. They may recite every day of their life—without, however, making a burden of it—the Little Crown of the Blessed Virgin, composed of three Our Fathers and twelve Hail Marys, in honor of Our Lady's twelve privileges and grandeurs. This is a very ancient practice and it has its foundation in Holy Scripture. St. John saw a woman crowned with twelve stars, clothed with the sun, and with the moon under her feet (*Apoc.* 12:1); and this woman, according to the interpreters, was the most holy Virgin.[8]

235. There are many ways of saying this Crown well, but it would take too long to enter upon them. The Holy Ghost will teach them to those who are the most faithful to this devotion. Nevertheless, to say it quite simply, we should begin by saying: "Grant that I may praise thee, holy Virgin; give me strength against thy enemies." After that, we should say the Apostles' Creed, then an Our Father with four Hail Marys and then one Glory be to the Father; then another Our Father, four Hail Marys, and Glory be to the Father, and so on with the rest; and at the end we should say the *Sub Tuum Praesidium* ("We fly to thy patronage . . .").[9]

III. The Wearing of Little Chains

236. It is a most glorious and praiseworthy thing, and very useful to those who have thus made themselves slaves of Jesus in Mary, that they should wear, as a sign of their loving slavery, little iron chains, blessed with the proper blessing.[10]

It is perfectly true that these external insignia are not essential, and a person who has embraced this devotion may very well go without them; nevertheless, I cannot refrain from warmly praising those who, after having shaken off the shameful chains of the slavery of the devil, in which Original Sin, and perhaps actual sin, had bound them, have voluntarily surrendered themselves to the glorious slavery of Jesus Christ, and glory with St. Paul in being in chains for Christ (*Eph.* 3:1; *Philem.* 9), chains a thousand times more glorious and precious, though of iron, than all the golden ornaments of emperors.

237. Once there was nothing more infamous on earth than the cross, and now that wood is the most glorious boast of Christianity. Let us say the same of the irons of slavery. There was nothing more ignominious among the ancients; there is nothing more shameful even now among the heathens. But among Christians, there is nothing more illustrious than the chains of Jesus; for they unchain us and preserve us from the infamous fetters of sin and the devil. They set us at liberty and chain us to Jesus and Mary; not by compulsion and constraint, like galley-slaves, but by charity and love, like children. "I will draw them to Me," says God by the mouth of the prophet, "by the chains of love." (*Osee* 11:14). These chains are as strong as death (*Cant.* 8:6), and in a certain sense even stronger than death in those who are faithful in carrying these glorious chains to their death. For though death destroys their bodies by bringing them to corruption, it does not destroy the chains of their slavery, which, being of iron, do not corrode so easily. Perhaps, on the day of the resurrection of the body, at the last judgment, these chains shall be around their bones, and shall be a part of their glory, and be transmuted into chains of light and splendor. Happy then, a thousand times happy, the illustrious slaves of Jesus who wear their chains even to the tomb!

238. The following are the reasons for wearing these little chains:

First, to remind the Christian of the vows and promises of his Baptism, of the perfect renewal he has made of them by this devotion, and of the strict obligation under which he is to be faithful to them. As man, who shapes his course more often by the senses than by pure faith, easily forgets his obligations toward God unless he has some outward thing to remind him of them, these little chains serve marvelously to remind the Christian of the chains of sin and the slavery of the devil from which Baptism has delivered him, and of the dependence on Jesus which he has vowed to Him in Baptism, and of the ratification of it which he has made by the renewal of his vows. One of the reasons why so few Christians think of their baptismal vows, and live with as much license as if they had promised no more to God than the heathen, is that they do not wear any external sign to remind them of their vows.

239. Secondly, to show that we are not ashamed of the servitude and slavery of Jesus Christ, and that we renounce the slavery of the world, of sin and of the devil.

Thirdly, to protect ourselves against the chains of sin and of the devil; for we must wear either "the chains of sinners or the chains of charity and salvation."

240. O my dear brother, let us break the chains of sin and sinners, of the world and worldliness, of the devil and his ministers; and let us cast far from us their depressing yoke. (*Ps.* 2:3). Let us put our feet, to use the terms of the Holy Ghost, into His glorious fetters and our necks into His chains. (*Ecclus.* 6:25). Let us shoulder and carry the Divine Wisdom [that is, Jesus Christ] and let us never weary of His chains. (*Ecclus.* 6:26). You will remark that the Holy Ghost, before saying these words, prepares a soul for them, lest it should reject His important counsel. See His words: "Hearken, My son, and receive a counsel of understanding and reject not My counsel." (*Ecclus.* 6:24).

241. You would wish, my very dear friend, that I should here unite myself to the Holy Ghost to give you the same counsel as His: "His chains are chains of salvation." (*Ecclus.* 6:31). As Jesus Christ on the cross must draw all to Himself, whether they will it or not, He will draw the reprobate by the chains of their sins, that He may chain them like galley-slaves and devils to His eternal anger and revengeful justice. But He will, and particularly in these latter times, draw the predestinate by the chains of charity: "I will draw all things to Myself" (*Jn.* 12:32); "I will draw them with the bands of love." (*Osee* 11:4).

242. These loving slaves of Jesus Christ, "the chained of Christ" (*Eph.* 3:1; *Philem.* 9), can wear their chains on their feet or on their arms, around their body or around their neck. Father Vincent Caraffa, seventh Superior General of the Jesuits, who died in the odor of sanctity in the year 1643, used to wear an iron band around his feet as a mark of his servitude; and he said that his only regret was that he could not publicly drag a chain. Mother Agnes of Jesus, of whom we have spoken before,[11] used to wear an iron chain around her body. Others have worn it around their neck in penance for the pearl necklaces which they had worn in the world; while others have worn it around their arms to remind themselves, in their manual labors, that they were slaves of Jesus Christ.

IV. Special Devotion to the Mystery of the Incarnation

243. Those who undertake this holy slavery should have a special devotion to the great mystery of the Incarnation of the Word (March 25th).[12] Indeed, the Incarnation is the mystery proper of this practice, inasmuch as it is a devotion inspired by the Holy Ghost: first, to honor and imitate the ineffable dependence which God the Son was pleased to have on Mary, for His Father's glory and our salvation—which dependence particularly appears in this mystery wherein Jesus is a captive and a slave in the bosom of the divine Mary, and depends on her for all things; secondly, to thank God for the incomparable graces He has given Mary, and particularly for having chosen her to be His most holy Mother, which choice was made in this mystery. These are the two principal ends of the slavery of Jesus in Mary.

244. Have the goodness to observe that I generally say, "the slave of Jesus in Mary," "the slavery of Jesus in Mary." I might, in good truth, as many have done before,[13] say the "slave of Mary," "the slavery of the holy Virgin"; but I think it better to say "the slave of Jesus in Mary," as Father Tronson, Superior General of the Seminary of St. Sulpice, renowned for his rare prudence and consummate piety, counseled to

an ecclesiastic who consulted him on the subject. The following were the reasons:

245. First, as we are living in an age of intellectual pride, and there are all around us numbers of puffed-up scholars and conceited and critical spirits who have plenty to say against the best established and most solid practices of piety, it is better for us not to give them any needless occasion of criticism. Hence it is better for us to say, "the slavery of Jesus in Mary," and call ourselves the slaves of Jesus Christ rather than the slaves of Mary, taking the denomination of our devotion rather from its Last End, which is Jesus Christ, than from the road and the means to the end, which is Mary; though I repeat that in truth we may do either, as I have done myself. For example, a man who goes from Orleans to Tours by way of Amboise may very well say that he is going to Amboise, or that he is going to Tours; that he is a traveler to Amboise and a traveler to Tours; with this difference, however, that Amboise is but his straight road to Tours and that Tours is only the last end and term of his journey.

246. A second reason is that the principal mystery we celebrate and honor in this devotion is the mystery of the Incarnation, wherein we can see Jesus only in Mary, and incarnate in her bosom. Hence it is more to the purpose to speak of the slavery of Jesus in Mary, and of Jesus residing and reigning in Mary, according to that beautiful prayer of so many great men: "O Jesus, living in Mary, come and live in us in Thy spirit of sanctity," etc.[14]

247. Another reason is that this manner of speaking sets forth still more the intimate union between Jesus and Mary. They are so intimately united that the one is altogether in the other. Jesus is altogether in Mary and Mary is altogether in Jesus; or rather, she exists no more, but Jesus alone is in her, and it were easier to separate the light from the sun than Mary from Jesus; so that we might call Our Lord, "Jesus of Mary," and our Blessed Lady, "Mary of Jesus."

248. Time would not permit me to stop now to explain the excellences and grandeurs of the mystery of Jesus living and reigning in Mary;

in other words, of the Incarnation of the Word. I will content myself with saying these few words: We have here the first mystery of Jesus Christ—the most hidden, the most exalted and the least known. It is in this mystery that Jesus, in His Mother's womb—which is for that very reason called by the saints "the cabinet of the secrets of God"[15]—has, in concert with Mary, chosen all the elect. It is in this mystery that He has wrought all the other mysteries of His life by the acceptance which He made of them. "When He cometh into the world, He saith: . . . Behold, I come to do Thy will, O God." (*Heb.* 10:5-9). Hence this mystery is an abridgement of all mysteries and contains the will and grace of all. Finally, this mystery is the throne of the mercy, of the liberality and of the glory of God. It is the throne of His mercy for us because, as we cannot approach Jesus but through Mary, we can see Jesus and speak to Him only by means of her. Jesus, who always hears His dear Mother, always grants His grace and mercy to poor sinners. "Let us go therefore with confidence to the throne of grace." (*Heb.* 4:16). It is the throne of His liberality toward Mary, because while the New Adam dwelt in that true terrestrial paradise, He worked so many miracles in secret that neither angels nor men can comprehend them. It is on this account that the saints call Mary the "magnificence of God"[16]—as if God were magnificent only in Mary. (*Is.* 33:21). It is the throne of His glory for His Father, because it is in Mary that Jesus Christ has calmed His Father, angered against men, and that He has made restitution of the glory which sin ravished from Him, and that, by the sacrifice He made of His own will and of Himself, He has given Him more glory than ever the sacrifices of the Old Law could give—an infinite glory, which He had never before received from man.

V. Devotion to the Hail Mary and to the Rosary

249. Those who adopt this slavery ought also to have a great devotion to saying the Hail Mary (the Angelical Salutation). Few Christians, however enlightened, know the real value, merit, excellence, and

necessity of the Hail Mary. It was necessary for the Blessed Virgin to appear several times to great and enlightened saints to show them the merit of it. She did so to St. Dominic, St. John Capistran and Blessed Alan de la Roche. They have composed entire works on the wonders and efficacy of that prayer for converting souls. They have loudly proclaimed and openly preached that, salvation having begun with the Hail Mary, the salvation of each one of us in particular is attached to that prayer. They tell us that it is that prayer which made the dry and barren earth bring forth the fruit of life; and that it is that prayer well said which makes the word of God germinate in our souls, and bring forth Jesus Christ, the Fruit of Life. They tell us that the Hail Mary is a heavenly dew for watering the earth, which is the soul, to make it bring forth its fruit in season; and that a soul which is not watered by that prayer bears no fruit, and brings forth only thorns and brambles, and is ready to be cursed. (*Heb.* 6:8).

250. Listen to what Our Lady revealed to Blessed Alan de la Roche, as he has recorded in his book on the dignity of the Rosary: "Know, my son, and make all others know, that it is a probable and proximate sign of eternal damnation to have an aversion, a lukewarmness, or a negligence in saying the Angelical Salutation, which has repaired the whole world."[17] These words are at once terrible and consoling, and we should find it hard to believe them if we had not that holy man for a guarantee, and St. Dominic before him, and many great men since. But we have also the experience of several ages; for it has always been remarked that those who wear the outward sign of reprobation, like all impious heretics and proud worldlings, hate or despise the Hail Mary and the Rosary. Heretics still learn and say the Our Father, but not the Hail Mary nor the Rosary. They abhor it; they would rather wear a serpent than a Rosary. The proud also, although Catholics, have the same inclinations as their father Lucifer; and so have only contempt or indifference for the Hail Mary, and look at the Rosary as at a devotion which is good only for the ignorant and for those who cannot read. On the contrary, it is an equally universal experience that those who have

otherwise great marks of predestination about them love and relish the Hail Mary, and delight in saying it. We always see that the more a man is for God, the more he likes that prayer. This is what Our Lady also said to Blessed Alan, after the words which I have just quoted.

251. I do not know how it is, nor why, but nevertheless I know well that it is true; nor have I any better secret of knowing whether a person is for God than to examine if he likes to say the Hail Mary and the Rosary. I say, if he likes; for it may happen that a person may be under some natural inability to say it, or even a supernatural one; yet, nevertheless, he likes it always, and always inspires the same liking in others.

252. O predestinate souls, slaves of Jesus in Mary, learn that the Hail Mary is the most beautiful of all prayers after the Our Father. It is the most perfect compliment which you can give to Mary, because it is the compliment which the Most High sent her by an archangel, in order to win her heart; and it was so powerful over her heart by the secret charms of which it is so full, that in spite of her profound humility she gave her consent to the Incarnation of the Word. It is by this compliment also that you will infallibly win her heart, if you say it as you ought.

253. The Hail Mary well said—that is, with attention, devotion, and modesty—is, according to the saints, the enemy of the devil which puts him to flight, and the hammer which crushes him. It is the sanctification of the soul, the joy of the angels, the melody of the predestinate, the canticle of the New Testament, the pleasure of Mary, and the glory of the most Holy Trinity. The Hail Mary is a heavenly dew which fertilizes the soul. It is the chaste and loving kiss which we give to Mary. It is a vermilion rose which we present to her; a precious pearl we offer her; a chalice of divine ambrosial nectar which we proffer to her. All these are comparisons of the saints.

254. I pray you urgently, by the love I bear you in Jesus and Mary, not to content yourselves with saying the Little Crown of the Blessed Virgin, but to say five decades, or even, if you have time, fifteen decades

of the Rosary every day. At the moment of your death you will bless the day and the hour in which you followed my advice. Having thus sown in the blessings of Jesus and Mary, you will reap eternal blessings in Heaven. "He who soweth in blessings, shall also reap blessings." (*2 Cor.* 9:6).

VI. Devotion to the Magnificat

255. To thank God for the graces He has given to Our Lady, those who adopt this devotion will often say the Magnificat, as Blessed Mary d'Oignies did, and many other saints. It is the only prayer, the only work, which the holy Virgin composed, or rather, which Jesus composed in her; for He spoke by her mouth. It is the greatest sacrifice of praise which God ever received from a pure creature in the law of grace. It is, on the one hand, the most humble and grateful, and on the other hand, the most sublime and exalted, of all canticles. There are in that canticle mysteries so great and hidden that the angels do not know them. The pious and erudite Gerson employed a great part of his life in composing works upon the most difficult subjects; and yet it was only at the close of his career, and even with trembling, that he undertook to comment on the Magnificat, so as to crown all his other works. He wrote a folio volume on it, bringing forward many admirable things about that beautiful and divine canticle. Among other things, he says that Our Lady often repeated it herself, and especially for thanksgiving after Communion. The learned Benzonius [Rutilio], in explaining the Magnificat, relates many miracles wrought by virtue of it, and says that the devils tremble and fly when they hear these words: "He hath showed might in His arm; He hath scattered the proud in the conceit of their heart." (*Lk.* 1:51).

VII. Contempt of and Flight from the World

256. Those faithful servants of Mary who adopt this devotion ought always greatly to despise, to hate and to eschew the corrupted world, and to make use of those practices of contempt of the world which we have given in the first part of this treatise.[18]

—ARTICLE TWO—

Interior Practices

257. Besides the external practices of the devotion which we have been describing so far, and which we must not omit through negligence or contempt, so far as the state and condition of each one will allow him to observe them, there are some very sanctifying interior practices for those whom the Holy Ghost calls to high perfection.

These may be expressed in four words: to do all our actions *by* Mary, *with* Mary, *in* Mary and *for* Mary; so that we may do them all the more perfectly *by* Jesus, *with* Jesus, *in* Jesus and *for* Jesus.

I. All by Mary

258. We must do all our actions *by* Mary; that is to say, we must obey her in all things, and in all things conduct ourselves by her spirit, which is the Holy Spirit of God. "Those who are led by the Spirit of God are the children of God." (*Rom.* 8:14). Those who are led by the spirit of Mary are the children of Mary, and consequently the children of God, as we have shown;[19] and among so many clients of the Blessed Virgin, none are true or faithful but those who are led by her spirit. I have said that the spirit of Mary was the Spirit of God, because she was never led by her own spirit, but always by the Spirit of God, who has rendered Himself so completely master of her that He has become her own spirit.

It is on this account that St. Ambrose says: "Let the soul of Mary be in each of us to magnify the Lord, and the spirit of Mary be in each of us to rejoice in God."[20] A soul is happy indeed when, like the good Jesuit lay-brother, Alphonse Rodriguez, who died in the odor of sanctity,[21] it is all possessed and overruled by the spirit of Mary, a spirit meek and strong, zealous and prudent, humble and courageous, pure and fruitful.

259. In order that the soul may let itself be led by Mary's spirit, it must first of all renounce its own spirit and its own lights and wills before it does anything. For example: It should do so before prayers, before saying or hearing Mass and before communicating; because the darkness of our own spirit, and the malice of our own will and operation, if we follow them, however good they may appear to us, will be an obstacle to the spirit of Mary. Secondly, we must deliver ourselves to the spirit of Mary to be moved and influenced by it in the manner she chooses. We must put ourselves and leave ourselves in her virginal hands, like a tool in the grasp of a workman, like a lute in the hands of a skillful player. We must lose ourselves and abandon ourselves to her, like a stone one throws into the sea. This can be done simply, and in an instant, by one glance of the mind, by one little movement of the will, or even verbally, in saying, for example, "I renounce myself, I give myself to thee, my dear Mother." We may not, perhaps, feel any sensible sweetness in this act of union, but it is not on that account the less real. It is just as if we were to say with equal sincerity, though without any sensible change in ourselves, what—may it please God—we never shall say: "I give myself to the devil"; we should not the less truly belong to the devil because we did not *feel* we belonged to him. Thirdly, we must, from time to time, both during and after the action, renew the same act of offering and of union. The more often we do so, the sooner we shall be sanctified, and attain to union with Jesus Christ, which always follows necessarily on our union with Mary, because the spirit of Mary is the spirit of Jesus.

II. All with Mary

260. We must do all our actions *with* Mary; that is to say, we must in all our actions regard Mary as an accomplished model of every virtue and perfection which the Holy Ghost has formed in a pure creature for us to imitate according to our little measure. We must therefore in every action consider how Mary has done it, or how she would have done it, had she been in our place. For that end we must examine and meditate on the great virtues which she practiced during her life, and particularly, first of all, her lively faith, by which she believed without hesitation the angel's word, and believed faithfully and constantly up to the foot of the cross; secondly, her profound humility, which made her hide herself, hold her peace, submit to everything, and put herself the last of all; and, thirdly, her altogether divine purity, which never has had, and never can have, its equal under Heaven; and so on with all of her other virtues.

Let us remember, I repeat, that Mary is the great and exclusive mold of God,[22] proper to making living images of God at small cost and in a little time; and that a soul which has found that mold, and has lost itself in it, is presently changed into Jesus Christ, whom that mold represents to the life.

III. All in Mary

261. We must do our actions *in* Mary. Thoroughly to understand this practice, we must first know that our Blessed Lady is the true terrestrial paradise of the New Adam, and that the ancient paradise was but a figure of her. There are, then, in this earthly paradise, riches, beauties, rarities and inexplicable sweetnesses, which Jesus Christ, the New Adam, has left there; it was in this paradise that He took His complacence for nine months, worked His wonders and displayed His riches with the magnificence of a God. This most holy place is composed only of a virginal and immaculate earth, of which the New Adam

was formed, and on which He was nourished, without any spot or stain, by the operation of the Holy Ghost, who dwelt there. It is in this earthly paradise that there is the true tree of life, which has borne Jesus Christ, the Fruit of Life, and the tree of the knowledge of good and evil, which has given light unto the world. There are in this divine place trees planted by the hand of God, and watered by His divine unction, which have borne and daily bear fruits of a divine taste. There are flower-beds adorned with beautiful and varied blossoms of virtues, diffusing odors which delight the very angels. There are meadows green with hope, impregnable towers of strength, and the most charming houses of confidence. It is only the Holy Ghost who can make us know the hidden truth of these figures of material things. There is in this place an air of perfect purity; a fair sun, without shadow, of the Divinity; a fair day, without night, of the Sacred Humanity; a continual burning furnace of love, where all the iron that is cast into it is changed, by excessive heat, to gold. There is a river of humility which springs from the earth, and which, dividing itself into four branches, waters all that enchanted place; and these are the four cardinal virtues.

262. The Holy Ghost, by the mouth of the Fathers, also styles the Blessed Virgin the Eastern Gate, by which the High Priest, Jesus Christ, enters the world and leaves it. (*Ezech.* 44:2-3). By it He came the first time, and by it He will come the second. The sanctuary of the Divinity, the repose of the Most Holy Trinity, the throne of God, the city of God, the altar of God, the temple of God, the world of God—all these different epithets and encomiums are most substantially true with reference to the different marvels and graces which the Most High has wrought in Mary. Oh, what riches! What glory! What pleasure! What happiness, to be able to enter into and dwell in Mary, where the Most High has set up the throne of His supreme glory!

263. But how difficult it is for sinners like ourselves to have the permission, the capacity and the light to enter into a place so high and so holy, which is guarded, not by one of the Cherubim like the old earthly paradise (*Gen.* 3:24), but by the Holy Ghost Himself,

who is its absolute Master. He Himself has said of it: "My sister, My spouse, is a garden enclosed, a garden enclosed, a fountain sealed up." (*Cant.* 4:12). Mary is shut, Mary is sealed. The miserable children of Adam and Eve, driven from the earthly paradise, cannot enter into this one except by a particular grace of the Holy Ghost, which they must merit.

264. After we have obtained this illustrious grace by our fidelity, we must remain in the fair interior of Mary with complacency, repose there in peace, lean our weight there in confidence, hide ourselves there with assurance, and lose ourselves there without reserve. Thus, in that virginal bosom, (1) the soul shall be nourished with the milk of grace and maternal mercy; (2) it shall be delivered from its troubles, fears and scruples; and (3) it shall be in safety against all its enemies—the world, the devil and sin—who never have entrance there. It is on this account that Mary says that they who work in her shall not sin (*Ecclus.* 24:30); that is to say, those who dwell in Mary in spirit shall fall into no considerable fault. Lastly, (4) the soul shall be formed in Jesus Christ and Jesus Christ in it, because her bosom is, as the holy Fathers say,[23] the chamber of the divine sacraments, where Jesus Christ and all the elect have been formed. "This man and that man is born in her."[24]

IV. *All for Mary*

265. Finally we must do all our actions *for* Mary. As we have given ourselves up entirely to her service, it is but just to do everything for her as servants and slaves. It is not that we take her for the last end of our services, for that is Jesus Christ alone; but we take her for our proximate end, our mysterious means and our easy way to go to Him. Like good servants and slaves, we must not remain idle, but, supported by her protection, we must undertake and achieve great things for this august sovereign. We must defend her privileges when they are disputed; we must stand up for her glory when it is attacked; we must draw all the world, if we can, to her service, and to this true and solid devotion;

we must speak and cry out against those who abuse her devotion to outrage her Son, and we must at the same time establish this veritable devotion; we must pretend to no recompense for our little services, except the honor of belonging to so sweet a Queen, and the happiness of being united through her to Jesus her Son by an indissoluble tie, in time and in eternity.

Glory to Jesus in Mary!
Glory to Mary in Jesus!
Glory to God alone!

V. Manner of Practicing This Devotion When We Go to Holy Communion

1. Before Holy Communion.

266. (1) You must humble yourself most profoundly before God. (2) You must renounce your corrupt interior and your dispositions, however good your self-love may make them look. (3) You must renew your consecration by saying: "I am all thine, my dear Mistress, with all that I have." (4) You must implore that good Mother to lend you her heart, that you may receive her Son there with the same dispositions as her own. You will explain to her that it touches her Son's glory to be put into a heart so sullied and so inconstant as yours, which would not fail either to lessen His glory or to destroy it. But if she will come and dwell with you, in order to receive her Son, she can do so by the dominion which she has over all hearts; and her Son will be well received by her, without stain, without danger of being outraged or unnoticed: "God is in the midst thereof, it shall not be moved." (*Ps.* 45:6). You will tell her confidently that all you have given her of your goods is little enough to honor her; but that by Holy Communion you wish to make her the same present as the Eternal Father gave her, and that you will honor her more by that than if you gave her all the goods in the

world; and finally, that Jesus, who loves her in a most special manner, still desires to take His pleasure and repose in her, even in your soul, though it be far filthier and poorer than the stable where He did not hesitate to come, simply because she was there. You will ask her for her heart, by these tender words: "I take thee for my all. Give me thy heart, O Mary."[25]

2. At Holy Communion.

267. After the Our Father, just before receiving Jesus Christ, you say three times: "Lord, I am not worthy." Say the first one to the Eternal Father, telling Him you are not worthy, because of your evil thoughts and ingratitude toward so good a Father, to receive His only Son; but that He is to behold Mary, His handmaid—"Behold the handmaid of the Lord" (*Lk.* 1:38)—who acts for you and who gives you a singular confidence and hope with His Majesty: "For thou singularly hast settled me in hope." (*Ps.* 4:10).

268. You will say to the Son: "Lord, I am not worthy"; telling Him that you are not worthy to receive Him because of your idle and evil words and your infidelity to His service; but that nevertheless you pray Him to have pity on you, because you are about to bring Him into the house of His own Mother and yours, and that you will not let Him go without His coming to lodge with her: "I held Him; and I will not let Him go, till I bring Him into my Mother's house and into the chamber of her that bore me." (*Cant.* 3:4). You will pray to Him to rise, and come to the place of His repose and into the ark of His sanctification: "Arise, Lord, into Thy resting place: Thou and the ark which Thou hast sanctified." (*Ps.* 131:8). Tell Him you put no confidence at all in your own merits, your own strength and your own preparations, as Esau did; but that you trust only in Mary, your dear Mother, as the little Jacob did in Rebecca. Tell Him that, sinner and Esau that you are, you dare to approach His sanctity, supported and adorned as you are with the virtues of His holy Mother.

269. You will say to the Holy Ghost: "Lord, I am not worthy"; telling Him that you are not worthy to receive this masterpiece of His charity, because of the lukewarmness and iniquity of your actions, and because of your resistance to His inspirations; but that all your confidence is in Mary, His faithful spouse. You will say, with St. Bernard: "She is my greatest security; she is the source of all my hope."[26] You can even pray Him to come Himself in Mary, His inseparable spouse, telling Him that her bosom is as pure and her heart as burning as ever; and that, without His descent into your soul, neither Jesus nor Mary will be formed nor worthily lodged.

3. After Holy Communion.

270. After Holy Communion, inwardly recollected and holding your eyes shut, you will introduce Jesus into the heart of Mary. You will give Him to His Mother, who will receive Him lovingly, will place Him honorably, will adore Him profoundly, will love Him perfectly, will embrace Him closely, and will render to Him, in spirit and in truth, many homages which are unknown to us in our thick darkness.

271. Or else you will keep yourself profoundly humbled in your heart, in the presence of Jesus residing in Mary. Or else you will sit like a slave at the gate of the King's palace, where He is speaking with the Queen; and while they talk to each other without need of you, you will go in spirit to Heaven and over all the earth, praying all creatures to thank, adore and love Jesus and Mary in your place: "Come, let us adore."* (*Ps.* 94:6).

272. Or else you will yourself ask of Jesus, in union with Mary, the coming of His kingdom on earth, through His holy Mother; or

---

* With reference to Mary, St. Louis De Montfort is obviously using the word "adore" (French *adorer*) in its secondary meaning, that is, to give homage and veneration to, rather than to denote that worship which is due to God alone. See Chap. 1, §14. —*Publisher*, 1999.

you will sue for divine wisdom, or for divine love, or for the pardon of your sins, or for some other grace; but always by Mary and in Mary; saying, while you look aside at yourself: "Lord, look not at my sins";[27] "but let Your eyes look at nothing in me but the virtues and merits of Mary."[28] And then, remembering your sins, you will add: "It is I who have committed these sins" (cf. *Matt.* 13:28); or you will say: "Deliver me from the unjust and deceitful man" (*Ps.* 42:1); or else: "My Jesus, You must increase in my soul, and I must decrease" (*Jn.* 3:30); Mary, you must increase within me, and I must be still less than I have been. "O Jesus and Mary, increase in me, and multiply yourselves outside in others also." (Cf. *Gen.* 1:22 ff.).

273. There are an infinity of other thoughts which the Holy Ghost furnishes, and will furnish you, if you are thoroughly interior, mortified and faithful to this grand and sublime devotion which I have been teaching you. But always remember that the more you allow Mary to act in your Communion, the more Jesus will be glorified; and you will allow Mary to act for Jesus and Jesus to act in Mary in the measure that you humble yourself and listen to them in peace and in silence, without troubling yourself about seeing, tasting or feeling; for the just man lives throughout on faith, and particularly in Holy Communion, which is an action of faith: "My just man liveth by faith." (*Heb.* 10:38).

NOTES

1. Cf. no. 119.
2. *Homilia 2a in evangelium.*
3. St. Louis De Montfort's wish has been realized. The Archconfraternity of Mary, Queen of All Hearts, has been canonically erected at Rome and has many affiliated confraternities in different countries throughout the world. See page 211.
4. These words seem to refer to some other work by St. Louis De Montfort which would have been used as an introduction to this treatise. Such might have been *L'amour de la divine Sagesse*; cf. chapter VII and XVI. Or, St. Louis may be referring to this treatise (*True Devotion to Mary*).
5. St. Bernard, Inter opera. Meditation on the knowledge of our human condition.
6. St. Augustine.
7. Cf. no. 266 and following.

8. For example, St. Augustine, *Tract. de Symbolo ad Catechumenos*, lib. IV, cap. I; St. Bernard, *Sermo super Signum magnum*, no. 3.

9. "We fly to thy patronage, O holy Mother of God; despise not our petitions in our necessities, but deliver us always from all dangers, O glorious and blessed Virgin."

10. It might be objected that certain decrees of the Roman Congregations have absolutely forbidden the use of little chains. There is nothing in these decrees concerning the private use of chains, especially if worn as a sign of slavery of Jesus in Mary, which is precisely what St. Louis De Montfort teaches. See *Analecta Juris Pontificii*, First Series, col. 757. However, there is no obligation to wear such chains. The Montfort Fathers do not distribute any special chain as a sign of the Holy Slavery of Jesus in Mary. The ordinary chain which members of the Confraternity of Mary, Queen of All Hearts wear with their medal may serve—and most fittingly so—as a sign of their holy servitude to Jesus and His Blessed Mother.

11. Cf. no. 170.

12. Members of the Confraternity can gain a plenary indulgence on the feast of the Annunciation, March 25th.

13. For instance, Father Boudon, in his book referred to in no. 159.

14. Cf. page 195.

15. St. Ambrose, *De Instit. Virg.* (caput VII, no. 50).

16. Cf. no. 6, note 2.

17. *Lib. de Dignitate Rosarii*, caput II.

18. Cf. no. 227 (note 4).

19. Cf. nos. 29, 30.

20. Cf. no. 217.

21. Canonized by Leo XIII, Jan. 15, 1888. St. Alphonsus Rodriguez (1531-1617) is not to be confused with Father Alphonsus Rodriguez (d. 1616), the author of *Christian Perfection*.

22. Cf. nos. 218, 219, sqq.

23. Cf. no. 248.

24. *Ps.* 86:5. Cf. no. 32.

25. Adaptation of two texts, *Jn.* 19:27 and *Prov.* 23:26.

26. *De Aquaeductu*, no. 7.

27. Prayer before Communion, Roman Missal.

28. *Ps.* 16:2, applied to the Blessed Virgin.

—SUPPLEMENT—

Preparation for Consecration

Consecration

Little Crown

Rosary

Confraternity

The Magnificat

My soul doth magnify the Lord.

And my spirit hath rejoiced in God my Saviour.

Because He hath regarded the humility of His hand-maid; for behold, from henceforth all generations shall call me blessed.

Because He that is mighty hath done great things to me; and holy is His name.

And His mercy is from generation to generations, to them that fear Him.

He hath showed might in His arm; He hath scattered the proud in the conceit of their heart.

He hath put down the mighty from their seat; and hath exalted the humble.

He hath filled the hungry with good things; and the rich He hath sent empty away.

He hath received Israel His servant, being mindful of His mercy.

As He spoke to our fathers, to Abraham and to his seed forever. Amen.

Glory be to the Father, etc.

PREPARATION FOR CONSECRATION TO JESUS THROUGH MARY

———— • ————

St. Louis De Montfort advises us to prepare for the consecration by exercises which certainly are not compulsory, but which assure its great efficacy because of the purity and other dispositions which they tend to develop in our souls.

Two different periods are assigned for these exercises: a preliminary period of twelve days during which we endeavor "to free ourselves from the spirit of the world"; and a second period of three weeks: the first devoted to the knowledge of ourselves, the second to that of the Blessed Virgin and the third to that of Jesus Christ.

These periods mentioned by St. Louis De Montfort do not constitute a rigorous and unchangable division. According to circumstances, they may be lengthened or shortened. The faithful often take but three days to prepare for the annual renewal of their consecration.

The object of this consecration is to cast off the spirit of the world, which is contrary to that of Jesus Christ, in order to acquire fully the spirit of Jesus Christ through the Blessed Virgin. Hence the practices suggested by St. Louis De Montfort: renouncement of the world, knowledge of self, of the Blessed Virgin and of Jesus Christ.

First Period

—TWELVE PRELIMINARY DAYS—
Renouncement of the World

"The first part of the preparation should be employed in casting off the spirit of the world, which is contrary to that of Jesus Christ."

The spirit of the world consists essentially in the denial of the supreme dominion of God, a denial which is manifested in practice by sin and disobedience; thus it is principally opposed to the spirit of Christ, which is also that of Mary.

It manifests itself by the concupiscence of the flesh, by the concupiscence of the eyes and by the pride of life; by disobedience to God's laws and the abuse of created things. Its works are, first, sin in all its forms; and then all else by which the devil leads to sin; works which bring error and darkness to the mind, and seduction and corruption to the will. Its pomps are the splendor and the charms employed by the devil to render sin alluring in persons, places and things.

Prayers to be said every day:
   Veni Creator and *Ave Maris Stella.*
Reading suitable for the twelve days:
   Gospel according to St. Matthew, chapters 5, 6, 7.
   Imitation of Christ, Book I, chapters 13, 18, 25; Book III, chapters 10, 40.
Spiritual Exercises:
   Examine your conscience, pray, practice renouncement, mortification, purity of heart; this purity is the indispensable condition for contemplating God in Heaven, to see Him on earth and to know Him by the light of faith.

Veni Creator

Come, O Creator Spirit blest!
And in our souls take up Thy rest;
Come with Thy grace and heavenly aid,
To fill the hearts which Thou hast made.

Great Paraclete! To Thee we cry,
O highest gift of God most high!
O font of life! O fire of love!
And sweet anointing from above.

Thou in Thy sevenfold gifts art known,
The finger of God's hand we own;
The promise of the Father, Thou!
Who dost the tongue with power endow.

Kindle our senses from above,
And make our hearts o'erflow with love;
With patience firm and virtue high
The weakness of our flesh supply.

Far from us drive the foe we dread,
And grant us Thy true peace instead;
So shall we not, with Thee for guide,
Turn from the path of life aside.

Oh, may Thy grace on us bestow
The Father and the Son to know,
And Thee, through endless times confessed,
Of both, the eternal Spirit blest.

All glory while the ages run
Be to the Father and the Son
Who rose from death; the same to Thee,
O Holy Ghost, eternally. Amen.

Ave Maris Stella

Hail, bright star of ocean,
　　God's own Mother blest,
Ever sinless Virgin,
　　Gate of heavenly rest.

Taking that sweet *Ave*
　　Which from Gabriel came,
Peace confirm within us,
　　Changing Eva's name.

Break the captives' fetters,
　　Light on blindness pour,
All our ills expelling,
　　Every bliss implore.

Show thyself a Mother;
　　May the Word Divine,
Born for us thy Infant,
　　Hear our prayers through thine.

Virgin all excelling,
　　Mildest of the mild,
Freed from guilt, preserve us,
　　Pure and undefiled.

Keep our life all spotless,
　　Make our way secure,
Till we find in Jesus
　　Joy forevermore.

Through the highest Heaven
　　To the Almighty Three,
Father, Son and Spirit,
　　One same glory be. Amen.

Gospel According to Matthew Ch. 5
Christ's sermon upon the mount. The eight beatitudes.

1 And seeing the multitudes, he went up into a mountain, and when he was set down, his disciples came unto him. *2* And opening his mouth, he taught them, saying: *3* Blessed are the poor in spirit: for theirs is the kingdom of heaven. *4* Blessed are the meek: for they shall possess the land. *5* Blessed are they that mourn: for they shall be comforted.

6 Blessed are they that hunger and thirst after justice: for they shall have their fill. *7* Blessed are the merciful: for they shall obtain mercy. *8* Blessed are the clean of heart: for they shall see God. *9* Blessed are the peacemakers: for they shall be called children of God. *10* Blessed are they that suffer persecution for justice' sake: for theirs is the kingdom of heaven.

11 Blessed are ye when they shall revile you, and persecute you, and speak all that is evil against you, untruly, for my sake: *12* Be glad and rejoice, for your reward is very great in heaven. For so they persecuted the prophets that were before you. *13* You are the salt of the earth. But if the salt lose its savour, wherewith shall it be salted? It is good for nothing any more but to be cast out, and to be trodden on by men. *14* You are the light of the world. A city seated on a mountain cannot be hid. *15* Neither do men light a candle and put it under a bushel, but upon a candlestick, that it may shine to all that are in the house.

16 So let your light shine before men, that they may see your good works, and glorify your Father who is in heaven. *17* Do not think that I am come to destroy the law, or the prophets. I am not come to destroy, but to fulfill. *18* For amen I say unto you, till heaven and earth pass, one jot, or one tittle shall not pass of the law, till all be fulfilled. *19* He therefore that shall break one of these least commandments, and shall so teach men, shall be called the least in the kingdom of heaven. But he that shall do and teach, he shall be called great in the kingdom of heaven. *20* For I tell you, that unless your justice abound more than that of the scribes and Pharisees, you shall not enter into the kingdom of heaven.

21 You have heard that it was said to them of old: Thou shalt not kill. And whosoever shall kill shall be in danger of the judgment. *22* But I say to you, that whosoever is angry with his brother, shall be in danger of the judgment. And whosoever shall say to his brother, Raca, shall be in danger of the council. And whosoever shall say, Thou Fool, shall be in danger of hell fire. *23* If therefore thou offer thy gift at the altar, and there thou remember that thy brother hath any thing against thee; *24* Leave there thy offering before the altar, and go first to be reconciled to thy brother: and then coming thou shalt offer thy gift. *25* Be at agreement with thy adversary betimes, whilst thou art in the way with him: lest perhaps the adversary deliver thee to the judge, and the judge deliver thee to the officer, and thou be cast into prison.

26 Amen I say to thee, thou shalt not go out from thence till thou repay the last farthing. *27* You have heard that it was said to them of old: Thou shalt not commit adultery. *28* But I say to you, that whosoever shall look on a woman to lust after her, hath already committed adultery with her in his heart. *29* And if thy right eye scandalize thee, pluck it out and cast it from thee. For it is expedient for thee that one of thy members should perish, rather than that thy whole body be cast into hell. *30* And if thy right hand scandalize thee, cut it off, and cast it from thee: for it is expedient for thee that one of thy members should perish, rather than that thy whole body be cast into hell.

31 And it hath been said, whosoever shall put away his wife, let him give her a bill of divorce. *32* But I say to you, that whosoever shall put away his wife, excepting for the cause of fornication, maketh her to commit adultery: and he that shall marry her that is put away, committeth adultery. *33* Again you have heard that it was said to them of old, Thou shalt not forswear thyself: but thou shalt perform thy oaths to the Lord. *34* But I say to you not to swear at all, neither by heaven, for it is the throne of God: *35* Nor by the earth, for it is his footstool: nor by Jerusalem, for it is the city of the great king:

36 Neither shalt thou swear by thy head, because thou canst not make one hair white or black. *37* But let your speech be yea, yea: no, no: and that which is over and above these, is of evil. *38* You have heard that it hath been said, An eye for an eye, and a tooth for a tooth. *39* But I say to you not to resist evil: but if one strike thee on thy right cheek, turn to him also the other: *40* And if a man will contend with thee in judgment, and take away thy coat, let go thy cloak also unto him.

41 And whosoever will force thee one mile, go with him other two, *42* Give to him that asketh of thee and from him that would borrow of thee turn not away. *43* You have heard that it hath been said, Thou shalt love thy neighbour, and hate thy enemy. *44* But I say to you, Love your enemies: do good to them that hate you: and pray for them that persecute and calumniate you: *45* That you may be the children of your Father who is in heaven, who maketh his sun to rise upon the good, and bad, and raineth upon the just and the unjust.

46 For if you love them that love you, what reward shall you have? do not even the publicans this? *47* And if you salute your brethren only, what do you more? do not also the heathens this? *48* Be you therefore perfect, as also your heavenly Father is perfect.

Gospel According to Matthew Chapter 6:
A continuation of the sermon on the mount.

1 Take heed that you do not your justice before men, to be seen by them: otherwise you shall not have a reward of your Father who is in heaven. *2* Therefore when thou dost an almsdeed, sound not a trumpet before thee, as the hypocrites do in the synagogues and in the streets, that they may be honoured by men. Amen I say to you, they have received their reward. *3* But when thou dost alms, let not thy left hand know what thy right hand doth. *4* That thy alms may be in secret, and thy Father who seeth in secret will repay thee. *5* And when ye pray, you shall not be as the hypocrites, that love to stand and pray in the synagogues and corners of the streets, that they may be seen by men: Amen I say to you, they have received their reward.

6 But thou when thou shalt pray, enter into thy chamber, and having shut the door, pray to thy Father in secret: and thy Father who seeth in secret will repay thee. *7* And when you are praying, speak not much, as the heathens. For they think that in their much speaking they may be heard. *8* Be not you therefore like to them, for your Father knoweth what is needful for you, before you ask him. *9* Thus therefore shall you pray: Our Father who art in heaven, hallowed be thy name. *10* Thy kingdom come. Thy will be done on earth as it is in heaven.

11 Give us this day our supersubstantial bread. *12* And forgive us our debts, as we also forgive our debtors. *13* And lead us not into temptation. But deliver us from evil. Amen. *14* For if you will forgive men their offences, your heavenly Father will forgive you also your offences. *15* But if you will not forgive men, neither will your Father forgive you your offences.

16 And when you fast, be not as the hypocrites, sad. For they disfigure their faces, that they may appear unto men to fast. Amen I say to you, they have received their reward. *17* But thou, when thou fastest anoint thy head, and wash thy face; *18* That thou appear not to men to fast, but to thy Father who is in secret: and thy Father who seeth in secret, will repay thee. *19* Lay not up to yourselves treasures on earth: where the rust, and moth consume, and where thieves break through and steal. *20* But lay up to yourselves treasures in heaven: where neither the rust nor moth doth consume, and where thieves do not break through, nor steal.

21 For where thy treasure is, there is thy heart also. *22* The light of thy body is thy eye. If thy eye be single, thy whole body shall be lightsome. *23* But if thy eye be evil thy whole body shall be darksome. If then the light that is in thee, be darkness: the darkness itself how great shall it be! *24* No man can serve two masters. For either he will hate the one, and love the other: or he will sustain the one, and despise the other. You cannot serve God and mammon. *25* Therefore I say to you, be not solicitous for your life, what you shall eat, nor for your body, what you shall put on. Is not the life more than the meat: and the body more than the raiment?

26 Behold the birds of the air, for they neither sow, nor do they reap, nor gather into barns: and your heavenly Father feedeth them. Are not you of much more value than they? *27* And which of you by taking thought, can add to his stature one cubit? *28* And for raiment why are you solicitous? Consider the lilies of the field, how they grow: they labour not, neither do they spin. *29* But I say to you, that not even Solomon in all his glory was arrayed as one of these. *30* And if the grass of the field, which is today, and tomorrow is cast into the oven, God doth so clothe: how much more you, O ye of little faith?

31 Be not solicitous therefore, saying, What shall we eat: or what shall we drink, or wherewith shall we be clothed? *32* For after all these things do the heathens seek. For your Father knoweth that you have need of all these things. *33* Seek ye therefore first the kingdom of God, and his justice, and all these things shall be added unto you. *34* Be not therefore solicitous for tomorrow; for the morrow will be solicitous for itself. Sufficient for the day is the evil thereof.

Gospel According to Matthew Chapter 7:
The third part of the sermon on the mount.

1 Judge not, that you may not be judged, *2* For with what judgment you judge, you shall be judged: and with what measure you mete, it shall be measured to you again. *3* And why seest thou the mote that is in thy brother's eye; and seest not the beam that is in thy own eye? *4* Or how sayest thou to thy brother: Let me cast the mote out of thy eye; and behold a beam is in thy own eye? *5* Thou hypocrite, cast out first the beam out of thy own eye, and then shalt thou see to cast out the mote out of thy brother's eye.

6 Give not that which is holy to dogs; neither cast ye your pearls before swine, lest perhaps they trample them under their feet, and turning upon you, they tear you. *7* Ask, and it shall be given you: seek, and you shall find: knock, and it shall be opened to you. *8* For every one that asketh, receiveth: and he that seeketh, findeth: and to him that knocketh, it shall be opened. *9* Or what man is there among you, of whom if his son shall ask bread, will he reach him a stone? *10* Or if he shall ask him a fish, will he reach him a serpent?

11 If you then being evil, know how to give good gifts to your children: how much more will your Father who is in heaven, give good things to them that ask him? *12* All things therefore whatsoever you would that men should do to you, do you also to them. For this is the law and the prophets. *13* Enter ye in at the narrow gate: for wide is the gate, and broad is the way that leadeth to destruction, and many there are who go in thereat. *14* How narrow is the gate, and strait is the way that leadeth to life: and few there are that find it! *15* Beware of false prophets, who come to you in the clothing of sheep, but inwardly they are ravening wolves.

16 By their fruits you shall know them. Do men gather grapes of thorns, or figs of thistles? *17* Even so every good tree bringeth forth good fruit, and the evil tree bringeth forth evil fruit. *18* A good tree cannot bring forth evil fruit, neither can an evil tree bring forth good fruit. *19* Every tree that bringeth not forth good fruit, shall be cut down, and shall be cast into the fire. *20* Wherefore by their fruits you shall know them.

21 Not every one that saith to me, Lord, Lord, shall enter into the kingdom of heaven: but he that doth the will of my Father who is in heaven, he shall enter into the kingdom of heaven. *22* Many will say to me in that day: Lord, Lord, have not we prophesied in thy name, and cast out devils in thy name, and done many miracles in thy name? *23* And then will I profess unto them, I never knew you: depart from me, you that work iniquity. *24* Every one therefore that heareth these my words, and doth them, shall be likened to a wise man that built his house upon a rock, *25* And the rain fell, and the floods came, and the winds blew, and they beat upon that house, and it fell not, for it was founded on a rock.

26 And every one that heareth these my words, and doth them not, shall be like a foolish man that built his house upon the sand, *27* And the rain fell, and the floods came, and the winds blew, and they beat upon that house, and it fell, and great was the fall thereof. *28* And it came to pass when Jesus had fully ended these words, the people were in admiration at his doctrine. *29* For he was teaching them as one having power, and not as the scribes and Pharisees.

Imitation of Christ, Book I, Chapter 13:
Of Resisting Temptations

AS LONG as we live in this world we cannot be without tribulation and temptation.

Hence it is written in Job: "The life of man upon earth is a warfare." (*Job* 7:1).

Therefore ought everyone to be solicitous about his temptations, and to watch in prayer, lest the devil, who never sleeps, but "goeth about seeking whom he may devour," find room to deceive him. (*1 Ptr.* 5:8).

No man is so perfect and holy as not to have sometimes temptations, and we cannot be wholly without them.

2. Yet temptations are often very profitable to a man, although they be troublesome and grievous, for in them a man is humbled, purified, and instructed.

All the saints have passed through many tribulations and temptations, and have profited by them; and they who could not support temptations, have become reprobates, and fallen away.

There is no order so holy, nor place so retired, where there are not temptations and adversities.

3. A man is never entirely secure from temptations as long as he lives, because we have within us the source of temptation, having been born in concupiscence.

When one temptation or tribulation is over, another comes on; and we shall have always something to suffer, because we have lost the good of our original happiness.

Many seek to fly temptations, and fall more grievously into them.

By flight alone we cannot overcome; but by patience and true humility we are made stronger than our enemies.

He who only declines them outwardly, and does not pluck out the root, will profit little; nay, temptations will sooner return to him, and he will find himself in a worse condition.

By degrees, and by patience, with longanimity, thou shalt by God's grace better overcome them than by harshness and thine own importunity.

In temptation often take counsel, and deal not roughly with one that is tempted; but comfort him as thou wouldst wish to be done to thyself.

4. Inconstancy of mind, and small confidence in God, is the beginning of all evil temptations.

For as a ship without a rudder is tossed to and fro by the waves, so the man who is remiss, and who quits his resolution, is many ways tempted.

Fire tries iron, and temptation tries a just man.

We often know not what we can do; but temptation discovers what we are.

However, we must be watchful, especially in the beginning of temptation, because then the enemy is easier overcome, if he is not suffered to come in at all at the door of the soul, but is kept out and resisted at his first knock.

Whence a certain man said: "Withstand the beginning, after-remedies come too late."

For first a bare thought comes to the mind; then a strong imagination; afterwards delight, and evil motion and consent.

And thus, by little and little, the wicked enemy gets full entrance, when he is not resisted in the beginning.

And the longer a man is negligent in resisting, so much the weaker does he daily become in himself, and the enemy becomes stronger against him.

5. Some suffer great temptations in the beginning of their conversion, and some in the end.

And some there are who are much troubled, in a manner, all their lifetime.

Some are but lightly tempted, according to the wisdom and equity of the ordinance of God, who weighs the state and merits of men, and pre-ordains all for the salvation of the elect.

6. We must not, therefore, despair when we are tempted, but pray to God with so much the more fervor that He may vouchsafe to help us in all tribulations; who, no doubt, according to the saying of St. Paul, will "make such issue with the temptation, that you may be able to bear it." (*1 Cor.* 10:13).

Let us, therefore, humble our souls under the hand of God in all temptations and tribulations: for the humble in spirit He will save and exalt.

7. In temptations and tribulations a man is proved as to what progress he has made; and in them there is a greater merit, and his virtue appears more conspicuous.

Nor is it much if a man be devout and fervent when he feels no trouble; but if in the time of adversity he bears up with patience, there will be hope of a great advancement.

Some are preserved from great temptations, and are often overcome in little daily ones; that, being humbled, they may never presume on themselves in great things, who are weak in such small occurrences.

Practical Reflections

Temptations serve to free us from all lurking inclinations to vanity or self-love, and from at all depending upon ourselves, because they make us feel the weight of our own miseries, give us a disgust for all earthly gratifications, and oblige us to rely solely upon God. They serve also to humble us by the experience they afford us of our own weakness, and of the depth of our natural corruption. They serve, in a word, to convince us of our inability to do the least good, or to avoid the smallest sin, without the assistance of God.

Prayer

I am sensible, O Jesus, that in the time of temptation, of myself, I cannot but offend Thee, and that, carried along by my natural inclination for evil, I am in danger of ruining myself. But I know, also, that Thou canst, and Thine Apostle assures me Thou wilt, defend me against the most violent assaults of my passions. Wherefore, mistrusting myself, and relying upon Thee, I will exclaim, "Lord, save me, or I perish"; I will stretch out my hand to Thee as St. Peter did, and confidently hope that Thou wilt not let me perish. Amen.

Imitation of Christ, Book I, Chapter 18: Of the Examples of the Holy Fathers

LOOK upon the lively examples of the holy Fathers, in whom true perfection and religion were most shining, and thou wilt see how little, and almost nothing, that is which we do.

Alas, what is our life, if compared to theirs?

The saints and friends of Christ served the Lord in hunger and thirst, in cold and nakedness, in labor and weariness, in watchings and fastings, in prayers and holy meditations, in persecutions and many reproaches. (*Heb.* 11:3–7).

2. Ah, how many and how grievous tribulations have the Apostles, martyrs, confessors, virgins, and all the rest undergone, who have been willing to follow Christ's footsteps!

For they hated their lives in this world, that they might possess them for eternity. (*John* 12:25).

Oh, how strict and mortified a life did the holy Fathers lead in the desert! What long and grievous temptations did they endure! How often were they molested by the enemy! What frequent and fervent prayers did they offer to God! What rigorous abstinence did they go through! What great zeal and fervor had they for their spiritual progress! How strong a war did they wage for overcoming vice! How pure and upright was their intention to God!

They labored all the day, and in the night they gave themselves to prayer: though even whilst they were at work they ceased not from mental prayer.

3. They spent all their time profitably: every hour seemed short which they spent with God, and through the great sweetness of divine contemplation they forgot even the necessity of their bodily refreshment.

They renounced all riches, dignities, honors, friends, and kindred; they desired to have nothing of this world; they scarcely allowed themselves the necessaries of life; the serving the body, even in necessity, was irksome to them.

They were poor, therefore, as to earthly things, but very rich in grace and virtue.

Outwardly they were in want, but inwardly they were refreshed with divine graces and consolations.

4. They were strangers to the world, but near and familiar friends to God.

They seemed to themselves as nothing, and were despised by this world; but in the eyes of God they were very precious and beloved.

They stood in true humility, they lived in simple obedience, they walked in charity and patience; and therefore they daily advanced in spirit, and obtained great favor with God.

They were given as an example for all religious, and ought more to excite us to make good progress, than the number of the lukewarm to grow slack.

5. Oh, how great was the fervor of all religious in the beginning of their holy institution!

Oh, how great was their devotion in prayer! How great their zeal for virtue! What great discipline was in force among them! What great reverence and obedience in all, flourished under the rule of a superior!

The footsteps remaining, still bear witness that they were truly perfect and holy men, who, waging war so stoutly, trod the world under their feet.

Now he is thought great who is not a transgressor, and who can with patience endure what he hath undertaken.

6. Ah, the lukewarmness and negligence of our state, that we so quickly fall away from our former fervor, and are now even weary of living through sloth and tepidity.

Would to God that advancement in virtues was not wholly asleep in thee who hast so often seen many examples of the devout!

Practical Reflections

Nothing can so powerfully excite us to live holily as the example of those who are holy. Example convinces us of the possibility of virtue, makes it practicable and easy, and offers it to us already illustrated in others, and, as it were, prepared for our exercise. For, when we read the lives or witness the examples of the saints, we naturally say to ourselves: See what men like ourselves have done, and suffered, and forsaken, for the Kingdom of Heaven, which is equally the object of our hopes. But what have we done to obtain it? Why do we not exert ourselves as they did to become worthy of the same recompense? Alas! I have reason to apprehend that when I shall appear before God, He will compare my life with my faith, with my religion, and with the examples of holy men who have lived in the same state of life as myself, and confronting me with these witnesses, will say to me: See what thou shouldst have done, and how thou hast neglected it; judge thou thyself: what dost thou deserve?

Prayer

Enter not, O Lord, into judgment with Thy servant; for my life, when compared with the conduct of the saints, can never justify me. Grant me the grace which Thou, my Saviour, didst merit for me, of attending to the discharge of my duties, of entering into the spirit of religion, of observing its rules and maxims, and of conforming my life to my faith, that so, when I appear before Thee, I may be clothed in the robes of Thy justice, supported by Thy mercy, and animated with Thy love. Amen.

Imitation of Christ, Book I, Chapter 25: Of the Fervent Amendment Of Our Whole Life

BE VIGILANT and diligent in God's service, and often think with thyself to what end thou camest hither, and why thou didst leave the world: Was it not that thou mightest live in God and become a spiritual man?

Be fervent, therefore, in thy spiritual progress, for thou shalt shortly receive the reward of thy labors; and then grief and fear shall no more come near thee.

Thou shalt labor now a little and thou shalt find great rest; yea, everlasting joy.

If thou continue faithful and fervent in working, God will doubtless be faithful and liberal in rewarding.

Thou must preserve a good and firm hope of winning the victory; but must not think thyself secure, lest thou grow negligent or proud.

2. When a certain person in anxiety of mind was often wavering between hope and fear, and, on a time, being overwhelmed with grief, had prostrated himself in prayer in the church before a certain altar, he revolved these things within himself saying: "If I did but know that I should still persevere"; and presently he heard within himself this answer from God: "And if thou didst know this what wouldst thou do? Do now what thou wouldst then do, and thou shalt be very secure."

And immediately, being comforted and strengthened, he committed himself to the divine will, and his anxious wavering ceased.

Neither had he a mind anymore to search curiously, to know what should befall him hereafter; but rather studied to inquire what was the will of God, "well pleasing and perfect" (*Rom.* 12:2), for the beginning and accomplishment of every good work.

3. "Trust in the Lord, and do good," saith the Prophet, "and dwell in the land, and thou shalt be fed with its riches." (*Ps.* 36:3).

There is one thing which keeps many back from spiritual progress and fervent amendment of life: and that is, dread of difficulty, or the labor which must be gone through in the conflict.

And they indeed advance most of all others in virtue, who strive manfully to overcome those things which they find more troublesome or contrary to them.

For there a man makes greater progress and merits greater grace where he overcomes himself more and mortifies himself in spirit.

4. But all men have not equal difficulties to overcome and mortify.

Yet he that is diligent and zealous, although he may have more passions to fight against, will be able to make a greater progress than another who has fewer passions but is withal less fervent in the pursuit of virtue.

Two things particularly conduce to a great amendment: these are, forcibly to withdraw one's self from that to which nature is viciously inclined, and earnestly to labor for that good which one wants most.

Study likewise to fly more carefully and to overcome those faults which most frequently displease thee in others.

5. Turn all occasions to thy spiritual profit: so that if thou see or hear any good examples thou mayest be spurred on to imitate them.

But if thou observe anything that is reprehensible take heed thou commit not the same; or if thou at any time hast done it, labor to amend it quickly.

As thine eye observeth others so art thou also observed by others.

Oh, how sweet and comfortable is it to see brethren fervent and devout, regular and well disciplined! (*Ps.* 132:1).

How sad a thing and how afflicting to see them walk disorderly, and practice nothing of what they are called to!

How hurtful it is to neglect the intent of our vocation and turn our minds to things that are not our business.

6. Be mindful of the resolution thou hast taken, and set before thee the image of the crucifix.

Well mayest thou be ashamed if thou hast looked upon the life of Jesus Christ, that thou hast not yet studied to conform thyself more to His pattern, although thou hast been long in the way of God.

A religious man, who exercises himself seriously and devoutly in the most holy life and Passion of Our Lord, shall find there abundantly all things profitable and necessary for him; nor need he seek any better model than that of Jesus.

Oh, if our crucified Jesus did but come into our heart, how quickly and sufficiently learned should we be!

7. A fervent religious man bears and takes all things well that are commanded him.

A negligent and lukewarm religious man has trouble upon trouble, and on every side suffers anguish, because he has no comfort within and is hindered from seeking any without.

A religious man that lives not in discipline lies open to dreadful ruin.

He that seeks to be more loose and remiss will always be uneasy, for one thing or other will always displease him.

8. How do so many other religious do who live under strict monastic discipline?

They seldom go abroad, they live very retired, their diet is very poor, their habit coarse, they labor much, they speak little, they watch long, they rise early, they spend much time in prayer, they read often and keep themselves in all discipline.

Consider the Carthusians, the Cistercians, and the monks and nuns of divers Orders, how every night they rise to sing psalms to the Lord.

It would, therefore, be a shame for thee to be sluggish at so holy a time, when such multitudes of religious begin with joy to give praise to God.

9. Oh, that we had nothing else to do but to praise the Lord our God with our whole heart and mouth!

Oh, that thou didst never want to eat, nor drink, nor sleep, but couldst always praise God and be employed solely in spiritual exercises!

Thou wouldst then be much more happy than now whilst thou art under the necessity of serving the flesh.

Would there were no such necessities, but only the spiritual refreshments of the soul, which, alas, we taste too seldom.

10. When a man is come to this, that he seeks comfort from nothing created, then he begins perfectly to relish God; then likewise will he be well content, however matters happen to him.

Then will he neither rejoice for much, nor be sorrowful for little, but will commit himself wholly and confidently to God, who is to him all in all; to whom nothing perishes or dies, but all things live to Him and serve Him at a nod without delay.

11. Always remember thine end and that time once lost never returns. Without care and diligence thou shalt never acquire virtues.

If thou begin to grow lukewarm thou wilt begin to be uneasy.

But if thou give thyself to fervor thou shalt find great peace, and the grace of God and love of virtue will make thee feel less labor.

A fervent and diligent man is ready for all things.

It is a greater task to resist vices and passions than to toil at bodily labors.

He that does not shun small defects by little and little falls into greater. (*Ecclus.* 19:1).

Thou shalt always rejoice in the evening if thou spend the day profitably.

Watch over thyself, stir up thyself, admonish thyself, and whatever becometh of others neglect not thyself.

The greater violence thou offerest to thyself the greater progress thou shalt make.

Practical Reflections

According to our zeal for advancement, we take advantage of the good we see to practice it, and carry us to God. To advance in virtue we must overcome and renounce ourselves in all things and die to the insatiable desires of our heart. It is certain that we can merit in the service of God only in proportion as we do violence to ourselves. Wherefore, let us fight against and subdue the irregular inclinations which allure us to sin or to relaxation of our fervor: by this means we shall secure our salvation. A vigorous, constant, and generous effort to overcome ourselves, forwards us more in the ways of perfection and salvation than all those fruitless desires by which we would give ourselves to God, yet we do not what we would. The more we die to ourselves, the more do we live to God; and the more we refuse to gratify ourselves, so much the more do we please Him. How delightful must the life of that Christian be whose desires are so regulated that his chief happiness is in denying himself, and pleasing God! How sure a means of obtaining a happy eternity!

Prayer

Thou knowest, O Jesus, the extreme difficulty we experience in subduing and subjecting ourselves to Thee: suffer not this difficulty to hinder us from accomplishing it. It is just we should prefer Thy glory, and Thy holy will, to our own will and gratification, and hence we are resolved to do so. Strengthen us in this resolution, and make us faithful; grant that all in us may yield to Thee, that, advancing daily in virtue, and leading a supernatural and through Thy merits an acceptable life, we may become worthy of Thy grace here, and of Thine eternal glory hereafter. Amen.

Imitation of Christ, Book III, Chapter 10: It Is Sweet to Serve God, Despising this World

Disciple
NOW will I speak, O Lord, and will not be silent; I will say in the hearing of my God, my Lord and my King that is on high.

Oh, how great is the multitude of Thy sweetness, O Lord, which Thou hast hidden for them that fear Thee. (*Ps.* 30:20). But what art

Thou to those that love Thee? What to those that serve Thee with their whole heart?

Unspeakable indeed in the sweetness of Thy contemplation, which Thou bestowest on those that love Thee.

In this most of all hast Thou shown me the sweetness of Thy love, that when I had no being Thou hast made me, and when I strayed far from Thee Thou hast brought me back again, that I might serve Thee, and Thou hast commanded me to love Thee.

2. O Fountain of everlasting love, what shall I say of Thee?

How can I ever forget Thee who hast vouchsafed to remember me, even after I was corrupted and lost.

Thou hast, beyond all hope, showed mercy to Thy servant, and beyond all my desert bestowed Thy grace and friendship upon me.

What returns shall I make to Thee for this favor? for it is a favor not granted to all to forsake all things and renounce the world and choose a monastic life.

Can it be much to serve Thee whom the whole creation is bound to serve?

It ought not to seem much to serve Thee, but this seems rather great and wonderful to me, that Thou vouchsafest to receive one so wretched and unworthy into Thy service and to associate him to Thy beloved servants.

3. Behold all things are Thine which I have and with which I serve Thee.

Although, on the contrary, Thou dost rather serve me than I Thee.

Lo! Heaven and earth, which Thou hast created for the service of man, are ready at Thy beck and daily do whatever Thou hast commanded them.

And this is yet but little, for Thou hast also appointed the angels for the service of man. (*Heb.* 1:14).

But what is above all this is that Thou Thyself hast vouchsafed to serve man and hast promised that Thou wilt give him Thyself.

4. What shall I give Thee for so many thousands of favors? Oh, that I could serve Thee all the days of my life!

Oh, that I were able, if it were but for one day, to serve Thee worthily!

Indeed Thou art worthy of all service, of all honor, and of eternal praise!

Thou art truly my Lord and I am Thy poor servant, who am bound with all my strength to serve Thee and ought never to grow weary of praising Thee.

This is my will, this is my desire, and whatever is wanting to me do Thou vouchsafe to supply.

5. It is a great honor, a great glory to serve Thee and to despise all things for Thee.

For they who willingly subject themselves to Thy most holy service shall have great grace.

They shall find the most sweet consolations of the Holy Ghost who, for the love of Thee, have cast away all carnal delights.

They shall gain great freedom of mind who, for Thy name, enter upon the narrow way and neglect all worldly care.

6. O pleasant and delightful service of God, which makes a man truly free and holy!

O sacred state of religious bondage, which makes men equal to angels, pleasing to God, terrible to the devils and commendable to all the faithful.

O service worthy to be embraced and always wished for, which leads to the supreme good and procures a joy that will never end.

Practical Reflections

To judge ourselves unworthy of every grace; to correspond with those we receive; to refer to God all the glory of our fidelity in His service; often to thank Him for His goodness in seeking us when we go astray, and receiving us again after we have sinned; to hope all things from His mercy, and to place ourselves entirely in His hands, is what should be done by every Christian soul who knows what Jesus Christ is to him, and what he ought to be to Jesus Christ.

How fortunate are we in not being able to find in ourselves any real cause for feelings of vanity or self-complacency, for this obliges us to forsake ourselves, and abide only in God! Ah, how does the sense of our miseries establish us in the heart of the God of mercy! And how does the experience of our inability to do good, and our inclination for evil, oblige us to adhere to God, and to have continual recourse to Him.

Prayer

How can I forget Thee, O Lord, Who hast so often preserved me from Hell, into which I might have precipitated myself by my irregular or useless life? Cure me of that vain complacency and swelling pride which would persuade me that there is something of good in me. It is in Thee, O Lord, it is all from Thee: for without Thee I can do nothing but offend Thee. Suffer me not to exalt myself before Thee by voluntary pride, lest I draw upon myself the same chastisement with which Thou didst visit the first angels. I would rather be despised by men and loved by Thee, then be esteemed by them and reproved by Thee. Grant that I may do Thee justice by referring all that is good to Thee, and to myself naught but the evil I have committed, that I may thus obtain Thy merciful pardon. Amen.

Imitation of Christ, Book III, Chapter 40: Man Hath No Good of Himself, and Cannot Glory in Anything

Disciple

LORD, what is man that Thou art mindful of him; or the son of man that Thou visitest him? (*Ps.* 8:3).

What hath man deserved that Thou shouldst give him Thy grace? Lord, what cause have I to complain if Thou forsake me? or what can I justly allege if Thou refuse to grant my petition? This, indeed, I may truly think and say, Lord, I am nothing, I can do nothing, I have nothing of myself that is good; but I fail and am defective in all things, and ever tend to nothing. And unless I am supported and interiorly instructed by Thee, I become quite tepid and dissolute.

2. But Thou, O Lord, art always the same and endurest forever; always good, just, and holy; doing all things well, justly, and holily; and disposing them in wisdom. (*Wis.* 12:13). But I, who am more inclined to go back than to advance, continue not always in one state; for seven different seasons are changed over me. (*Dan.* 4:15).

Yet it quickly becomes better when it pleaseth Thee, and Thou stretchest out Thy helping hand; for Thou alone without man's aid can assist me, and so strengthen me that my countenance shall be no more changed in various ways, but my heart shall be converted and take its rest in Thee alone.

3. Wherefore, if I did but well know how to cast away from me all human comfort, either for the sake of devotion, or through the necessity of seeking Thee, because there is no man that can comfort me, then might I justly depend on Thy grace, and rejoice in the gift of new consolation.

4. Thanks be to Thee, from whom all proceeds, as often as it goes well with me.

But, for my part, I am but mere vanity, and nothing in Thy sight; an inconstant and weak man.

What have I then to glory in? or why do I desire to be esteemed? Is it not for nothing? and this is most vain. Truly vainglory is an evil plague, a very great vanity, because it draws us away from true glory, and robs us of heavenly grace. For whilst a man takes complacency in himself, he displeaseth Thee; whilst he seeks after the praises of men, he is deprived of true virtues.

5. But true glory and holy joy is to glory in Thee and not in one's self; to rejoice in Thy name, and not to be delighted in one's own virtue, nor in any creature, save only for Thy sake. Let Thy name be praised, not mine; let Thy work be extolled, not mine; let Thy holy name be blessed, but to me let nothing be attributed of the praises of men.

Thou art my glory, Thou art the joy of my heart. In Thee will I glory and rejoice all the day; but for myself I will glory in nothing but in my infirmities. (*2 Cor.* 12:5).

6. Let the Jews seek the glory which one man receives from another; I will seek that which is from God alone. (*John* 5:44). All

human glory, all temporal honor, all worldly grandeur, compared to Thine eternal glory is but vanity and foolishness. O my truth and my mercy, O my God, O blessed Trinity! to Thee alone be all praise, honor, power, and glory, for endless ages of ages. (*Deut.* 26:19).

Practical Reflections

I am sensible of my natural corruption, which renders me incapable of all supernatural good and prone to all evil: but I cast myself on the mercies of a God who can bring much out of little, as He produced all things out of nothing; since it is not sufficient for me to know my own nothingness, and that I ought to glory in nothing, save only in my infirmities; I should also (for this is most important) be guided by an humble diffidence in myself, and a firm confidence in God, to whom nothing is impossible. When I find no consolation in man, then it is I feel indeed the happy necessity of having recourse to God, and of depending upon Him: happy that, all being wanting to me without Thee, O Lord, I should find my all in Thee! Well might holy Job thus express himself: Thine eyes are upon me, and I shall be no more. For when I think of Thee, my God! I feel within me an ardent desire of pleasing Thee; and everything disappears from before me, when Thou dost present Thyself to my soul.

Prayer

Do Thou, O God, reign absolutely over my soul, and may all that it contains yield and be immolated to Thee? Grant that, by corresponding with Thy holy grace, I may be enabled to suffer the loss of all human and natural satisfaction, to seek in Thee alone my consolation, and to sacrifice my whole self to Thee. O great God! Who knowest my condition, Who art able and willing to assist me, have compassion on the excess of my miseries! withdraw me from myself, raise me above all visible things, grant that, quitting and renouncing myself, I may desire and seek only Thee. Amen.

Second Period

—FIRST WEEK—
Knowledge of Self

"During the first week they should employ all their prayers and pious actions in asking for a knowledge of themselves and for contrition of their sins; and they should do this in a spirit of humility." (See no. 228).

During this week, we shall consider not so much the opposition that exists between the spirit of Jesus and ours, as the miserable and humiliating state to which our sins have reduced us. Moreover, the True Devotion being an easy, short, sure and perfect way to arrive at that union with Our Lord which is Christian perfection, we shall enter seriously upon this way, strongly convinced of our misery and helplessness. But how attain this without a knowledge of ourselves?

Prayers:
> *Litany of the Holy Ghost. Ave Maris Stella*, page 150. *Litany of the Blessed Virgin.*

Reading:
> Gospel according to St. Matthew, chapters 24, 25.
> Gospel of St. Luke, chapters 11, 13, 16, 17, 18.
> *Imitation of Christ*, Book I, chapter 24; Book II, chapter 5; Book III, chapters 7, 8, 13, 20, 30, 47.
> *True Devotion*, nos. 78-82, 227, 228.

Spiritual Exercises:
> Prayers, examens, reflection, acts of renouncement of our own will, of contrition for our sins, of contempt of self—all performed at the feet of Mary, for it is from her we hope for light to know ourselves, and it is near her that we shall be able to measure the abyss of our miseries without despairing.

Litany of the Holy Ghost
(For private use only.)

Lord, have mercy on us.
  Christ, have mercy on us.
Lord, have mercy on us.

Father all powerful, *have mercy on us.*
Jesus, Eternal Son of the Father, Redeemer of the world, *save us.*
Spirit of the Father and the Son, boundless life of both, *sanctify us.*
Holy Trinity, *hear us.*

Holy Ghost, Who proceedest from the Father and the Son, *enter our hearts.*
Holy Ghost, Who art equal to the Father and the Son, *enter our hearts.*

Promise of God the Father, *have mercy on us.*
Ray of heavenly light, *have mercy on us.*
Author of all good, *etc.*
Source of heavenly water,
Consuming fire,
Ardent charity,
Spiritual unction,
Spirit of love and truth,
Spirit of wisdom and understanding,
Spirit of counsel and fortitude,
Spirit of knowledge and piety,
Spirit of the fear of the Lord,
Spirit of grace and prayer,
Spirit of peace and meekness,
Spirit of modesty and innocence,
Holy Ghost, the Comforter,

Holy Ghost, the Sanctifier,
Holy Ghost, Who governest the Church,
Gift of God, the Most High,
Spirit Who fillest the universe,
Spirit of the adoption of the children of God,
Holy Ghost, *inspire us with horror of sin.*
Holy Ghost, *come and renew the face of the earth.*
Holy Ghost, *shed Thy light in our souls.*
Holy Ghost, *engrave Thy law in our hearts.*
Holy Ghost, *inflame us with the flame of Thy love.*
Holy Ghost, *open to us the treasures of Thy graces.*
Holy Ghost, *teach us to pray well.*
Holy Ghost, *enlighten us with Thy heavenly inspirations.*
Holy Ghost, *lead us in the way of salvation.*
Holy Ghost, *grant us the only necessary knowledge.*
Holy Ghost, *inspire in us the practice of good.*
Holy Ghost, *grant us the merits of all virtues.*
Holy Ghost, *make us persevere in justice.*
Holy Ghost, *be Thou our everlasting reward.*

Lamb of God, Who takest away the sins of the world, *Send us Thy Holy Ghost.*

Lamb of God, Who takest away the sins of the world, *Pour down into our souls the gifts of the Holy Ghost.*

Lamb of God, Who takest away the sins of the world, *Grant us the Spirit of wisdom and piety.*

V. Come, Holy Ghost! Fill the hearts of Thy faithful,
R. *And enkindle in them the fire of Thy love.*

Let Us Pray

Grant, O merciful Father, that Thy Divine Spirit may enlighten, inflame and purify us, that He may penetrate us with His heavenly dew and make us fruitful in good works, through Our Lord Jesus Christ, Thy Son, Who with Thee, in the unity of the same Spirit, liveth and reigneth forever and ever. R. *Amen.*

Litany of the Blessed Virgin Mary

Lord, have mercy on us.
   Christ, have mercy on us.
Lord, have mercy on us. Christ, hear us.
   Christ, graciously hear us.
God the Father of Heaven, *have mercy on us.*
God the Son, Redeemer of the world, *have mercy on us.*
God the Holy Ghost, *have mercy on us.*
Holy Trinity, One God, *have mercy on us.*

Holy Mary, *pray for us.*
Holy Mother of God, *pray for us.*
Holy Virgin of virgins, *etc.*
Mother of Christ,
Mother of divine grace,
Mother most pure,
Mother most chaste,
Mother inviolate,
Mother undefiled,
Mother most amiable,
Mother most admirable,
Mother of good counsel,
Mother of our Creator,
Mother of our Saviour,

Mother of the Church,
Virgin most prudent,
Virgin most venerable,
Virgin most renowned,
Virgin most powerful,
Virgin most merciful,
Virgin most faithful,
Mirror of justice,
Seat of wisdom,
Cause of our joy,
Spiritual vessel,
Vessel of honor,
Singular vessel of devotion,
Mystical rose,
Tower of David,
Tower of ivory,
House of gold,
Ark of the covenant,
Gate of Heaven,
Morning star,
Health of the sick,
Refuge of sinners,
Comforter of the afflicted,
Help of Christians,
Queen of angels,
Queen of patriarchs,
Queen of prophets,
Queen of Apostles,
Queen of martyrs,
Queen of confessors,
Queen of virgins,
Queen of all saints,
Queen conceived without Original Sin,

Queen assumed into Heaven,
Queen of the most holy Rosary,
Queen of peace,

Lamb of God, Who takest away the sins of the world, *Spare us, O Lord.*
Lamb of God, Who takest away the sins of the world, *Graciously hear us, O Lord.*
Lamb of God, Who takest away the sins of the world, *Have mercy on us.*

V. Pray for us, O holy Mother of God,
R. *That we may be made worthy of the promises of Christ.*

Let Us Pray

Grant, we beseech Thee, O Lord God, unto us Thy servants, that we may rejoice in continual health of mind and body, and by the glorious intercession of Blessed Mary, ever virgin, may be delivered from present sadness, and enter into the joy of Thine eternal gladness. Through Christ Our Lord. R. *Amen.*

Gospel According to St. Matthew, Chapter 24:
Christ foretells the destruction of the temple, with the signs that shall come before it, and before the last judgment. We must always watch.

1 And Jesus being come out of the temple, went away. And his disciples came to shew him the buildings of the temple. *2* And he answering, said to them: Do you see all these things? Amen I say to you there shall not be left here a stone upon a stone that shall not be destroyed. *3* And when he was sitting on mount Olivet, the disciples came to him privately, saying: Tell us when shall these things be? and what shall be the sign of thy coming, and of the consummation of the world? *4* And Jesus answering, said to them: Take heed that no man seduce you: *5* For many will come in my name saying, I am Christ: and they will seduce many.

6 And you shall hear of wars and rumours of wars. See that ye be not troubled. For these things must come to pass, but the end is not yet. *7* For nation shall rise against nation, and kingdom against kingdom; and there shall be pestilences, and famines, and earthquakes in places: *8* Now all these are the beginnings of sorrows. *9* Then shall they deliver you up to be afflicted, and shall put you to death: and you shall be hated by all nations for my name's sake. *10* And then shall many be scandalized: and shall betray one another: and shall hate one another.

11 And many false prophets shall rise, and shall seduce many. *12* And because iniquity hath abounded, the charity of many shall grow cold. *13* But he that shall persevere to the end, he shall be saved. *14* And this gospel of the kingdom, shall be preached in the whole world, for a testimony to all nations, and then shall the consummation come. *15* When therefore you shall see the *abomination of desolation*, which was spoken of by Daniel the prophet, standing in the holy place: he that readeth let him understand.

16 Then they that are in Judea, let them flee to the mountains: *17* And he that is on the housetop, let him not come down to take any thing out of his house: *18* And he that is in the field, let him not go back to take his coat. *19* And woe to them that are with child, and that give suck in those days. *20* But pray that your flight be not in the winter, or on the sabbath.

21 For there shall be then great tribulation, such as hath not been from the beginning of the world until now, neither shall be. *22* And unless those days had been shortened, no flesh should be saved: but for the sake of the elect those days shall be shortened. *23* Then if any man shall say to you: Lo here is Christ, or there, do not believe him. *24* For there shall arise false Christs and false prophets, and shall shew great signs and wonders, insomuch as to deceive (if possible) even the elect. *25* Behold I have told it to you, beforehand.

26 If therefore they shall say to you: Behold he is in the desert, go ye not out: Behold he is in the closets, believe it not. *27* For as lightning cometh out of the east, and appeareth even into the west: so shall also the coming of the Son of man be. *28* Wheresoever the body shall be, there shall the eagles also be gathered together. *29* And immediately after the tribulation of those days, the sun shall be darkened and the moon shall not give her light, and the stars shall fall from heaven, and the powers of heaven shall be moved: *30* And then shall appear the sign of the Son of man in heaven: and then shall all tribes of the earth mourn: and they shall see the Son of man coming in the clouds of heaven with much power and majesty.

31 And he shall send his angels with a trumpet, and a great voice: and they shall gather together his elect from the four winds, from the farthest parts of the heavens to the utmost bounds of them. *32* And from the fig tree learn a parable: When the branch thereof is now tender, and the leaves come forth, you know that summer is nigh. *33* So you also, when you shall see all these things, know ye that it is nigh, even at the doors. *34* Amen I say to you, that this generation shall not pass, till all these things be done. *35* Heaven and earth shall pass, but my words shall not pass.

36 But of that day and hour no one knoweth, not the angels of heaven, but the Father alone. *37* And as in the days of Noe, so shall also the coming of the Son of man be. *38* For as in the days before the flood, they were eating and drinking, marrying and giving in marriage, even till that day in which Noe entered into the ark, *39* And they knew not till the flood came, and took them all away; so also shall the coming of the Son of man be. *40* Then two shall be in the field: one shall be taken, and one shall be left.

41 Two women shall be grinding at the mill: one shall be taken, and one shall be left. *42* Watch ye therefore, because ye know not what hour your Lord will come. *43* But this know ye, that if the goodman of the house knew at what hour the thief would come, he would certainly watch, and would not suffer his house to be broken open. *44* Wherefore be you also ready, because at what hour you know not the Son of man will come. *45* Who, thinkest thou, is a faithful and wise servant, whom his lord hath appointed over his family, to give them meat in season.

46 Blessed is that servant, whom when his lord shall come he shall find so doing. *47* Amen I say to you, he shall place him over all his goods. *48* But if that evil servant shall say in his heart: My lord is long a coming: *49* And shall begin to strike his fellow servants, and shall eat and drink with drunkards: *50* The lord of that servant shall come in a day that he hopeth not, and at an hour that he knoweth not:

51 And shall separate him, and appoint his portion with the hypocrites. There shall be weeping and gnashing of teeth.

Gospel According to St. Matthew, Chapter 25:
The parable of the ten virgins, and of the talents:
the description of the last judgment.

1 Then shall the kingdom of heaven be like to ten virgins, who taking their lamps went out to meet the bridegroom and the bride. *2* And five of them were foolish, and five wise. *3* But the five foolish, having taken their lamps, did not take oil with them: *4* But the wise took oil in their vessels with the lamps. *5* And the bridegroom tarrying, they all slumbered and slept.

6 And at midnight there was a cry made: Behold the bridegroom cometh, go ye forth to meet him. *7* Then all those virgins arose and trimmed their lamps. *8* And the foolish said to the wise: Give us of your oil, for our lamps are gone out. *9* The wise answered, saying: Lest perhaps there be not enough for us and for you, go ye rather to them that sell, and buy for yourselves. *10* Now whilst they went to buy, the bridegroom came: and they that were ready, went in with him to the marriage, and the door was shut.

11 But at last come also the other virgins, saying: Lord, Lord, open to us. *12* But he answering said: Amen I say to you, I know you not. *13* Watch ye therefore, because you know not the day nor the hour.

14 For even as a man going into a far country, called his servants, and delivered to them his goods; *15* And to one he gave five talents, and to another two, and to another one, to every one according to his proper ability: and immediately he took his journey.

16 And he that had received the five talents, went his way, and traded with the same, and gained other five. *17* And in like manner he that had received the two, gained other two. *18* But he that had received the one, going his way digged into the earth, and hid his lord's money. *19* But after a long time the lord of those servants came, and reckoned with them. *20* And he that had received the five talents coming, brought other five talents, saying: Lord, thou didst deliver to me five talents, behold I have gained other five over and above.

21 His lord said to him: Well done, good and faithful servant, because thou hast been faithful over a few things, I will place thee over many things: enter thou into the joy of thy lord. *22* And he also that had received the two talents came and said: Lord, thou deliveredst two talents to me: behold I have gained other two. *23* His lord said to him: Well done, good and faithful servant: because thou hast been faithful over a few things, I will place thee over many things: enter thou into the joy of thy lord. *24* But he that had received the one talent, came and said: Lord, I know that thou art a hard man; thou reapest where thou hast not sown, and gatherest where thou hast not strewed. *25* And being afraid I went and hid thy talent in the earth: behold here thou hast that which is thine.

26 And his lord answering, said to him: Wicked and slothful servant, thou knewest that I reap where I sow not, and gather where I have not strewed: *27* Thou oughtest therefore to have committed my money to the bankers, and at my coming I should have received my own with usury. *28* Take ye away therefore the talent from him, and give it to him that hath ten talents. *29* For to every one that hath shall be given, and he shall abound: but from him that hath not, that also which he seemeth to have shall be taken away. *30* And the unprofitable servant cast ye out into the exterior darkness. There shall be weeping and gnashing of teeth.

31 And when the Son of man shall come in his majesty, and all the angels with him, then shall he sit upon the seat of his majesty: *32* And all nations shall be gathered together before him, and he shall separate them one from another, as the shepherd separateth the sheep from the goats: *33* And he shall set the sheep on his right hand, but the goats on his left. *34* Then shall the king say to them that shall be on his right hand: Come, ye blessed of my Father, possess you the kingdom prepared for you from the foundation of the world. *35* For I was hungry, and you gave me to eat; I was thirsty, and you gave me to drink; I was a stranger, and you took me in:

36 Naked, and you covered me: sick, and you visited me: I was in prison, and you came to me. *37* Then shall the just answer him, saying: Lord, when did we see thee hungry, and fed thee; thirsty, and gave thee drink? *38* And when did we see thee a stranger, and took thee in? or naked, and covered thee? *39* Or when did we see thee sick or in prison, and came to thee? *40* And the king answering, shall say to them: Amen I say to you, as long as you did it to one of these my least brethren, you did it to me.

41 Then he shall say to them also that shall be on his left hand: Depart from me, you cursed, into everlasting fire which was prepared for the devil and his angels. *42* For I was hungry, and you gave me not to eat: I was thirsty, and you gave me not to drink. *43* I was a stranger, and you took me not in: naked, and you covered me not: sick and in prison, and you did not visit me. *44* Then they also shall answer him, saying: Lord, when did we see thee hungry, or thirsty, or a stranger, or naked, or sick, or in prison, and did not minister to thee? *45* Then he shall answer them, saying: Amen I say to you, as long as you did it not to one of these least, neither did you do it to me.

46 And these shall go into everlasting punishment: but the just, into life everlasting.

Gospel According to St. Luke, Chapter 11:
Christ teaches his disciples to pray. Casts out a dumb devil. Confutes
the Pharisees; and pronounces woes against them for their hypocrisy.

1 And it came to pass, that as he was in a certain place praying, when he ceased, one of his disciples said to him: Lord, teach us to pray, as John also taught his disciples. *2* And he said to them: When you pray, say: Father, hallowed be thy name. Thy kingdom come. *3* Give us this day our daily bread. *4* And forgive us our sins, for we also forgive every one that is indebted to us. And lead us not into temptation. *5* And he said to them: Which of you shall have a friend, and shall go to him at midnight, and shall say to him: Friend, lend me three loaves,

6 Because a friend of mine is come off his journey to me, and I have not what to set before him. *7* And he from within should answer, and say: Trouble me not, the door is now shut, and my children are with me in bed; I cannot rise and give thee. *8* Yet if he shall continue knocking, I say to you, although he will not rise and give him, because he is his friend; yet, because of his importunity, he will rise, and give him as many as he needeth. *9* And I say to you, Ask, and it shall be given you: seek, and you shall find: knock, and it shall be opened to you. *10* For every one that asketh, receiveth; and he that seeketh, findeth; and to him that knocketh, it shall be opened.

11 And which of you, if he ask his father bread, will he give him a stone? or a fish, will he for a fish give him a serpent? *12* Or if he shall ask an egg, will he reach him a scorpion? *13* If you then, being evil, know how to give good gifts to your children, how much more will your Father from heaven give the good Spirit to them that ask him? *14* And he was casting out a devil, and the same was dumb: and when he had cast out the devil, the dumb spoke: and the multitudes were in admiration at it: *15* But some of them said: He casteth out devils by Beelzebub, the prince of devils.

16 And others tempting, asked of him a sign from heaven. *17* But he seeing their thoughts, said to them: Every kingdom divided against itself, shall be brought to desolation, and house upon house shall fall. *18* And if Satan also be divided against himself, how shall his kingdom stand? because you say, that through Beelzebub I cast out devils. *19* Now if I cast out devils by Beelzebub; by whom do your children cast them out? Therefore they shall be your judges. *20* But if I by the finger of God cast out devils; doubtless the kingdom of God is come upon you.

21 When a strong man armed keepeth his court, those things are in peace which he possesseth. *22* But if a stronger than he come upon him, and overcome him; he will take away all his armour wherein he trusted, and will distribute his spoils. *23* He that is not with me, is against me; and he that gathereth not with me, scattereth. *24* When the unclean spirit is gone out of a man, he walketh through places without water, seeking rest; and not finding, he saith: I will return into my house whence I came out. *25* And when he is come, he findeth it swept and garnished.

26 Then he goeth and taketh with him seven other spirits more wicked than himself, and entering in they dwell there. And the last state of that man becomes worse than the first. *27* And it came to pass, as he spoke these things, a certain woman from the crowd, lifting up her voice, said to him: Blessed is the womb that bore thee, and the paps that gave thee suck. *28* But he said: Yea rather, blessed are they who hear the word of God, and keep it. *29* And the multitudes running together, he began to say: This generation is a wicked generation: it asketh a sign, and a sign shall not be given it, but the sign of Jonas the prophet. *30* For as Jonas was a sign to the Ninivites; so shall the Son of man also be to this generation.

31 The queen of the south shall rise in the judgment with the men of this generation, and shall condemn them: because she came from the ends of the earth to hear the wisdom of Solomon; and behold more than Solomon here. *32* The men of Ninive shall rise in the judgment with this generation, and shall condemn it; because they did penance at the preaching of Jonas; and behold more than Jonas here. *33* No man lighteth a candle, and putteth it in a hidden place, nor under a bushel; but upon a candlestick, that they that come in, may see the light. *34* The light of thy body is thy eye. If thy eye be single, thy whole body will be lightsome: but if it be evil, thy body also will be darksome. *35* Take heed therefore, that the light which is in thee, be not darkness.

36 If then thy whole body be lightsome, having no part of darkness; the whole shall be lightsome; and as a bright lamp, shall enlighten thee. *37* And as he was speaking, a certain Pharisee prayed him, that he would dine with him. And he going in, sat down to eat. *38* And the Pharisee began to say, thinking within himself, why he was not washed before dinner. *39* And the Lord said to him: Now you Pharisees make clean the outside of the cup and of the platter; but your inside is full of rapine and iniquity. *40* Ye fools, did not he that made that which is without, make also that which is within?

41 But yet that which remaineth, give alms; and behold, all things are clean unto you. *42* But woe to you, Pharisees, because you tithe mint and rue and every herb; and pass over judgment, and the charity of God. Now these things you ought to have done, and not to leave the other undone. *43* Woe to you, Pharisees, because you love the uppermost seats in the synagogues, and salutations in the marketplace. *44* Woe to you, because you are as sepulchres that appear not, and men that walk over are not aware. *45* And one of the lawyers answering, saith to him: Master, in saying these things, thou reproachest us also.

46 But he said: Woe to you lawyers also, because you load men with burdens which they cannot bear, and you yourselves touch not the packs with one of your fingers. *47* Woe to you who build the monuments of the prophets: and your fathers killed them. *48* Truly you bear witness that you consent to the doings of your fathers: for they indeed killed them, and you build their sepulchres. *49* For this cause also the wisdom of God said: I will send to them prophets and apostles; and some of them they will kill and persecute. *50* That the blood of all the prophets which was shed from the foundation of the world, may be required of this generation, *51* From the blood of Abel unto the blood of Zacharias, who was slain between the altar and the temple: Yea I say to you, It shall be required of this generation. *52* Woe to you lawyers, for you have taken away the key of knowledge: you yourselves have not entered in, and those that were entering in, you have hindered. *53* And as he was saying these things to them, the Pharisees and the lawyers began violently to urge him, and to oppress his mouth about many things, *54* Lying in wait for him, and seeking to catch something from his mouth, that they might accuse him.

Gospel According to St. Luke, Chapter 13:
The necessity of penance. The barren fig tree.
The cure of the infirm woman, etc.

1 And there were present, at that very time, some that told him of the Galileans, whose blood Pilate had mingled with their sacrifices. *2* And he answering, said to them: Think you that these Galileans were sinners above all the men of Galilee, because they suffered such things? *3* No, I say to you: but unless you shall do penance, you shall all likewise perish. *4* Or those eighteen upon whom the tower fell in Siloe, and slew them: think you, that they also were debtors above all the men that dwelt in Jerusalem? *5* No, I say to you; but except you do penance, you shall all likewise perish.

6 He spoke also this parable: A certain man had a fig tree planted in his vineyard, and he came seeking fruit on it, and found none. *7* And he said to the dresser of the vineyard: Behold, for these three years I come seeking fruit on this fig tree, and I find none. Cut it done therefore: why cumbereth it the ground? *8* But he answering, said to him: Lord, let it alone this year also, until I dig about it, and dung it. *9* And if happily it bear fruit: but if not, then after that thou shalt cut it down. *10* And he was teaching in their synagogue on their sabbath.

11 And behold there was a woman, who had a spirit of infirmity eighteen years: and she was bowed together, neither could she look upwards at all. *12* Whom when Jesus saw, he called her unto him, and said to her: Woman, thou art delivered from thy infirmity.

13 And he laid his hands upon her, and immediately she was made straight, and glorified God. *14* And the ruler of the synagogue (being angry that Jesus had healed on the sabbath) answering, said to the multitude: Six days there are wherein you ought to work. In them therefore come, and be healed; and not on the sabbath day. *15* And the Lord answering him, said: Ye hypocrites, doth not every one of you, on the sabbath day, loose his ox or his ass from the manger, and lead them to water?

16 And ought not this daughter of Abraham, whom Satan hath bound, lo, these eighteen years, be loosed from this bond on the sabbath day? *17* And when he said these things, all his adversaries were ashamed: and all the people rejoiced for all the things that were gloriously done by him. *18* He said therefore: To what is the kingdom of God like, and whereunto shall I resemble it? *19* It is like to a grain of mustard seed, which a man took and cast into his garden, and it grew and became a great tree, and the birds of the air lodged in the branches thereof. *20* And again he said: Whereunto shall I esteem the kingdom of God to be like?

21 It is like to leaven, which a woman took and hid in three measures of meal, till the whole was leavened. *22* And he went through the cities and towns teaching, and making his journey to Jerusalem. *23* And a certain man said to him: Lord, are they few that are saved? But he said to them: *24* Strive to enter by the narrow gate; for many, I say to you, shall seek to enter, and shall not be able. *25* But when the master of the house shall be gone in, and shall shut the door, you shall begin to stand without, and knock at the door, saying: Lord, open to us. And he answering, shall say to you: I know you not, whence you are.

26 Then you shall begin to say: We have eaten and drunk in thy presence, and thou hast taught in our streets. *27* And he shall say to you: I know you not, whence you are: depart from me, all ye workers of iniquity. *28* There shall be weeping and gnashing of teeth, when you shall see Abraham and Isaac and Jacob, and all the prophets, in the kingdom of God, and you yourselves thrust out. *29* And there shall come from the east and the west, and the north and the south; and shall sit down in the kingdom of God. *30* And behold, they are last that shall be first; and they are first that shall be last.

31 The same day, there came some of the Pharisees, saying to him: Depart, and get thee hence, for Herod hath a mind to kill thee. *32* And he said to them: Go and tell that fox, Behold, I cast out devils, and do cures today and tomorrow, and the third day I am consummated. *33* Nevertheless I must walk today and tomorrow, and the day following, because it cannot be that a prophet perish, out of Jerusalem. *34* Jerusalem, Jerusalem, that killest the prophets, and stonest them that are sent to thee, how often would I have gathered thy children as the bird doth her brood under her wings, and thou wouldest not? *35* Behold your house shall be left to you desolate. And I say to you, that you shall not see me till the time come, when you shall say: Blessed is he that cometh in the name of the Lord.

Gospel According to St. Luke, Chapter 16:
The parable of the unjust steward: of the rich man and Lazarus.

1 And he said also to his disciples: There was a certain rich man who had a steward: and the same was accused unto him, that he had wasted his goods. *2* And he called him, and said to him: How is it that I hear this of thee? give an account of thy stewardship: for now thou canst be steward no longer. *3* And the steward said within himself: What shall I do, because my lord taketh away from me the stewardship? To dig I am not able; to beg I am ashamed. *4* I know what I will do, that when I shall be removed from the stewardship, they may receive me into their houses. *5* Therefore calling together every one of his lord's debtors, he said to the first: How much dost thou owe my lord?

6 But he said: An hundred barrels of oil. And he said to him: Take thy bill and sit down quickly, and write fifty. *7* Then he said to another: And how much dost thou owe? Who said: An hundred quarters of wheat. He said to him: Take thy bill, and write eighty. *8* And the lord commended the unjust steward, forasmuch as he had done wisely: for the children of this world are wiser in their generation than the children of light. *9* And I say to you: Make unto you friends of the mammon of iniquity; that when you shall fail, they may receive you into everlasting dwellings. *10* He that is faithful in that which is least, is faithful also in that which is greater: and he that is unjust in that which is little, is unjust also in that which is greater.

11 If then you have not been faithful in the unjust mammon; who will trust you with that which is the true? *12* And if you have not been faithful in that which is another's; who will give you that which is your own? *13* No servant can serve two masters: for either he will hate the one, and love the other; or he will hold to the one, and despise the other. You cannot serve God and mammon. *14* Now the Pharisees, who were covetous, heard all these things: and they derided him. *15* And he said to them: You are they who justify yourselves before men, but God knoweth your hearts; for that which is high to men, is an abomination before God.

16 The law and the prophets were until John; from that time the kingdom of God is preached, and every one useth violence towards it. *17* And it is easier for heaven and earth to pass, than one tittle of the law to fall. *18* Every one that putteth away his wife, and marrieth another, committeth adultery: and he that marrieth her that is put away from her husband, committeth adultery. *19* There was a certain rich man, who was clothed in purple and fine linen; and feasted sumptuously every day. *20* And there was a certain beggar, named Lazarus, who lay at his gate, full of sores,

21 Desiring to be filled with the crumbs that fell from the rich man's table, and no one did give him; moreover the dogs came, and licked his sores. *22* And it came to pass, that the beggar died, and was carried by the angels into Abraham's bosom. And the rich man also died: and he was buried in hell. *23* And lifting up his eyes when he was in torments, he saw Abraham afar off, and Lazarus in his bosom: *24* And he cried, and said: Father Abraham, have mercy on me, and send Lazarus, that he may dip the tip of his finger in water, to cool my tongue: for I am tormented in this flame. *25* And Abraham said to him: Son, remember that thou didst receive good things in thy lifetime, and likewise Lazareth evil things, but now he is comforted; and thou art tormented.

26 And besides all this, between us and you, there is fixed a great chaos: so that they who would pass from hence to you, cannot, nor from thence come hither. *27* And he said: Then, father, I beseech thee, that thou wouldst send him to my father's house, for I have five brethren, *28* That he may testify unto them, lest they also come into this place of torments. *29* And Abraham said to him: They have Moses and the prophets; let them hear them. *30* But he said: No, father Abraham: but if one went to them from the dead, they will do penance.

31 And he said to him: If they hear not Moses and the prophets, neither will they believe, if one rise again from the dead.

Gospel According to St. Luke, Chapter 17:
Lessons of avoiding scandal: of the efficacy of faith, etc.
The ten lepers. The manner of the coming of Christ.

1 And he said to his disciples: It is impossible that scandals should not come: but woe to him through whom they come. *2* It were better for him, that a millstone were hanged about his neck, and he cast into the sea, than that he should scandalize one of these little ones. *3* Take heed to yourselves. If thy brother sin against thee, reprove him: and if he do penance, forgive him. *4* And if he sin against thee seven times in a day, and seven times in a day be converted unto thee, saying, I repent; forgive him. *5* And the apostles said to the Lord: Increase our faith.

6 And the Lord said: If you had faith like to a grain of mustard seed, you might say to this mulberry tree, Be thou rooted up, and be thou transplanted into the sea: and it would obey you. *7* But which of you having a servant ploughing, or feeding cattle, will say to him, when he is come from the field: Immediately go, sit down to meat: *8* And will not rather say to him: Make ready my supper, and gird thyself, and serve me, whilst I eat and drink, and afterwards thou shalt eat and drink? *9* Doth he thank that servant, for doing the things which he commanded him? *10* I think not. So you also, when you shall have done all these things that are commanded you, say: We are unprofitable servants; we have done that which we ought to do.

11 And it came to pass, as he was going to Jerusalem, he passed through the midst of Samaria and Galilee. *12* And as he entered into a certain town, there met him ten men that were lepers, who stood afar off; *13* And lifted up their voice, saying: Jesus, master, have mercy on us. *14* Whom when he saw, he said: Go, shew yourselves to the priests. And it came to pass, as they went, they were made clean. *15* And one of them, when he saw that he was made clean, went back, with a loud voice glorifying God.

16 And he fell on his face before his feet, giving thanks: and this was a Samaritan. *17* And Jesus answering, said, Were not ten made clean? and where are the nine? *18* There is no one found to return and give glory to God, but this stranger. *19* And he said to him: Arise, go thy way; for thy faith hath made thee whole. *20* And being asked by the Pharisees, when the kingdom of God should come? he answered them, and said: The kingdom of God cometh not with observation:

21 Neither shall they say: Behold here, or behold there. For lo, the kingdom of God is within you. *22* And he said to his disciples: The days will come, when you shall desire to see one day of the Son of man; and you shall not see it. *23* And they will say to you: See here, and see there. Go ye not after, nor follow them: *24* For as the lightening that lighteneth from under heaven, shineth unto the parts that are under heaven, so shall the Son of man be in his day. *25* But first he must suffer many things, and be rejected by this generation.

26 And as it came to pass in the days of Noe, so shall it be also in the days of the Son of man. *27* They did eat and drink, they married wives, and were given in marriage, until the day that Noe entered into the ark: and the flood came and destroyed them all. *28* Likewise as it came to pass, in the days of Lot: they did eat and drink, they bought and sold, they planted and built. *29* And in the day that Lot went out of Sodom, it rained fire and brimstone from heaven, and destroyed them all. *30* Even thus shall it be in the day when the Son of man shall be revealed.

31 In that hour, he that shall be on the housetop, and his goods in the house, let him not go down to take them away: and he that shall be in the field, in like manner, let him not return back. *32* Remember Lot's wife. *33* Whosoever shall seek to save his life, shall lose it: and whosoever shall lose it, shall preserve it. *34* I say to you: in that night there shall be two men in one bed; the one shall be taken, and the other shall be left. *35* Two women shall be grinding together: the one shall be taken, and the other shall be left: two men shall be in the field; the one shall be taken, and the other shall be left.

36 They answering, say to him: Where, Lord? *37* Who said to them: Wheresoever the body shall be, thither will the eagles also be gathered together.

Gospel According to St. Luke, Chapter 18:
We must pray always. The Pharisee and the publican. The danger of riches. The blind man is restored to sight.

1 And he spoke also a parable to them, that we ought always to pray, and not to faint, *2* Saying: There was a judge in a certain city, who feared not God, nor regarded man. *3* And there was a certain widow in that city, and she came to him, saying: Avenge me of my adversary. *4* And he would not for a long time. But afterwards he said within himself: Although I fear not God, nor regard man, *5* Yet because this widow is troublesome to me, I will avenge her, lest continually coming she weary me.

6 And the Lord said: Hear what the unjust judge saith. *7* And will not God revenge his elect who cry to him day and night: and will he have patience in their regard? *8* I say to you, that he will quickly revenge them. But yet the Son of man, when he cometh, shall he find, think you, faith on earth? *9* And to some who trusted in themselves as just, and despised others, he spoke also this parable: *10* Two men went up into the temple to pray: the one a Pharisee, and the other a publican.

11 The Pharisee standing, prayed thus with himself: O God, I give thee thanks that I am not as the rest of men, extortioners, unjust, adulterers, as also is this publican. *12* I fast twice in a week: I give tithes of all that I possess. *13* And the publican, standing afar off, would not so much as lift up his eyes towards heaven; but struck his breast, saying: O God, be merciful to me a sinner. *14* I say to you, this man went down into his house justified rather than the other: because every one that exalteth himself, shall be humbled: and he that humbleth himself, shall be exalted. *15* And they brought unto him also infants, that he might touch them. Which when the disciples saw, they rebuked them.

16 But Jesus, calling them together, said: Suffer children to come to me, and forbid them not: for of such is the kingdom of God. *17* Amen, I say to you: Whosoever shall not receive the kingdom of God as a child, shall not enter into it. *18* And a certain ruler asked him, saying: Good master, what shall I do to possess everlasting life? *19* And Jesus said to him: Why dost thou call me good? None is good but God alone. *20* Thou knowest the commandments: Thou shalt not kill: Thou shalt not commit adultery: Thou shalt not steal: Thou shalt not bear false witness: Honour thy father and mother.

21 Who said: All these things have I kept from my youth. *22* Which when Jesus had heard, he said to him: Yet one thing is wanting to thee: sell all whatever thou hast, and give to the poor, and thou shalt have treasure in heaven: and come, follow me. *23* He having heard these things, became sorrowful; for he was very rich. *24* And Jesus seeing him become sorrowful, said: How hardly shall they that have riches enter into the kingdom of God. *25* For it is easier for a camel to pass through the eye of a needle, than for a rich man to enter into the kingdom of God.

26 And they that heard it, said: Who then can be saved? *27* He said to them: The things that are impossible with men, are possible with God. *28* Then Peter said: Behold, we have left all things, and have followed thee. *29* Who said to them: Amen, I say to you, there is no man that hath left house, or parents, or brethren, or wife, or children, for the kingdom of God's sake, *30* Who shall not receive much more in this present time, and in the world to come life everlasting.

31 Then Jesus took unto him the twelve, and said to them: Behold, we go up to Jerusalem, and all things shall be accomplished which were written by the prophets concerning the Son of man. *32* For he shall be delivered to the Gentiles, and shall be mocked, and scourged, and spit upon: *33* And after they have scourged him, they will put him to death; and the third day he shall rise again. *34* And they understood none of these things, and this word was hid from them, and they understood not the things that were said. *35* Now it came to pass, when he drew nigh to Jericho, that a certain blind man sat by the way side, begging.

36 And when he heard the multitude passing by, he asked what this meant. *37* And they told him, that Jesus of Nazareth was passing by. *38* And he cried out, saying: Jesus, son of David, have mercy on me. *39* And they that went before, rebuked him, that he should hold his peace: but he cried out much more: Son of David, have mercy on me. *40* And Jesus standing, commanded him to be brought unto him. And when he was come near, he asked him,

41 Saying: What wilt thou that I do to thee? But he said: Lord, that I may see. *42* And Jesus said to him: Receive thy sight: thy faith hath made thee whole. *43* And immediately he saw, and followed him, glorifying God. And all the people, when they saw it, gave praise to God.

Imitation of Christ, Book I, Chapter 24:
Of Judgment, and the Punishment of Our Sins

IN ALL things look to thine end (Ecclus. 7:40), and how thou shalt be able to stand before a severe Judge, from whom nothing is hidden, who takes no bribes, nor receives excuses, but will judge that which is just.

O most wretched and foolish sinner, what answer wilt thou make to God, who knows all thine evils? thou who art sometimes afraid of the looks of an angry man.

Why dost thou not provide for thyself against the Day of Judgment, when no man can be excused or defended by another, but everyone shall have enough to do to answer for himself?

At present thy labor is profitable; thy tears are acceptable, thy sighs will be heard, thy sorrow is satisfactory, and may purge away thy sins.

2. A patient man hath a great and wholesome purgatory, who, receiving injuries, is more concerned at the person's sin than his own wrong; who willingly prays for his adversaries, and from his heart forgives offenses; who delays not to ask forgiveness of others; who is easier moved to compassion than to anger; who frequently useth violence to himself, and labors to bring the flesh wholly under subjection to the spirit.

It is better now to purge away our sins and to cut up our vices than to reserve them to be purged hereafter.

Truly we deceive ourselves through the inordinate love we bear to our flesh.

3. What other things shall the fire feed on but thy sins?

The more thou sparest thyself now and followest the flesh the more grievously shalt thou suffer hereafter and the more fuel dost thou lay up for that fire.

In those things which a man has more sinned shall he be more heavily punished.

There the slothful shall be pricked forward with burning goads, and the glutton will be tormented with extreme hunger and thirst.

There the luxurious and the lovers of pleasure shall be covered all over with burning pitch and stinking brimstone, and the envious like mad dogs shall howl for grief.

4. There is no vice which will not there have its proper torment.

There the proud shall be filled with all confusion, and the covetous be straitened with most miserable want.

There one hour of suffering will be more sharp than a hundred years here spent in the most rigid penance.

There is no rest, no comfort for the damned; but here there is sometimes intermission of labor, and we receive comfort from our friends.

Be careful at present and sorrowful for thy sins, that in the Day of Judgment thou mayest be secure with the blessed.

"For then shall the just stand with great constancy against those that have afflicted and oppressed them." (*Wis.* 5:1).

Then will he stand to judge who now humbly submits himself to the judgment of men.

Then the poor and the humble shall have great confidence and the proud shall fear on every side.

5. Then will it appear that he was wise in this word who learned for Christ's sake to be a fool and despised.

Then all tribulation suffered with patience will be pleasing "and all iniquity shall stop her mouth." (*Ps.* 106:42).

Then every devout person shall rejoice and the irreligious shall be sad.

Then the flesh that has been mortified shall triumph more than if it had always been pampered in delights.

Then shall the mean habit shine and fine clothing appear contemptible.

Then shall the poor cottage be more commended than the gilded palace.

Then constant patience shall more avail than all the power of the world.

Then simple obedience shall be more prized than all worldly craftiness.

6. Then a pure and good conscience shall be a greater subject of joy than learned philosophy.

Then the contempt of riches shall weigh more than all the treasures of worldlings.

Then wilt thou be more comforted that thou hast prayed devoutly than that thou hast fared daintily.

Then wilt thou rejoice more that thou hast kept silence than that thou hast made long discourses or talked much.

Then will holy works be of greater value than many fair words.

Then will a strict life and hard penance be more pleasing than all the delights of the earth.

Learn, at present, to suffer in little things, that then thou mayest be delivered from more grievous sufferings.

Try first here what thou canst suffer hereafter.

If thou canst now endure so little how wilt thou be able to bear everlasting torments?

If a little suffering now makes thee so impatient what will hell-fire do hereafter?

Surely thou canst not have both joys—take thy pleasure in this world and afterwards reign with Christ.

7. If to this day thou hadst always lived in honors and pleasures what would it avail thee if thou wert now in a moment to die?

All then is vanity but to love God and to serve Him alone. (*Eccles.* 1:2; *Deut.* 10:20).

For he that loves God with his whole heart neither fears death, nor punishment, nor judgment, nor Hell; because perfect love gives secure access to God.

But he that is yet delighted with sin no wonder if he be afraid of death and judgment.

It is good, however, that if love, as yet, reclaim thee not from evil, at least the fear of Hell restrain thee.

But he that lays aside the fear of God will not be able to continue long in good, but will quickly fall into the snares of the devil.

Practical Reflections

How powerfully do the fear of God's judgments and the dread of a miserable eternity act as a restraint upon our passions, arrest the sallies of temper, and oblige us to withdraw from the allurements and pleasures of sin! To what end (let us say to ourselves in time of temptation) is the criminal pleasure of this sin of revenge, impurity, anger, injustice, or lying? To afford myself a momentary gratification. And should I die immediately after having yielded, without repentance, without the Sacraments (which may happen, and which does happen to thousands), where will this sinful enjoyment terminate? In a miserable eternity. A momentary pleasure, an eternity of pain! No, I will not expose myself to the danger of being miserable forever for the sake of a moment of pleasure. How true it is, according to the Wise Man, that to avoid sin, at least habitual sin, we must remember our last end. Did we frequently and seriously reflect that we must one day give an exact account of our consciences, of the conduct of our whole lives, of all our sins, to a Judge who knoweth and remembereth all things, who would not be terrified at the apprehension of Judgment, and of the terrible account we are then to give, and would not watch over himself, and endeavor to correct all his faults? Let us be convinced that the sure way to avoid condemnation in the next life is to condemn and punish ourselves in this.

Prayer

O Sovereign Judge of the living and the dead! Who, at the moment of our death, will decide our eternal doom, remember that Thou art our Saviour as well as our Judge, and that as much as our sins have provoked Thee to wrath, Thy sacred Wounds have inclined Thee to mercy. Look, therefore, on those Wounds inflicted on Thee for our sins, and on the Blood which Thou hast shed for their expiation, and by those precious pledges of salvation we conjure Thee to pardon our manifold transgressions. Amen.

Imitation of Christ, Book II, Chapter 5:
Of the Consideration of One's Self

WE CANNOT trust much to ourselves, because we often want grace and understanding.

There is but little light in us and this we quickly lose through negligence.

Many times also we perceive not that we are so blind interiorly.

We often do ill and do worse in excusing it.

We are sometimes moved with passion, and we mistake it for zeal.

We blame little things in others and pass over great things in ourselves.

We are quick enough at perceiving and weighing what we suffer from others, but we mind not what others suffer from us.

He that would well and duly weigh his own deeds would have no room to judge hardly of others.

2. An internal man prefers the care of himself before all other cares, and he that diligently attends to himself is easily silent with regard to others.

Thou wilt never be internal and devout unless thou pass over in silence other men's concerns and particularly look to thyself.

If thou attend wholly to thyself and to God, thou wilt be little moved with what thou perceivest without thee.

Where art thou when thou art not present to thyself? And when thou hast run over all things, what profit will it be to thee if thou hast neglected thyself? (*Matt.* 16:26).

If thou desirest to have peace and true union thou must set all the rest aside and turn thine eyes upon thyself alone.

3. Thou wilt then make great progress if thou keep thyself free from all temporal care.

But if thou set a value upon anything temporal thou wilt fail exceedingly.

Let nothing be great in thine eyes, nothing high, nothing pleasant, nothing agreeable to thee, except it be purely God or of God.

Look upon all the comfort which thou meetest with from any creature as vain.

A soul that loveth God despiseth all things that are less than God.

None but God, eternal and incomprehensible, who filleth all things, can afford true comfort to the soul and true joy to the heart.

Practical Reflections

Useless reflections upon ourselves and upon exterior things occasion us to lose much time, many graces, and much merit. Did we but endeavor to substitute a respectful remembrance of God, in place of a vain and hurtful attention to ourselves and to creatures, we should be always well employed. To consider God as within us, and ourselves as existing in God: to live under the eye of Jesus Christ by means of recollection, in His hands by resignation, and at His feet by humility and a sincere acknowledgment of our miseries, is to live really as Christians; for we can only be such in proportion as we are devoted to Jesus Christ. Why then are we so much and so frequently attracted by news, curiosities, and vanity, and so little interested with God, our duties, and our salvation? It is because we are indifferent to the things of eternity, and too much attached to those which pass away with time. Let us, therefore, begin to be now what we hope to be forever—occupied only with God, in God, and for God.

Prayer

Correct in me, O Lord, that indolence of mind in which I squander away my time with trifles, and that uselessness of thought which withdraws me from the enjoyment of Thy presence, and distracts my attention in the time of prayer; or if, when I recite my prayers, I cannot always think of Thee, grant that my distractions may not be voluntary, so that whilst they divert my mind, they may never withdraw my heart from Thee. Teach me, O Lord, before prayer, to prepare my soul, that, urged by my many necessities, and by a desire of pleasing Thee, I may fulfill this important duty with a becoming sense of Thine awful presence, and of the subject on which I seek relief from Thy bounty and mercy. Amen.

Imitation of Christ, Book III, Chapter 7:
Grace Is to Be Hid under the Guardianship of Humility

MY SON, it is more profitable and more safe for thee to hide the grace of devotion and not to be elevated with it, not to speak much of it, not to consider it much, but rather to despise thyself the more and to be afraid of it, as given to one unworthy.

Thou must not depend too much on this affection which may be quickly changed into the contrary.

When thou hast grace think with thyself how miserable and poor thou art wont to be when thou art without it.

Nor does the progress of a spiritual life consist so much in having the grace of consolation, as in bearing the want of it with humility, resignation, and patience, so as not to grow remiss in thine exercise of prayer at that time, nor to suffer thyself to omit any of thine accustomed good works.

But that thou willingly do what lies in thee, according to the best of thy ability and understanding, and take care not wholly to neglect thyself through the dryness or anxiety of mind which thou feelest.

2. For there are many who when things succeed not well with them presently grow impatient or slothful.

Now the way of man is not always in his own power (*Jer.* 10:23), but it belongs to God to give and to comfort when He will, and as much as He will, and to whom He will, and as it shall please Him and no more.

Some, wanting discretion, have ruined themselves upon occasion of the grace of devotion, because they were desirous of doing more than they could, not weighing well the measure of their own weakness, but following rather the inclinations of the heart than the dictates of reason.

And because they presumptuously undertook greater things than were pleasing to God, therefore they quickly lost His grace.

They became needy and were left in a wretched condition, who had built themselves a nest in Heaven to the end, that being thus humbled and impoverished they might learn not to trust to their own wings, but to hide themselves under Mine. (*Ps.* 90:4).

Those who are yet but novices and unexperienced in the way of the Lord, if they will not govern themselves by the counsel of discreet persons, will be easily deceived and overthrown.

3. And if they will rather follow their own judgment than believe others who have more experience, their future is full of danger if they continue to refuse to lay down their own conceits.

They that are wise in their own eyes seldom humbly suffer themselves to be ruled by others. (*Prov.* 3:7; *Rom.* 11:25).

It is better to have little knowledge with humility and a weak understanding, than greater treasures of learning with self-conceit.

It is better for thee to have less than much, which may puff thee up with pride.

He is not so discreet as he ought to be who gives himself up wholly to joy, forgetting his former poverty and the chaste fear of God, which apprehends the loss of that grace which is offered.

Neither is he so virtuously wise who, in the time of adversity or any tribulation whatsoever, carries himself in a desponding way and conceives and reposes less confidence in Me than he ought.

4. He who is too secure in time of peace will often be found too much dejected and fearful in time of war.

If thou couldst but always continue humble and little in thine own eyes and keep thy spirit in due order and subjection, thou wouldst not fall so easily into dangers and offenses.

It is a good counsel that when thou hast conceived the spirit of fervor, thou shouldst meditate how it will be with thee when that light shall leave thee.

Which, when it shall happen, remember that the light may return again, which, for thine instruction and My glory I have withdrawn from thee for a time.

5. Such a trial is oftentimes more profitable than if thou wert always to have prosperity according to thy will.

For a man's merits are not to be estimated by his having many visions or consolations, nor by his knowledge in scriptures, nor by his being placed in a more elevated station.

But by his being grounded in true humility and replenished with divine charity; by his seeking always purely and entirely the honor of God; by his esteeming himself as nothing and sincerely despising himself, and being better pleased to be despised and humbled by others than to be the object of their esteem.

Practical Reflections

Man in the state of innocence would have perfect love, because all within him would have submitted without difficulty to His orders; but in the state of sin in which we now are we cannot serve Him without continually fighting against ourselves; nor can we love Him without hating ourselves; we can do but little for Him but what we do against ourselves. Hence we should humbly submit to the dryness, disgust, and irksomeness which we frequently experience in our exercises of piety; we should enter into the designs of Almighty God, make a merit of seeking to please Him without gratifying ourselves; and willingly consent to become victims of His love, and to sacrifice all for His honor. Did the truly Christian soul know how far a state of suffering may be made a holy and sanctifying state, a state of proved and purified love for God, in a word, a state in which we neither seek nor find ourselves in anything but purely God, how would that soul esteem it! What care would it not take to profit by it, that is, to suffer patiently, to support the Lord with courage, and to neglect nothing, whatever uneasiness might arise. Were we thoroughly persuaded of, and deeply impressed with a conviction of the continual merit of a life of dryness when supported without dejection, we should without doubt endeavor to correspond with the designs of God, who would thus oblige us not to seek ourselves in anything, but to endeavor only to please Him, and to make a real merit of His good pleasure. We should esteem ourselves happy in sacrificing to God the gratifications of our hearts, in yielding ourselves up to Him, and in doing our duty, even without the satisfaction of knowing that we please Him!

Prayer

Purify my heart, O Lord, from the pursuits of self-love, which is never satisfied with what is done for Thee unless it also be gratified by it. Grant that, in all my exercises of piety, I may seek rather to please Thee than to gratify myself: that dying daily to the natural life of my soul, in which consists true satisfaction, I may seek no other pleasure than fidelity in Thy service and exactness in following Thy holy will in all things; that so, approaching to Thee, my God, more by faith than by sense, I may do and suffer all for Thy love, notwithstanding my natural aversion and the deprivation of all the sweetness and sensible charms of piety, persuaded of the truth of what Thou didst once say to St. Gertrude, that Thou reservest until death the consolation of all we perform without consolation during life. Grant, therefore, that my whole employment and all my happiness may be to serve and to love Thee much more for Thyself than for my own gratification. Amen.

Imitation of Christ, Book III, Chapter 8: Of Acknowledging Our Unworthiness in the Sight of God

Disciple
I WILL speak to my Lord, I who am but dust and ashes. (*Gen.* 18:27). If I think anything better of myself, behold Thou standest against me and my sins bear witness to the truth, and I cannot contradict it.

But if I humble myself and acknowledge my own nothingness, and cast away all manner of esteem of myself and (as I really am) account myself to be mere dust, Thy grace will be favorable to me and Thy light will draw nigh to my heart; and all self-esteem, how small soever, will be sunk in the depth of my own nothingness and there lose itself forever.

It is there Thou showest me to myself, what I am, what I have been and what I am to come to; for I am nothing and I knew it not. (*Ps.* 72:22).

If I am left to myself, behold I am nothing and all weakness; but if Thou shouldst graciously look upon me, I presently become strong and am filled with a new joy.

And it is very wonderful that I am so quickly raised up and so graciously embraced by Thee; I, who by my own weight, am always sinking to the bottom.

2. It is Thy love that effects this, freely preventing me and assisting me in so many necessities, reserving me also from grievous dangers, and as I may truly say, delivering me from innumerable evils.

For by an evil loving of myself, I lost myself, and by seeking Thee alone and purely loving Thee, I found both myself and Thee, and by this love have more profoundly annihilated myself.

Because Thou, O most sweet Lord, art bountiful to me above all desert and above all I dare hope or ask for.

3. Blessed be Thou, O my God, for though I am unworthy of all good, yet Thy generosity and infinite goodness never ceaseth to do good, even to those who are ungrateful and that are turned away from Thee.

Oh, convert us unto Thee, that we may be thankful, humble, and devout; for Thou art our salvation, our power, and our strength. (*Ps.* 61:8).

Practical Reflections

When we perceive within ourselves any feelings of vanity or self-complacency, we need but consider, for one moment, the unfathomable depth of our corruption, and descend into the abyss of our miseries, to stifle them in their very birth. For how can we represent to ourselves that universal incapacity which we experience for supernatural good, our inclination for evil, how violently we are carried towards wickedness, the blindness of our understandings, the malice of our hearts and the fury of our passions, which are always revolting against reason; in a word, how can we consider what we really are, and not despise and humble ourselves beneath all creatures? And if we consider ourselves with reference to God; if we reflect what He is and what we are in His sight, a mere nothing, sinners, but sinners loaded with the numberless crimes we have committed, not knowing whether they have ever been pardoned; creatures so weak and feeble, so inconstant in good, and so constant in evil; alas! perhaps in the sight of God, living and dying in the state of sin, and worthy only of His eternal hatred; how, in the midst of such reflections, can we possibly consent to the least thought of vanity? How true it is that to esteem ourselves is not to know, but to forget what we are.

Prayer

Suffer not pride, O Lord, to deprive us of the sight and conviction of our manifold miseries. Oblige us to do justice to ourselves and to Thee, by referring the glory of all things to Thee, to Whom alone it belongs: and by giving to ourselves nothing but contempt, which is truly our desert and appropriate portion. How does a Christian who knows that he is all Thine, my Saviour, and that he carries within himself an inexhaustible source of malice and corruption, give Thee alone the honor of all the good he may do by the help of Thy grace, and attribute nothing to himself but the evil which he commits, since without Thee he is incapable of doing anything but sin! Fill my heart with this true humility, without which it is impossible ever to become worthy of Thy love. Amen.

Imitation of Christ, Book III, Chapter 13:
The Obedience of an Humble Subject,
After the Example of Jesus Christ

Christ

SON, he who strives to withdraw himself from obedience withdraws himself from grace, and he that seeks to have things for his own particular use loses such as are common.

If a man doth not freely and willingly submit himself to his superior, it is a sign that his flesh is not, as yet, perfectly obedient to him, but oftentimes rebels and murmurs.

Learn then to submit thyself readily to thy superior if thou desire to subdue thine own flesh.

For the outward enemy is sooner overcome if the inward man be not laid waste.

There is no more troublesome or worse enemy to the soul than thou art thyself, when not agreeing well with the Spirit.

Thou must, in good earnest, conceive a true contempt of thyself if thou wilt prevail over flesh and blood.

Because thou hast yet too inordinate a love for thyself, therefore art thou afraid to resign thyself wholly to the will of others.

2. But what great matter is it if thou, who art but dust and a mere nothing, submit thyself for God's sake to man, when I, the Almighty and the Most High, who created all things out of nothing, have for thy sake humbly subjected Myself to man?

I became the most humble and most abject of all, that thou mightest learn to overcome thy pride by My humility.

Learn, O dust, to obey; learn to humble thyself, thou that art but dirt and mire, and to cast thyself down under the feet of all men.

Learn to break thine own will and to yield thyself up to all subjection.

3. Conceive an indignation against thyself; suffer not the swelling of pride to live in thee, but make thyself so submissive and little, that all may trample on thee and tread thee underfoot as the dirt of the streets.

What hast thou, vain man, to complain of?

What answer canst thou make, O wretched sinner, to those that reproach thee, thou that hast so often offended God and many times deserved Hell?

But Mine eye hath spared thee (*1 Kgs.* 24:11), because thy soul was precious in My sight, that thou mightest know My love and mightest be always thankful for My favor and that thou mightest give thyself continually to true subjection and humility, and bear with patience to be despised by all.

Practical Reflections

We must not be satisfied with exteriorly submitting to obedience and in things that are easy, but we must obey with our whole heart, and in things the most difficult. For the greater the difficulty, the greater also is the merit of obedience. Can we refuse to submit to man for God's sake, when God, for love of us, submits to man, even to His very executioners?

Jesus Christ was willingly obedient during His whole life, and even unto the death of the Cross; and am I unwilling to spend my life in the exercise of obedience, and to make it my cross and my merit? Independence belongs to God, who has made man dependent upon others, that his subordination may be to him the means of his sanctification. I will therefore form myself upon the model of my submissive, dependent, and obedient Saviour, and dispose of nothing in myself, not even of my own will.

Prayer

O my Saviour, Who, in obedience to Thy Father, wast conceived in the womb of Mary, Who didst go down to Nazareth, and wast subject to Thy parents for thirty years, Who wouldst be born and live, and die in obedience, induce us to follow Thine example, to obey Thee in all things in the persons of our superiors, who hold Thy place in our regard. Grant that, doing willingly what is ordained us, and endeavoring to believe it best, we may spend our whole lives in continual obedience, and thus secure for ourselves Thy grace in time, and Thy glory for all eternity. Amen.

Imitation of Christ, Book III, Chapter 20:
The Confession of Our Own Infirmity And the Miseries of This Life

Disciple
I WILL confess against myself my injustice. (*Ps.* 21:5). I will confess to Thee, O Lord, my infirmity.

It is oftentimes a small thing which casts me down and troubles me.

I make a resolution to behave myself valiantly; but when a small temptation comes I am brought into great straits.

It is sometimes a very trifling thing from which proceeds a grievous temptation.

209

And when I think myself somewhat safe, I find myself sometimes, when I least apprehend it, almost overcome with a small blast.

2. Behold, then, O Lord, my abjection and frailty (*Ps.* 24:18), every way known to Thee.

Have pity on me and draw me out of the mire (*Ps.* 118:15), that I stick not fast therein, that I may not be utterly cast down forever.

This it is which often drives me back and confounds me in Thy sight, to find that I am so subject to fall and have so little strength to resist my passions.

And although I do not altogether consent, yet their assaults are troublesome and grievous to me, and it is exceedingly irksome to live thus always in a conflict.

Hence my infirmity is made known to me, because wicked thoughts do always much more easily rush in upon me than they can be cast out again.

3. Oh, that Thou, the most mighty God of Israel, the zealous lover of faithful souls, wouldst behold the labor and sorrow of Thy servant, and stand by me in all my undertakings.

Strengthen me with heavenly fortitude, lest the old man, the miserable flesh, not fully subject to the spirit, prevail and get the upper hand, against which we must fight as long as we breathe in this most wretched life.

Alas! what kind of life is this, where afflictions and miseries are never wanting; where all things are full of snares and enemies.

For when one tribulation or temptation is gone another cometh: yea, and whilst the first still lasts, many others come on and these unexpected.

4. How can a life be loved that hath such great bitterness, that is subject to so many calamities and miseries.

How can it be called life since it begets so many deaths and plagues?

And yet it is loved and many seek their delight in it.

Many blame the world that it is deceitful and vain, yet they are not willing to quit it, because the concupiscence of the flesh overmuch prevails.

But there are some things that draw them to love the world—others to despise it.

The concupiscence of the flesh, the concupiscence of the eyes, and the pride of life (*John* 2:16), draw to the love of the world; but the pains and miseries, which justly follow these things, breed a hatred and loathing of the world.

5. But alas! the pleasure of sin prevails over the worldly soul and under these briers she imagines there are delights (*Job* 30:7); because she has neither seen nor tasted the sweetness of God, nor the internal pleasures of virtue.

But they that perfectly despise the world and study to live to God under holy discipline, experience the divine sweetness that is promised for those who forsake all; and such clearly see how grievously the world is mistaken and how many ways it is imposed upon.

Practical Reflections

It is not sufficient to know and to feel our weaknesses and miseries, and our continual danger of perishing eternally by yielding to our passions; we should also at the sight of them humble ourselves before God, and place our whole confidence in Him. We should incessantly bewail our exile, and cast and support ourselves upon the bounty of God. We should never remain in the state of sin, tepidity, or infidelity in which our weakness too often engages us, but immediately arise after we have fallen and speedily return to our heavenly Father when we find we have gone astray.

This life is so replete with temptations, pains, and miseries, that it becomes insupportable to a soul that loves God, and is afraid of offending Him. How shall I live, does it exclaim, and not sin? Yet how shall I sin and still live? to be ever falling, and then rising again; ever resisting my passions, and fighting against the irregular desires of my heart, is this life? It is continual death. But let us not grow weary of repressing, of fighting, and conquering our predominant passions, for in this consists the merit of a supernatural life, of a life conducting to eternal happiness.

Prayer

I acknowledge, O God, that life would be unsatisfactory had I no trial of suffering for Thy sake. Grant, therefore, that, when weary of myself, and fatigued with the miseries of this life, I may commit them all to Thy most merciful providence. Support me by Thy bounty, and give me patience and fidelity to endure myself, and to suffer whatever Thou shalt appoint. Amen.

Imitation of Christ, Book III, Chapter 30: Of Asking the Divine Assistance, and of Confidence of Recovering Grace

Christ

SON, I am the Lord, who give strength in the day of trouble. (*Nahum* 1:7).

Come to Me when it is not well with thee.

This is that which most of all hinders heavenly comfort, that thou art slow in turning thyself to prayer.

For before thou earnestly prayest to Me thou seekest in the meantime many comforts and delightest thyself in outward things.

And hence it comes to pass that all things avail thee little till thou take notice that I am He that delivers those that trust in Me. Nor is there out of Me any powerful help, or profitable counsel, or lasting remedy.

But now having recovered spirit after the storm, grow thou strong again in the light of My tender mercies; for I am at hand to repair all, not only to the full, but even with abundance and above measure.

2. Is anything difficult to Me? or shall I be like one that promises and does not perform? (*Jer.* 32:27; *Num.* 23:19).

Where is thy faith? Stand firmly and with perseverance.

Have patience and be of good courage, comfort will come to thee in its proper season.

Wait for Me, wait, I will come and cure thee.

It is a temptation that troubles thee, and a vain fear that frightens thee.

What does that solicitude about future accidents bring thee but only sorrow upon sorrow? "Sufficient for the day is the evil thereof." (*Matt.* 6:34).

It is a vain and unprofitable thing to conceive either grief or joy for future things, which perhaps will never happen.

3. But it is incident to man to be deluded with such imaginations; and a sign of a soul that is yet weak and to be easily drawn away by the suggestions of the enemy.

For he cares not whether it be with things true or false that he abuses and deceives thee, whether he overthrow thee with the love of things present or the fear of things to come.

"Let not, therefore, thy heart be troubled and let it not be afraid." (*John* 14:27).

Believe in Me and trust in My mercy. When thou thinkest I am far from thee, I am often nearest to thee.

When thou judgest that almost all is lost, then oftentimes it is that thou art in the way of gaining the greatest merit.

All is not lost when anything falls out otherwise than thou wouldst have it.

Thou must not judge according to thy present feeling, nor give thyself up in such manner to any trouble, from whence soever it comes, nor take it so as if all hope were gone of being delivered out of it.

4. Think not thyself wholly forsaken, although for a time I have sent thee some tribulation, or withdrawn from thee the comfort which thou desirest; for this is the way to the Kingdom of Heaven.

And without doubt it is more expedient for thee, and for the rest of My servants, that thou be exercised by adversities than that thou shouldst have all things according to thine inclination.

I know thy secret thoughts; I know that it is very expedient for thy soul that thou shouldst sometimes be left without consolation, lest thou shouldst be puffed up with much success and shouldst take a complacence in thyself, imagining thyself to be what thou art not.

What I have given I can justly take away, and restore it again when I please.

5. When I give it, it is still Mine; when I take it away again I take not anything that is thine; for every good gift and every perfect gift is Mine. (*James* 1:17).

If I send thee affliction or any adversity, repine not, neither let thy heart be cast down.

I can quickly raise thee up again and turn all thy burden into joy.

Nevertheless, I am just and greatly to be praised when I deal thus with thee.

6. If thou think rightly and consider things in truth thou oughtst never to be so much dejected and troubled for any adversity, but rather to rejoice and give thanks.

Yea, even to account this as a special subject of joy, that afflicting thee with sorrows I spare thee not. (*Job* 6:10).

"As my Father hath loved me I also have loved you," said I to My beloved disciples (*John* 15:9), whom certainly I did not send to temporal joys, but to great conflicts; not to honors, but to contempt; not to idleness, but to labors; not to rest, but to "bring forth much fruit in patience." (*Luke* 8:13). Remember these words, O My son.

Practical Reflections

I am the Lord, saith the Almighty, by the mouth of one of His prophets, who give strength to souls in the day of trouble, and deliver those from danger who put their trust in Me. How consoling, how encouraging and supporting, are these words to a soul that, in the time of temptation and adversity, is faithful and constant to what God requires of it! This is what the Scripture calls to wait for and to support the Lord.

Believe in Me, says our blessed Saviour, and thy heart shall not be troubled nor fear. Wherefore, upon occasion of interior or exterior affliction, we should, in the first place, have recourse to God with confidence; secondly, we should resign ourselves to His blessed will; thirdly, we should not neglect any of our spiritual exercises; fourthly, we should subdue ourselves, restrain and renounce ourselves in all things, that we may act in concert with God; fifthly, we should consider it our welfare and our merit to be afflicted, tormented, and, as it were, annihilated for the honor of God's majesty; sixthly, we should be content to carry a crucified heart, a heart suffering and penetrated with bitterness and sorrow, in imitation of our crucified Jesus.

Prayer

No, Lord, I will not give up all as lost when Thou seemest to withdraw Thyself from me; but, on the contrary, I will believe all gained when my soul, though sinking under fatigue, and withered with bitterness, shall resign itself to Thy holy will, and live only in Thee, saying with the Prophet, I commit to Thee all my strength, for my soul is in Thy hands, and Thy mercy supports and encourages my heart to profit by the sense of my miseries. Abandon me not, O God, to the disorder of my passions, but be Thou their master by Thy grace, and keep me always in the possession of Thy love. Amen.

Imitation of Christ, Book III, Chapter 47:
All Grievous Things Are to Be Endured for Eternal Life

Christ

SON, be not dismayed with the labors which thou hast undertaken for Me; neither let the tribulations
   which befall thee quite cast thee down; but let My promise strengthen thee, and comfort thee in every event. (*Ps.* 118:71).

I am sufficient to reward thee beyond all measure. (*Gen.* 15:1).

Thou shalt not labor here long, nor shalt thou be always oppressed with sorrows.

Wait a little while and thou shalt see a speedy end of all thine evils. The hour will come when labor and trouble shall be no more.

All is little and short which passeth away with time. (*Wis.* 3:9).

2. Do thy part well; mind what thou art about; labor faithfully in My vineyard, I will be thy reward.

Write, read, sing, sigh, keep silence, pray, bear thy crosses manfully; eternal life is worthy of all these, and greater combats.

Peace shall come in one day, which is known to the Lord; and it shall not be a vicissitude of day and night, such as is at present; but everlasting light, infinite brightness, steadfast peace, and secure rest. (*Apoc.* 21:23).

Thou shalt not then say: Who shall deliver me from the body of this death? (*Rom.* 7:24). Nor shalt thou cry out: Woe is me, that my sojourning is prolonged. (*Ps.* 119:5). For death shall be no more, but never-failing health; no anxiety, but blessed delight; and a society sweet and lovely. Oh, if thou hadst seen the everlasting crown of the saints in Heaven, and in how great glory they now triumph who appeared contemptible heretofore to this world, and in a manner even unworthy of life, doubtless thou wouldst immediately cast thyself down to the very earth, and wouldst rather seek to be under the feet of all, than to have command over so much as one.

Neither wouldst thou covet the pleasant days of this life, but wouldst rather be glad to suffer tribulation for God's sake, and esteem it thy greatest gain to be reputed as nothing amongst men.

3. Ah, if thou didst but relish these things, and suffer them to penetrate deeply into thy heart, how wouldst thou dare so much as once to complain!

Are not all painful labors to be endured for everlasting life? It is no small matter to lose or gain the Kingdom of God. Lift up therefore thy face to Heaven. Behold, I, and all My saints with Me, who in this world have had a great conflict, do now rejoice, are now comforted, are now secure, are now at rest, and they shall for all eternity abide with Me in the Kingdom of My Father. (*Wis.* 5:1).

Practical Reflections

How hard is this saying, that salvation is only to be obtained by a life of continual suffering, by constantly fighting against and by ever renouncing and dying to ourselves! But how we are encouraged to submit to such a course by the hope and assurance of eternal happiness, which will be the reward we shall receive in exchange for the disappointments and miseries of this present time! Nothing will afford us such great consolation at the hour of death as the good use we have made of sufferings: then shall we find that we have done nothing purely for God but what we have done contrary to ourselves, and that a truly Christian life must necessarily be a life of crosses and self-denials.

Prayer

As, O God, we believe and hope for the good things of eternity, grant that we may so use the transitory miseries of this life as to obtain the permanent felicity of the next. At the hour of death, what shall we not wish to have done, to have suffered, and renounced for the sake of obtaining Heaven! Instill, O Lord, into our hearts something of the desires we shall then entertain to no purpose, that we may now really renounce and die to ourselves. Grant we may never consider anything as great but what is eternal, and regard all that passes away with time, as little and contemptible. O happiness! O joy! O eternal felicity! console us under the afflictions of our mortal course. And since we must of necessity repent either in time or for all eternity, suffer either in this life or in the next, grant us, we beseech Thee, O Jesus, patiently to endure all present evils, in hopes of obtaining future bliss and happiness. Amen.

—SECOND WEEK—
Knowledge of the Blessed Virgin

"They shall devote the second week to the knowledge of the Blessed Virgin." (See no. 229).

We must unite ourselves to Jesus through Mary—this is the characteristic of our devotion; therefore, Saint Louis De Montfort asks that the second week be employed in acquiring a knowledge of the Blessed Virgin.

Mary is our sovereign and our mediatrix, our Mother and our Mistress. Let us then endeavor to know the effects of this royalty, of this mediation, and of this maternity, as well as the grandeurs and prerogatives which are the foundation or consequences thereof. Our Mother is also a perfect mold wherein we are to be molded in order to make her intentions and dispositions ours. This we cannot achieve without studying the interior life of Mary; namely, her virtues, her sentiments, her actions, her participation in the mysteries of Christ and her union with Him.

Prayers:

> *Litany of the Holy Ghost,* page 174. *Ave Maris Stella,* page 150.
> *Litany of the Blessed Virgin,* page 176.
> *St. Louis De Montfort's Prayer to Mary.* Recitation of the *Rosary.*

Reading:

> Gospel according to St. Luke, chapters 1, 2. Gospel according to St. John, chapter 2.
> *True Devotion,* nos. 1-48, 90-93, 105-182, 213-225.
> *Secret of Mary,* nos. 23 and 24

Spiritual Exercises:

> Acts of love, pious affections for the Blessed Virgin, imitation of her virtues, especially her profound humility, her lively faith, her blind obedience, her continual mental prayer, her mortification in all things, her ardent charity, her heroic patience, her angelic sweetness, her divine wisdom, and her divine purity; "these being," as St. Louis De Montfort says, "the ten principal virtues of the Blessed Virgin."

St. Louis De Montfort's Prayer to Mary

Hail Mary, beloved Daughter of the Eternal Father! Hail Mary, admirable Mother of the Son! Hail Mary, faithful spouse of the Holy Ghost! Hail Mary, my dear Mother, my loving Mistress, my powerful sovereign! Hail my joy, my glory, my heart and my soul! Thou art all mine by mercy, and I am all thine by justice. But I am not yet sufficiently thine. I now give myself wholly to thee without keeping anything back for myself or others. If thou still seest in me anything which does not belong to thee, I beseech thee to take it and to make thyself the absolute Mistress of all that is mine. Destroy in me all that may be displeasing to God, root it up and bring it to nought; place and cultivate in me everything that is pleasing to thee.

May the light of thy faith dispel the darkness of my mind; may thy profound humility take the place of my pride; may thy sublime contemplation check the distractions of my wandering imagination; may thy continuous sight of God fill my memory with His presence; may the burning love of thy heart inflame the lukewarmness of mine; may thy virtues take the place of my sins; may thy merits be my only adornment in the sight of God and make up for all that is wanting in me. Finally, dearly beloved Mother, grant, if it be possible, that I may have no other spirit but thine to know Jesus and His divine will; that I may have no other soul but thine to praise and glorify the Lord; that I may have no other heart but thine to love God with a love as pure and ardent as thine. I do not ask thee for visions, revelations, sensible devotion or spiritual pleasures. It is thy privilege to see God clearly; it is thy privilege to enjoy heavenly bliss; it is thy privilege to triumph gloriously in Heaven at the right hand of thy Son and to hold absolute sway over angels, men and demons; it is thy privilege to dispose of all the gifts of God, just as thou willest.

Such is, O heavenly Mary, the "best part," which the Lord has given thee and which shall never be taken away from thee—and this thought fills my heart with joy. As for my part here below, I wish for no other than that which was thine: to believe sincerely without spiritual pleasures; to suffer joyfully without human consolation; to die continually to myself without respite; and to work zealously and unselfishly for thee until death as the humblest of thy servants. The only grace I beg thee to obtain for me is that every day and every moment of my life I may say: Amen, so be it—to all that thou didst do while on earth; Amen, so be it—to all that thou art now doing in Heaven; Amen, so be it—to all that thou art doing in my soul, so that thou alone mayest fully glorify Jesus in me for time and eternity. Amen.

Gospel According to St. Luke, Chapter 1:
The conception of John the Baptist, and of Christ:
the visitation and canticle of the Blessed Virgin:
the birth of the Baptist and the canticle of Zachary.

1 Forasmuch as many have taken in hand to set forth in order a narration of the things that have been accomplished among us; *2* According as they have delivered them unto us, who from the beginning were eyewitnesses and ministers of the word: *3* It seemed good to me also, having diligently attained to all things from the beginning, to write to thee in order, most excellent Theophilus, *4* That thou mayest know the verity of those words in which thou hast been instructed. *5* There was in the days of Herod, the king of Judea, a certain priest named Zachary, of the course of Abia; and his wife was of the daughters of Aaron, and her name Elizabeth.

6 And they were both just before God, walking in all the commandments and justifications of the Lord without blame. *7* And they had no son, for that Elizabeth was barren, and they both were well advanced in years. *8* And it came to pass, when he executed the priestly function in the order of his course before God, *9* According to the custom of the priestly office, it was his lot to offer incense, going into the temple of the Lord. *10* And all the multitude of the people was praying without, at the hour of incense.

11 And there appeared to him an angel of the Lord, standing on the right side of the altar of incense. *12* And Zachary seeing him, was troubled, and fear fell upon him. *13* But the angel said to him: Fear not, Zachary, for thy prayer is heard; and thy wife Elizabeth shall bear thee a son, and thou shalt call his name John: *14* And thou shalt have joy and gladness, and many shall rejoice in his nativity. *15* For he shall be great before the Lord; and shall drink no wine nor strong drink: and he shall be filled with the Holy Ghost, even from his mother's womb.

16 And he shall convert many of the children of Israel to the Lord their God. *17* And he shall go before him in the spirit and power of Elias; that he may turn the hearts of the fathers unto the children, and the incredulous to the wisdom of the just, to prepare unto the Lord a perfect people. *18* And Zachary said to the angel: Whereby shall I know this? for I am an old man, and my wife is advanced in years. *19* And the angel answering, said to him: I am Gabriel, who stand before God; and am sent to speak to thee, and to bring thee these good tidings. *20* And behold, thou shalt be dumb, and shalt not be able to speak until the day wherein these things shall come to pass, because thou hast not believed my words, which shall be fulfilled in their time.

21 And the people were waiting for Zachary; and they wondered that he tarried so long in the temple. *22* And when he came out, he could not speak to them: and they understood that he had seen a vision in the temple. And he made signs to them, and remained dumb. *23* And it came to pass, after the days of his office were accomplished, he departed to his own house. *24* And after those days, Elizabeth his wife conceived, and hid herself five months, saying: *25* Thus hath the Lord dealt with me in the days wherein he hath had regard to take away my reproach among men.

26 And in the sixth month, the angel Gabriel was sent from God into a city of Galilee, called Nazareth, *27* To a virgin espoused to a man whose name was Joseph, of the house of David; and the virgin's name was Mary. *28* And the angel being come in, said unto her: Hail, full of grace, the Lord is with thee: blessed art thou among women. *29* Who having heard, was troubled at his saying, and thought with herself what manner of salutation this should be. *30* And the angel said to her: Fear not, Mary, for thou hast found grace with God.

31 Behold thou shalt conceive in thy womb, and shalt bring forth a son; and thou shalt call his name Jesus. *32* He shall be great, and shall be called the Son of the most High; and the Lord God shall give unto him the throne of David his father; and he shall reign in the house of Jacob for ever. *33* And of his kingdom there shall be no end. *34* And Mary said to the angel: How shall this be done, because I know not man? *35* And the angel answering, said to her: The Holy Ghost shall come upon thee, and the power of the most High shall overshadow thee. And therefore also the Holy which shall be born of thee shall be called the Son of God.

36 And behold thy cousin Elizabeth, she also hath conceived a son in her old age; and this is the sixth month with her that is called barren: *37* Because no word shall be impossible with God. *38* And Mary said: Behold the handmaid of the Lord; be it done to me according to thy word. And the angel departed from her. *39* And Mary rising up in those days, went into the hill country with haste into a city of Juda. *40* And she entered into the house of Zachary, and saluted Elizabeth.

41 And it came to pass, that when Elizabeth heard the salutation of Mary, the infant leaped in her womb. And Elizabeth was filled with the Holy Ghost: *42* And she cried out with a loud voice, and said: Blessed art thou among women, and blessed is the fruit of thy womb. *43* And whence is this to me, that the mother of my Lord should come to me? *44* For behold as soon as the voice of thy salutation sounded in my ears, the infant in my womb leaped for joy. *45* And blessed art thou that hast believed, because those things shall be accomplished that were spoken to thee by the Lord.

46 And Mary said: My soul doth magnify the Lord. *47* And my spirit hath rejoiced in God my Saviour. *48* Because he hath regarded the humility of his handmaid; for behold from henceforth all generations shall call me blessed. *49* Because he that is mighty, hath done great things to me; and holy is his name. *50* And his mercy is from generation unto generations, to them that fear him.

51 He hath shewed might in his arm: he hath scattered the proud in the conceit of their heart. *52* He hath put down the mighty from their seat, and hath exalted the humble. *53* He hath filled the hungry with good things; and the rich he hath sent empty away. *54* He hath received Israel his servant, being mindful of his mercy: 55 As he spoke to our fathers: to Abraham and to his seed for ever.

56 And Mary abode with her about three months; and she returned to her own house. 57 Now Elizabeth's full time of being delivered was come, and she brought forth a son. 58 And her neighbours and kinsfolks heard that the Lord had shewed his great mercy towards her, and they congratulated with her. 59 And it came to pass, that on the eighth day they came to circumcise the child, and they called him by his father's name Zachary. 60 And his mother answering, said: Not so; but he shall be called John.

61 And they said to her: There is none of thy kindred that is called by this name. 62 And they made signs to his father, how he would have him called. 63 And demanding a writing table, he wrote, saying: John is his name. And they all wondered. 64 And immediately his mouth was opened and his tongue loosed, and he spoke, blessing God. 65 And fear came upon all their neighbours; and all these things were noised abroad over all the hill country of Judea.

66 And all they that had heard them laid them up in their heart, saying: What an one, think ye, shall this child be? For the hand of the Lord was with him. 67 And Zachary his father was filled with the Holy Ghost; and he prophesied, saying: 68 Blessed be the Lord God of Israel; because he hath visited and wrought the redemption of his people: 69 And hath raised up an horn of salvation to us, in the house of David his servant: 70 As he spoke by the mouth of his holy prophets, who are from the beginning:

71 Salvation from our enemies, and from the hand of all that hate us: 72 To perform mercy to our fathers, and to remember his holy testament, 73 The oath, which he swore to Abraham our father, that he would grant to us, 74 That being delivered from the hand of our enemies, we may serve him without fear, 75 In holiness and justice before him, all our days.

76 And thou, child, shalt be called the prophet of the Highest: for thou shalt go before the face of the Lord to prepare his ways: 77 To

give knowledge of salvation to his people, unto the remission of their sins: *78* Through the bowels of the mercy of our God, in which the Orient from on high hath visited us: *79* To enlighten them that sit in darkness, and in the shadow of death: to direct our feet into the way of peace. *80* And the child grew, and was strengthened in spirit; and was in the deserts until the day of his manifestation to Israel.

Gospel According to St. Luke, Chapter 2:
The birth of Christ: his presentation in the temple: Simeon's prophecy.
Christ, at twelve years of age, is found amongst the doctors.

1 And it came to pass, that in those days there went out a decree from Caesar Augustus, that the whole world should be enrolled. *2* This enrolling was first made by Cyrinus, the governor of Syria. *3* And all went to be enrolled, every one into his own city. *4* And Joseph also went up from Galilee, out of the city of Nazareth into Judea, to the city of David, which is called Bethlehem: because he was of the house and family of David, *5* To be enrolled with Mary his espoused wife, who was with child.

6 And it came to pass, that when they were there, her days were accomplished, that she should be delivered. *7* And she brought forth her firstborn son, and wrapped him up in swaddling clothes, and laid him in a manger; because there was no room for them in the inn. *8* And there were in the same country shepherds watching, and keeping the night watches over their flock. *9* And behold an angel of the Lord stood by them, and the brightness of God shone round about them; and they feared with a great fear. *10* And the angel said to them: Fear not; for, behold, I bring you good tidings of great joy, that shall be to all the people:

11 For, this day, is born to you a Saviour, who is Christ the Lord, in the city of David. *12* And this shall be a sign unto you. You shall find the infant wrapped in swaddling clothes, and laid in a manger. *13* And suddenly there was with the angel a multitude of the heavenly army, praising God, and saying: *14* Glory to God in the highest; and on earth peace to men of good will. *15* And it came to pass, after the angels departed from them into heaven, the shepherds said one to another: Let us go over to Bethlehem, and let us see this word that is come to pass, which the Lord hath shewed to us.

16 And they came with haste; and they found Mary and Joseph, and the infant lying in the manger. *17* And seeing, they understood of the word that had been spoken to them concerning this child. *18* And all that heard, wondered; and at those things that were told them by the shepherds. *19* But Mary kept all these words, pondering them in her heart. *20* And the shepherds returned, glorifying and praising God, for all the things they had heard and seen, as it was told unto them.

21 And after eight days were accomplished, that the child should be circumcised, his name was called JESUS, which was called by the angel, before he was conceived in the womb. *22* And after the days of her purification, according to the law of Moses, were accomplished, they carried him to Jerusalem, to present him to the Lord: *23* As it is written in the law of the Lord: Every male opening the womb shall be called holy to the Lord: *24* And to offer a sacrifice, according as it is written in the law of the Lord, a pair of turtledoves, or two young pigeons: *25* And behold there was a man in Jerusalem named Simeon, and this man was just and devout, waiting for the consolation of Israel; and the Holy Ghost was in him.

26 And he had received an answer from the Holy Ghost, that he should not see death, before he had seen the Christ of the Lord. *27* And he came by the Spirit into the temple. And when his parents brought in the child Jesus, to do for him according to the custom of the law, *28* He also took him into his arms, and blessed God, and said: *29* Now thou dost dismiss thy servant, O Lord, according to thy word in peace; *30* Because my eyes have seen thy salvation,

31 Which thou hast prepared before the face of all peoples: *32* A light to the revelation of the Gentiles, and the glory of thy people Israel. *33* And his father and mother were wondering at those things which were spoken concerning him. *34* And Simeon blessed them, and said to Mary his mother: Behold this child is set for the fall, and for the resurrection of many in Israel, and for a sign which shall be contradicted; *35* And thy own soul a sword shall pierce, that, out of many hearts, thoughts may be revealed.

36 And there was one Anna, a prophetess, the daughter of Phanuel, of the tribe of Aser; she was far advanced in years, and had lived with her husband seven years from her virginity. *37* And she was a widow until fourscore and four years; who departed not from the temple, by fastings and prayers serving night and day. *38* Now she, at the same hour, coming in, confessed to the Lord; and spoke of him to all that looked for the redemption of Israel. *39* And after they had performed all things according to the law of the Lord, they returned into Galilee, to their city Nazareth. *40* And the child grew, and waxed strong, full of wisdom; and the grace of God was in him.

41 And his parents went every year to Jerusalem, at the solemn day of the pasch, *42* And when he was twelve years old, they going up into Jerusalem, according to the custom of the feast, *43* And having fulfilled the days, when they returned, the child Jesus remained in Jerusalem; and his parents knew it not. *44* And thinking that he was in the company, they came a day's journey, and sought him among their kinsfolks and acquaintance. *45* And not finding him, they returned into Jerusalem, seeking him.

46 And it came to pass, that, after three days, they found him in the temple, sitting in the midst of the doctors, hearing them, and asking them questions. *47* And all that heard him were astonished at his wisdom and his answers. *48* And seeing him, they wondered. And his mother said to him: Son, why hast thou done so to us? behold thy father and I have sought thee sorrowing. *49* And he said to them: How is it that you sought me? did you not know, that I must be about my father's business? *50* And they understood not the word that he spoke unto them. *51* And he went down with them, and came to Nazareth, and was subject to them. And his mother kept all these words in her heart. *52* And Jesus advanced in wisdom, and age, and grace with God and men.

Gospel According to St. John, Chapter 2:
Christ changes water into wine. He casts the sellers out of the temple.

1 And the third day, there was a marriage in Cana of Galilee: and the mother of Jesus was there. *2* And Jesus also was invited, and his disciples, to the marriage. *3* And the wine failing, the mother of Jesus saith to him: They have no wine. *4* And Jesus saith to her: Woman, what is that to me and to thee? my hour is not yet come. *5* His mother saith to the waiters: Whatsoever he shall say to you, do ye.

6 Now there were set there six waterpots of stone, according to the manner of the purifying of the Jews, containing two or three measures apiece. *7* Jesus saith to them: Fill the waterpots with water. And they filled them up to the brim. *8* And Jesus saith to them: Draw out now, and carry to the chief steward of the feast. And they carried it. *9* And when the chief steward had tasted the water made wine, and knew not whence it was, but the waiters knew who had drawn the water; the chief steward calleth the bridegroom, *10* And saith to him: Every man at first setteth forth good wine, and when men have well drunk, then that which is worse. But thou hast kept the good wine until now.

11 This beginning of miracles did Jesus in Cana of Galilee; and manifested his glory, and his disciples believed in him. *12* After this he went down to Capharnaum, he and his mother, and his brethren, and his disciples: and they remained there not many days. *13* And the pasch of the Jews was at hand, and Jesus went up to Jerusalem. *14* And he found in the temple them that sold oxen and sheep and doves, and the changers of money sitting. *15* And when he had made, as it were, a scourge of little cords, he drove them all out of the temple, the sheep also and the oxen, and the money of the changers he poured out, and the tables he overthrew.

16 And to them that sold doves he said: Take these things hence, and make not the house of my Father a house of traffic. *17* And his disciples remembered, that it was written: The zeal of thy house hath eaten me up. *18* The Jews, therefore, answered, and said to him: What sign dost thou shew unto us, seeing thou dost these things?

19 Jesus answered, and said to them: Destroy this temple, and in three days I will raise it up. *20* The Jews then said: Six and forty years was this temple in building; and wilt thou raise it up in three days?

21 But he spoke of the temple of his body. *22* When therefore he was risen again from the dead, his disciples remembered, that he had said this, and they believed the scripture, and the word that Jesus had said. *23* Now when he was at Jerusalem, at the pasch, upon the festival day, many believed in his name, seeing his signs which he did. *24* But Jesus did not trust himself unto them, for that he knew all men, *25* And because he needed not that any should give testimony of man: for he knew what was in man.

Secret of Mary

23. The difficulty, then, is to find really and truly the most Blessed Virgin Mary in order to find all abundant grace. God, being the absolute Master, can confer directly by Himself that which He usually grants only through Mary. It would even be rash to deny that sometimes He does so. Nevertheless, St. Thomas teaches that in the order of grace, established by Divine Wisdom, God ordinarily communicates Himself to men only through Mary. Therefore, if we would go up to Him and be united with Him, we must use the same means He used to come down to us, to be made man and to impart His graces to us. That means is a true devotion [perfect devotion] to our Blessed Lady.

Our Sanctification By The Perfect Devotion To
The Blessed Virgin Mary
OR
The Holy Slavery of Love

A Perfect Means

Devotions to Mary

24. There are several true devotions to Our Lady: here I do not speak of those that are false.

1. Devotion without Special Practices

25. The first consists in fulfilling our Christian duties, avoiding mortal sin, acting more out of love than fear, praying to Our Lady now and then, honoring her as the Mother of God, yet without having any special devotion to her.

2. Devotion with Special Practices

26. The second consists in entertaining for Our Lady more perfect feelings of esteem and love, of confidence and veneration. It leads us to join the Confraternities of the Holy Rosary and of the Scapular, to recite the five decades or the fifteen decades of the Rosary, to honor Mary's images and altars, to publish her praises and to enroll ourselves in her sodalities. This devotion is good, holy and praiseworthy, if we keep ourselves free from sin; but it is not so perfect as the next, nor so efficient in severing our soul from creatures or in detaching us from ourselves, in order to be united with Jesus Christ.

3. The Perfect Devotion: The Holy Slavery of Love

27. The third devotion to Our Lady, known and practiced by very few persons, is the one I am now about to disclose to you, predestinate soul.

a. Nature And Scope Of The Holy Slavery Of Love

Nature

28. It consists in giving oneself entirely and as a slave to Mary, and to Jesus through Mary; and after that to do all that we do, with Mary, in Mary, through Mary and for Mary. I shall now explain these words.

Scope: Total Surrender

29. We should choose a special feast-day on which we give, consecrate and sacrifice to Mary voluntarily, lovingly and without constraint, entirely and without reserve: our body and soul, our exterior property, such as house, family and income; and also our interior and spiritual possessions; namely, our merits, graces, virtues and satisfactions.

It should be observed here that by this devotion the soul sacrifices to Jesus, through Mary, all that it holds most dear, things of which even no religious order would require the sacrifice; namely, the right to dispose of ourselves, of the value of our prayers and alms, of our mortifications and satisfactions. The soul leaves everything to be freely disposed of by Our Lady so that she may apply it all according to her own will for the greater glory of God, which she alone knows perfectly.

Surrender of the Value of Our Good Works

30. We leave to her disposal all the satisfactory and impetratory value of our good works, so that after we have made the sacrifice of them— although not by vow—we are no longer the masters of any good works we may do; but Our Lady may apply them, sometimes for the relief or the deliverance of a soul in Purgatory, sometimes for the conversion of a poor sinner, etc.

31. By this devotion we also place our merits in the hands of Our Lady, but only that she may preserve, augment and embellish them, because we cannot communicate to one another either the merits of sanctifying grace or those of glory. However, we give her all our prayers and good works, inasmuch as they have an impetratory and satisfactory value, that she may distribute and apply them to whom she pleases. If, after having thus consecrated ourselves to Our Lady, we desire to relieve a soul in Purgatory, to save a sinner, or to assist a friend by our prayers, our alms-deeds, our mortifications and sacrifices, we must humbly ask it of Our Lady, abiding, however, by her decision, which remains unknown to us; and we must be fully persuaded that the value of our actions, being dispensed by the same

hand which God Himself makes use of to distribute to us His graces and gifts, cannot fail to be applied for His greater glory.

Three Kinds of Slavery

32. I have said that this devotion consists in giving ourselves to Mary as slaves. But notice that there are three kinds of slavery. The first is the slavery of nature; in this sense all men, good and bad alike, are slaves of God. The second is the slavery of constraint; the devils and the damned are slaves of God in this second sense. The third is the slavery of love and of free will; and this is the one by which we must consecrate ourselves to God through Mary. It is the most perfect way for us human creatures to give ourselves to God our Creator.

Servant and Slave

33. Notice again, that there is a great difference between a servant and a slave. A servant claims wages for his services; a slave has a right to none. A servant is free to leave his master when he likes—he serves him only for a time; a slave belongs to his master for life and has no right to leave him. A servant does not give to his master the right of life and death over him; a slave gives himself up entirely, so that his master can put him to death without being molested by the law. It is easily seen, then, that he who is a slave by constraint is rigorously dependent on his master. Strictly speaking, a man must be dependent in that sense only on his Creator. Hence, we do not find that kind of slavery among Christians, but only among pagans.

Happiness of the Slave of Love

34. But happy and a thousand times happy is the generous soul that consecrates itself entirely to Jesus through Mary as a slave of love after it has shaken off by Baptism the tyrannical slavery of the devil!

—THIRD WEEK—
Knowledge of Jesus Christ

"During the third week, they shall apply themselves to the study of Jesus Christ." (See no. 230).

What is to be studied in Christ? First the Man-God, His grace and glory; then His rights to sovereign dominion over us; since, after having renounced Satan and the world, we have taken Jesus Christ for our Lord. What next shall be the object of our study? His exterior actions and also His interior life; namely, the virtues and acts of His Sacred Heart; His association with Mary in the mysteries of the Annunciation and Incarnation, during His infancy and hidden life, at the feast of Cana and on Calvary.

Prayers:
> *Litany of the Holy Ghost,* page 174. *Ave Maris Stella,* page 150.
> *Litany of the Holy Name of Jesus* or *Litany of the Sacred Heart.*
> *St. Louis De Montforts Prayer to Jesus. O Jesus Living in Mary.*

Reading:
> Gospel according to St. Matthew, chapters 26, 27. Gospel according to St. John, chapters 13 ff.
> *Imitation of Christ,* Book II, chapters 7, 11, 12; Book III, chapters 5, 6, 56; Book IV, chapters 1, 8, 13.
> *True Devotion,* nos. 60-67, 183, 212, 226-265.

Spiritual Exercises:
> Acts of love of God, thanksgiving for the blessings of Jesus, contrition and resolution.

Litany of the Holy Name of Jesus

Lord, have mercy on us.
Christ, have mercy on us.
Lord, have mercy on us. Jesus, hear us.
Jesus, graciously hear us.

God the Father of Heaven, *have mercy on us.*

God the Son, Redeemer of the world, *have mercy on us.*

God the Holy Ghost, *etc.*

Holy Trinity, One God,

Jesus, Son of the living God,

Jesus, splendor of the Father,

Jesus, brightness of eternal light,

Jesus, King of glory,

Jesus, sun of justice,

Jesus, Son of the Virgin Mary,

Jesus, most amiable,

Jesus, most admirable,

Jesus, mighty God,

Jesus, Father of the world to come,

Jesus, angel of great counsel,

Jesus, most powerful,

Jesus, most patient,

Jesus, most obedient,

Jesus, meek and humble of heart,

Jesus, lover of chastity,

Jesus, lover of us,

Jesus, God of peace,

Jesus, author of life,

Jesus, model of virtues,

Jesus, lover of souls,

Jesus, our God,

Jesus, our refuge,

Jesus, Father of the poor,

Jesus, treasure of the faithful,

Jesus, Good Shepherd,

Jesus, true light,

Jesus, eternal wisdom,

Jesus, infinite goodness,

Jesus, our way and our life,
Jesus, joy of angels,
Jesus, King of patriarchs,
Jesus, master of Apostles,
Jesus, teacher of Evangelists,
Jesus, strength of martyrs,
Jesus, light of confessors,
Jesus, purity of virgins,
Jesus, crown of all saints,
Be merciful, *spare us, O Jesus.*
Be merciful, *graciously hear us, O Jesus.*

From all evil, *Jesus, deliver us.*
From all sin, *Jesus, deliver us.*
From Thy wrath, *etc.*
From the snares of the devil,
From the spirit of fornication,
From everlasting death,
From the neglect of Thine inspirations,
Through the mystery of Thy holy Incarnation,
Through Thy nativity,
Through Thine infancy,
Through Thy most divine life,
Through Thy labors,
Through Thine agony and Passion,
Through Thy cross and dereliction,
Through Thy sufferings,
Through Thy death and burial,
Through Thy Resurrection,
Through Thine Ascension,
Through Thine institution of the most Holy Eucharist,
Through Thy joys,
Through Thy glory,

Lamb of God, Who takest away the sins of the world,
Spare us, O Jesus.
Lamb of God, Who takest away the sins of the world,
Graciously hear us, O Jesus.
Lamb of God, Who takest away the sins of the world,
Have mercy on us.
Jesus, hear us, *Jesus, graciously hear us.*

Let Us Pray

O Lord Jesus Christ, Who hast said: Ask and ye shall receive, seek and ye shall find, knock and it shall be opened unto you; grant, we beseech Thee, to us who ask the gift of Thy divine love, that we may ever love Thee with all our hearts, and in all our words and actions, and never cease from praising Thee.

Give us, O Lord, a perpetual fear and love of Thy holy Name; for Thou never failest to govern those whom Thou dost solidly establish in Thy love, Who livest and reignest world without end. R. *Amen.*

Litany of the Sacred Heart

Lord, have mercy on us.
Christ, have mercy on us.
Lord, have mercy on us. Christ, hear us.
Christ, graciously hear us.

God the Father of Heaven, *have mercy on us.*
God the Son, Redeemer of the world,
have mercy on us.
God the Holy Ghost, *etc.*
Holy Trinity, One God,
Heart of Jesus, Son of the Eternal Father,

Heart of Jesus, formed by the Holy Ghost in the womb of the Virgin Mother,

Heart of Jesus, substantially united with the Word of God,

Heart of Jesus, of infinite majesty,

Heart of Jesus, holy temple of God,

Heart of Jesus, tabernacle of the Most High,

Heart of Jesus, house of God and gate of Heaven,

Heart of Jesus, burning furnace of charity,

Heart of Jesus, abode of justice and love,

Heart of Jesus, full of goodness and love,

Heart of Jesus, abyss of all virtues,

Heart of Jesus, most worthy of all praise,

Heart of Jesus, King and center of all hearts,

Heart of Jesus, in Whom are all the treasures of wisdom and knowledge,

Heart of Jesus, in Whom dwells all the fullness of divinity,

Heart of Jesus, in Whom the Father was well pleased,

Heart of Jesus, of Whose fullness we have all received,

Heart of Jesus, desire of the everlasting hills,

Heart of Jesus, patient and most merciful,

Heart of Jesus, enriching all who invoke Thee,

Heart of Jesus, fountain of life and holiness,

Heart of Jesus, propitiation for our sins,

Heart of Jesus, loaded down with opprobrium,

Heart of Jesus, bruised for our offenses,

Heart of Jesus, obedient unto death,

Heart of Jesus, pierced with a lance,

Heart of Jesus, source of all consolation,

Heart of Jesus, our life and resurrection,

Heart of Jesus, our peace and reconciliation,

Heart of Jesus, victim for sin,

Heart of Jesus, salvation of those who trust in Thee,

Heart of Jesus, hope of those who die in Thee,
Heart of Jesus, delight of all the saints,

Lamb of God, Who takest away the sins of the world,
Spare us, O Lord.
Lamb of God, Who takest away the sins of the world,
Graciously hear us, O Lord.
Lamb of God, Who takest away the sins of the world,
Have mercy on us.

V. Jesus, meek and humble of heart,
R. *Make our hearts like unto Thine.*

Let Us Pray

Almighty and everlasting God, graciously regard the Heart of Thy well-beloved Son and the acts of praise and satisfaction which He renders Thee on behalf of sinners; appeased by worthy homage, pardon those who implore Thy mercy, in the name of the same Jesus Christ Thy Son, Who liveth and reigneth with Thee, world without end. R. *Amen.*

St. Louis De Montfort's Prayer to Jesus

O most loving Jesus, deign to let me pour forth my gratitude before Thee, for the grace Thou hast bestowed upon me in giving me to Thy holy Mother through the devotion of Holy Bondage, that she may be my advocate in the presence of Thy majesty and my support in my extreme misery. Alas, O Lord! I am so wretched that without this dear Mother I should be certainly lost. Yes, Mary is necessary for me at Thy side and everywhere: that she may appease Thy just wrath, because I have so often offended Thee; that, she may save me from the eternal punishment of Thy justice, which I deserve; that she may contemplate

Thee, speak to Thee, pray to Thee, approach Thee and please Thee; that she may help me to save my soul and the souls of others; in short, Mary is necessary for me that I may always do Thy holy will and seek Thy greater glory in all things. Ah, would that I could proclaim throughout the whole world the mercy that Thou hast shown to me! Would that everyone might know I should be already damned, were it not for Mary! Would that I might offer worthy thanksgiving for so great a blessing! Mary is in me. Oh, what a treasure! Oh, what a consolation! And shall I not be entirely hers? Oh, what ingratitude! My dear Saviour, send me death rather than such a calamity, for I would rather die than live without belonging entirely to Mary. With St. John the Evangelist at the foot of the Cross, I have taken her a thousand times for my own and as many times have given myself to her; but if I have not yet done it as Thou, dear Jesus, dost wish, I now renew this offering as Thou dost desire me to renew it. And if Thou seest in my soul or my body anything that does not belong to this august princess, I pray Thee to take it and cast it far from me, for whatever in me does not belong to Mary is unworthy of Thee.

O Holy Spirit, grant me all these graces. Plant in my soul the Tree of true Life, which is Mary; cultivate it and tend it so that it may grow and blossom and bring forth the fruit of life in abundance. O Holy Spirit, give me great devotion to Mary, Thy faithful spouse; give me great confidence in her maternal heart and an abiding refuge in her mercy, so that by her Thou mayest truly form in me Jesus Christ, great and mighty, unto the fullness of His perfect age. Amen.

O Jesus Living in Mary

O Jesus living in Mary,
Come and live in Thy servants,
In the spirit of Thy holiness,
In the fullness of Thy might,

In the truth of Thy virtues,
In the perfection of Thy ways,
In the communion of Thy mysteries;
Subdue every hostile power
In Thy spirit, for the glory of the Father. Amen.

Gospel According to St. Matthew, Chapter 26:
The Jews conspire against Christ. He is anointed by Mary.
The treason of Judas. The last supper. The prayer in the garden.
The apprehension of our Lord: His treatment in the house of Caiphas.

1 And it came to pass, when Jesus had ended all these words, he said to his disciples: *2* You know that after two days shall be the pasch, and the son of man shall be delivered up to be crucified: *3* Then were gathered together the chief priests and ancients of the people into the court of the high priest, who was called Caiphas: *4* And they consulted together, that by subtilty they might apprehend Jesus, and put him to death. *5* But they said: Not on the festival day, lest perhaps there should be a tumult among the people.

6 And when Jesus was in Bethania, in the house of Simon the leper, *7* There came to him a woman having an alabaster box of precious ointment, and poured it on his head as he was at table. *8* And the disciples seeing it, had indignation, saying: To what purpose is this waste? *9* For this might have been sold for much, and given to the poor. *10* And Jesus knowing it, said to them: Why do you trouble this woman? for she hath wrought a good work upon me.

11 For the poor you have always with you: but me you have not always. *12* For she in pouring this ointment upon my body, hath done it for my burial. *13* Amen I say to you, wheresoever this gospel shall be preached in the whole world, that also which she hath done, shall be told for a memory of her. *14* Then went one of the twelve, who was called Judas Iscariot, to the chief priests, *15* And said to them: What will you give me, and I will deliver him unto you? But they appointed him thirty pieces of silver.

239

16 And from thenceforth he sought opportunity to betray him. *17* And on the first day of the Azymes, the disciples came to Jesus, saying: Where wilt thou that we prepare for thee to eat the pasch? *18* But Jesus said: Go ye into the city to a certain man, and say to him: the master saith, My time is near at hand, with thee I make the pasch with my disciples. *19* And the disciples did as Jesus appointed to them, and they prepared the pasch. *20* But when it was evening, he sat down with his twelve disciples.

21 And whilst they were eating, he said: Amen I say to you, that one of you is about to betray me. *22* And they being very much troubled, began every one to say: Is it I, Lord? *23* But he answering, said: He that dippeth his hand with me in the dish, he shall betray me. *24* The Son of man indeed goeth, as it is written of him: but woe to that man by whom the Son of man shall be betrayed: it were better for him, if that man had not been born. *25* And Judas that betrayed him, answering, said: Is it I, Rabbi? He saith to him: Thou hast said it.

26 And whilst they were at supper, Jesus took bread, and blessed, and broke: and gave to his disciples, and said: Take ye, and eat. This is my body. *27* And taking the chalice, he gave thanks, and gave to them, saying: Drink ye all of this. *28* For this is my blood of the new testament, which shall be shed for many unto remission of sins. *29* And I say to you, I will not drink from henceforth of this fruit of the vine, until that day when I shall drink it with you new in the kingdom of my Father. *30* And a hymn being said, they went out unto mount Olivet.

31 Then Jesus said to them: All you shall be scandalized in me this night. For it is written: I will strike the shepherd, and the sheep of the flock shall be dispersed. *32* But after I shall be risen again, I will go before you into Galilee. *33* And Peter answering, said to him: Although all shall be scandalized in thee, I will never be scandalized. *34* Jesus said to him: Amen I say to thee, that in this night before the cock crow, thou wilt deny me thrice. *35* Peter saith to him: Yea, though I should die with thee, I will not deny thee. And in like manner said all the disciples.

36 Then Jesus came with them into a country place which is called Gethsemani; and he said to his disciples: Sit you here, till I go yonder and pray. *37* And taking with him Peter and the two sons of Zebedee, he began to grow sorrowful and to be sad. *38* Then he saith to them: My soul is sorrowful even unto death: stay you here, and watch with me. *39* And going a little further, he fell upon his face, praying, and saying: My Father, if it be possible, let this chalice pass from me. Nevertheless not as I will, but as thou wilt. *40* And he cometh to his disciples, and findeth them asleep, and he saith to Peter: What? Could you not watch one hour with me?

41 Watch ye, and pray that ye enter not into temptation. The spirit indeed is willing, but the flesh weak. *42* Again the second time, he went and prayed, saying: My Father, if this chalice may not pass away, but I must drink it, thy will be done. *43* And he cometh again and findeth them sleeping: for their eyes were heavy. *44* And leaving them, he went again: and he prayed the third time, saying the selfsame word. *45* Then he cometh to his disciples, and saith to them: Sleep ye now and take your rest; behold the hour is at hand, and the Son of man shall be betrayed into the hands of sinners.

46 Rise, let us go: behold he is at hand that will betray me. *47* As he yet spoke, behold Judas, one of the twelve, came, and with him a great multitude with swords and clubs, sent from the chief priests and the ancients of the people. *48* And he that betrayed him, gave them a sign, saying: Whomsoever I shall kiss, that is he, hold him fast. *49* And forthwith coming to Jesus, he said: Hail, Rabbi. And he kissed him. *50* And Jesus said to him: Friend, whereto art thou come? Then they came up, and laid hands on Jesus, and held him.

51 And behold one of them that were with Jesus, stretching forth his hand, drew out his sword: and striking the servant of the high priest, cut off his ear. *52* Then Jesus saith to him: Put up again thy sword into its place: for all that take the sword shall perish with the sword. *53* Thinkest thou that I cannot ask my Father, and he will give me presently more than twelve legions of angels? *54* How then shall the scriptures be fulfilled, that so it must be done? *55* In that same hour

Jesus said to the multitudes: You are come out as it were to a robber with swords and clubs to apprehend me. I sat daily with you, teaching in the temple, and you laid not hands on me.

56 Now all this was done, that the scriptures of the prophets might be fulfilled. Then the disciples all leaving him, fled. 57 But they holding Jesus led him to Caiphas the high priest, where the scribes and the ancients were assembled. 58 And Peter followed him afar off, even to the court of the high priest. And going in, he sat with the servants, that he might see the end. 59 And the chief priests and the whole council sought false witness against Jesus, that they might put him to death: 60 And they found not, whereas many false witnesses had come in. And last of all there came two false witnesses:

61 And they said: This man said, I am able to destroy the temple of God, and after three days to rebuild it. 62 And the high priest rising up, said to him: Answerest thou nothing to the things which these witness against thee? 63 But Jesus held his peace. And the high priest said to him: I adjure thee by the living God, that thou tell us if thou be the Christ the Son of God. 64 Jesus saith to him: Thou hast said it. Nevertheless I say to you, hereafter you shall see the Son of man sitting on the right hand of the power of God, and coming in the clouds of heaven. 65 Then the high priest rent his garments, saying: He hath blasphemed; what further need have we of witnesses? Behold, now you have heard the blasphemy:

66 What think you? But they answering, said: He is guilty of death. 67 Then did they spit in his face, and buffeted him: and others struck his face with the palms of their hands, 68 Saying: Prophesy unto us, O Christ, who is he that struck thee? 69 But Peter sat without in the court: and there came to him a servant maid, saying: Thou also wast with Jesus the Galilean. 70 But he denied before them all, saying: I know not what thou sayest.

71 And as he went out of the gate, another maid saw him, and she saith to them that were there: This man also was with Jesus of Nazareth. 72 And again he denied with an oath, I know not the man. 73 And after a little while they came that stood by, and said to Peter:

Surely thou also art one of them; for even thy speech doth discover thee. *74* Then he began to curse and to swear that he knew not the man. And immediately the cock crew. *75* And Peter remembered the word of Jesus which he had said: Before the cock crow, thou wilt deny me thrice. And going forth, he wept bitterly.

Gospel According to St. Matthew, Chapter 27:
The continuation of the history of the passion of Christ.
His death and burial.

1 And when morning was come, all the chief priests and ancients of the people took counsel against Jesus, that they might put him to death. *2* And they brought him bound, and delivered him to Pontius Pilate the governor. *3* Then Judas, who betrayed him, seeing that he was condemned, repenting himself, brought back the thirty pieces of silver to the chief priests and ancients, *4* Saying: I have sinned in betraying innocent blood. But they said: What is that to us? look thou to it. *5* And casting down the pieces of silver in the temple, he departed: and went and hanged himself with an halter.

6 But the chief priests having taken the pieces of silver, said: It is not lawful to put them into the corbona, because it is the price of blood. *7* And after they had consulted together, they bought with them the potter's field, to be a burying place for strangers. *8* For this cause the field was called Haceldama, that is, The field of blood, even to this day. *9* Then was fulfilled that which was spoken by Jeremias the prophet, saying: And they took the thirty pieces of silver, the price of him that was prized, whom they prized of the children of Israel. *10* And they gave them unto the potter's field, as the Lord appointed to me.

11 And Jesus stood before the governor, and the governor asked him, saying: Art thou the king of the Jews? Jesus saith to him: Thou sayest it. *12* And when he was accused by the chief priests and ancients, he answered nothing. *13* Then Pilate saith to him: Dost not thou hear how great testimonies they allege against thee? *14* And he answered him to never a word; so that the governor wondered exceedingly. *15* Now upon the solemn day the governor was accustomed to release to the people one prisoner, whom they would.

16 And he had then a notorious prisoner, that was called Barabbas. *17* They therefore being gathered together, Pilate said: Whom will you that I release to you, Barabbas, or Jesus that is called Christ? *18* For he knew that for envy they had delivered him. *19* And as he was sitting in the place of judgment, his wife sent to him, saying: Have thou nothing to do with that just man; for I have suffered many things this day in a dream because of him. *20* But the chief priests and ancients persuaded the people, that they should ask for Barabbas, and make Jesus away.

21 And the governor answering, said to them: Whether will you of the two to be released unto you? But they said, Barabbas. *22* Pilate saith to them: What shall I do then with Jesus that is called Christ? They say all: Let him be crucified. *23* The governor said to them: Why, what evil hath he done? But they cried out the more, saying: Let him be crucified. *24* And Pilate seeing that he prevailed nothing, but that rather a tumult was made; taking water washed his hands before the people, saying: I am innocent of the blood of this just man; look you to it. *25* And the whole people answering, said: His blood be upon us and upon our children.

26 Then he released to them Barabbas, and having scourged Jesus, delivered him unto them to be crucified. *27* Then the soldiers of the governor taking Jesus into the hall, gathered together unto him the whole band; *28* And stripping him, they put a scarlet cloak about him. *29* And platting a crown of thorns, they put it upon his head, and a reed in his right hand. And bowing the knee before him, they mocked him, saying: Hail, king of the Jews. *30* And spitting upon him, they took the reed, and struck his head.

31 And after they had mocked him, they took off the cloak from him, and put on him his own garments, and led him away to crucify him. *32* And going out, they found a man of Cyrene, named Simon: him they forced to take up his cross. *33* And they came to the place that is called Golgotha, which is the place of Calvary. *34* And they gave him wine to drink mingled with gall. And when he had tasted, he would not drink. *35* And after they had crucified him, they divided his garments, casting lots; that it might be fulfilled which was spoken by the prophet, saying: They divided my garments among them; and upon my vesture they cast lots.

36 And they sat and watched him. *37* And they put over his head his cause written: THIS IS JESUS THE KING OF THE JEWS. *38* Then were crucified with him two thieves: one on the right hand, and one on the left. *39* And they that passed by, blasphemed him, wagging their heads, *40* And saying: Vah, thou that destroyest the temple of God, and in three days dost rebuild it: save thy own self: if thou be the Son of God, come down from the cross.

41 In like manner also the chief priests, with the scribes and ancients, mocking, said: *42* He saved others; himself he cannot save. If he be the king of Israel, let him now come down from the cross, and we will believe him. *43* He trusted in God; let him now deliver him if he will have him; for he said: I am the Son of God. *44* And the selfsame thing the thieves also, that were crucified with him, reproached him with. *45* Now from the sixth hour there was darkness over the whole earth, until the ninth hour.

46 And about the ninth hour Jesus cried with a loud voice, saying: Eli, Eli, lamma sabacthani? that is, My God, my God, why hast thou forsaken me? *47* And some that stood there and heard, said: This man calleth Elias. *48* And immediately one of them running took a sponge, and filled it with vinegar; and put it on a reed, and gave him to drink. *49* And the others said: Let be, let us see whether Elias will come to deliver him. *50* And Jesus again crying with a loud voice, yielded up the ghost.

51 And behold the veil of the temple was rent in two from the top even to the bottom, and the earth quaked, and the rocks were rent. *52* And the graves were opened: and many bodies of the saints that had slept arose, *53* And coming out of the tombs after his resurrection, came into the holy city, and appeared to many. *54* Now the centurion and they that were with him watching Jesus, having seen the earthquake, and the things that were done, were sore afraid, saying: Indeed this was the Son of God. *55* And there were there many women afar off, who had followed Jesus from Galilee, ministering unto him:

56 Among whom was Mary Magdalen, and Mary the mother of James and Joseph, and the mother of the sons of Zebedee. *57* And when it was evening, there came a certain rich man of Arimathea, named Joseph, who also himself was a disciple of Jesus. *58* He went to Pilate, and asked the body of Jesus. Then Pilate commanded that the body should be delivered. *59* And Joseph taking the body, wrapped it up in a clean linen cloth. *60* And laid it in his own new monument, which he had hewed out in a rock. And he rolled a great stone to the door of the monument, and went his way.

61 And there was there Mary Magdalen, and the other Mary sitting over against the sepulchre. *62* And the next day, which followed the day of preparation, the chief priests and the Pharisees came together to Pilate, *63* Saying: Sir, we have remembered, that that seducer said, while he was yet alive: After three days I will rise again. *64* Command therefore the sepulchre to be guarded until the third day: lest perhaps his disciples come and steal him away, and say to the people: He is risen from the dead; and the last error shall be worse than the first. *65* Pilate saith to them: You have a guard; go, guard it as you know.

66 And they departing, made the sepulchre sure, sealing the stone, and setting guards.

Gospel According to St. John, Chapter 13:
Christ washes his disciples' feet: the treason of Judas:
the new commandment of love.

1 Before the festival day of the pasch, Jesus knowing that his hour was come, that he should pass out of this world to the Father: having loved his own who were in the world, he loved them unto the end.

2 And when supper was done, (the devil having now put into the heart of Judas Iscariot, the son of Simon, to betray him,) *3* Knowing that the Father had given him all things into his hands, and that he came from God, and goeth to God; *4* He riseth from supper, and layeth aside his garments, and having taken a towel, girded himself. *5* After that, he putteth water into a basin, and began to wash the feet of the disciples, and to wipe them with the towel wherewith he was girded.

6 He cometh therefore to Simon Peter. And Peter saith to him: Lord, dost thou wash my feet? *7* Jesus answered, and said to him: What I do thou knowest not now; but thou shalt know hereafter. *8* Peter saith to him: Thou shalt never wash my feet. Jesus answered him: If I wash thee not, thou shalt have no part with me. *9* Simon Peter saith to him: Lord, not only my feet, but also my hands and my head. *10* Jesus saith to him: He that is washed, needeth not but to wash his feet, but is clean wholly. And you are clean, but not all.

11 For he knew who he was that would betray him; therefore he said: You are not all clean. *12* Then after he had washed their feet, and taken his garments, being set down again, he said to them: Know you what I have done to you? *13* You call me Master, and Lord; and you say well, for so I am. *14* If then I being your Lord and Master, have washed your feet; you also ought to wash one another's feet. *15* For I have given you an example, that as I have done to you, so you do also.

16 Amen, amen I say to you: The servant is not greater than his lord; neither is the apostle greater than he that sent him. *17* If you know these things, you shall be blessed if you do them. *18* I speak not of you all: I know whom I have chosen. But that the scripture may be fulfilled: He that eateth bread with me, shall lift up his heel against me. *19* At present I tell you, before it come to pass: that when it shall come to pass, you may believe that I am he. *20* Amen, amen I say to you, he that receiveth whomsoever I send, receiveth me; and he that receiveth me, receiveth him that sent me.

21 When Jesus had said these things, he was troubled in spirit; and he testified, and said: Amen, amen I say to you, one of you shall betray me. *22* The disciples therefore looked one upon another, doubting of whom he spoke. *23* Now there was leaning on Jesus' bosom one of his disciples, whom Jesus loved. *24* Simon Peter therefore beckoned to him, and said to him: Who is it of whom he speaketh? *25* He therefore, leaning on the breast of Jesus, saith to him: Lord, who is it?

26 Jesus answered: He it is to whom I shall reach bread dipped. And when he had dipped the bread, he gave it to Judas Iscariot, the son of Simon. *27* And after the morsel, Satan entered into him. And Jesus said to him: That which thou dost, do quickly. *28* Now no man at the table knew to what purpose he said this unto him. *29* For some thought, because Judas had the purse, that Jesus had said to him: Buy those things which we have need of for the festival day: or that he should give something to the poor. *30* He therefore having received the morsel, went out immediately. And it was night.

31 When he therefore was gone out, Jesus said: Now is the Son of man glorified, and God is glorified in him. *32* If God be glorified in him, God also will glorify him in himself; and immediately will he glorify him. *33* Little children, yet a little while I am with you. You shall seek me; and as I said to the Jews: Whither I go you cannot come; so I say to you now. *34* A new commandment I give unto you: That you love one another, as I have loved you, that you also love one another. *35* By this shall all men know that you are my disciples, if you have love one for another.

36 Simon Peter saith to him: Lord, whither goest thou? Jesus answered: Whither I go, thou canst not follow me now; but thou shalt follow hereafter. *37* Peter saith to him: Why cannot I follow thee now? I will lay down my life for thee. *38* Jesus answered him: Wilt thou lay down thy life for me? Amen, amen I say to thee, the cock shall not crow, till thou deny me thrice.

Imitation of Christ, Book II, Chapter 7: Of the Love of Jesus above All Things

BLESSED is he who knows what it is to love Jesus and to despise himself for the sake of Jesus.

We must quit what we love for this Beloved, because Jesus will be loved alone above all things.

The love of things created is deceitful and inconstant.

The love of Jesus is faithful and enduring. He that cleaveth to creatures shall fall with them.

He that embraceth Jesus shall stand firm forever.

Love Him and keep Him for thy friend, who, when all go away, will not leave thee nor suffer thee to perish in the end.

Thou must at last be separated from all things else, whether thou wilt or not.

2. Keep thyself with Jesus both in life and death and commit thyself to His care, who alone can help thee when all others fail.

Thy Beloved is of such a nature that He will admit of no other, but will have thy heart to Himself, and sit there like a king upon his own throne.

If thou couldst but purge thyself well from affection to creatures, Jesus would willingly dwell with thee.

Thou wilt find all that in a manner lost, which thou hast placed in men out of Jesus.

Do not trust or rely upon a frail reed; "for all flesh is grass and all the glory thereof shall fade as the flower of the field." (*Is.* 40:6).

3. Thou wilt soon be deceived if thou only regard the outward show of men.

For if thou seek thy comfort and thy gain in others, thou wilt often meet with loss.

If in all things thou seek Jesus, doubtless thou wilt find Jesus.

But if thou seek thyself thou wilt indeed find thyself, to thine own ruin.

For a man does himself more harm if he seek not Jesus, than the whole world and all his enemies could do him.

Practical Reflections

Apply thy whole mind to know Jesus Christ, thy whole heart to love Him, and all thy care to follow Him, since for this alone thou art a Christian. What difficulty canst thou have in loving a Man God, who assumed humanity only for love of thee and for thy salvation! Be then resolved to study and to contemplate Him in all His actions, to penetrate into His designs, to enter into His dispositions and the purport of His mysteries; and endeavor to do, to suffer, and to live as He did; for the whole merit of a Christian in this life consists in conformity in all things with Jesus Christ; and, in the next, it will constitute his never-ending happiness. If he endeavor to participate here in the humble and suffering life of his Redeemer, he will hereafter partake of His glorious immortality.

Prayer

As, O Jesus, I can have no pretensions to Heaven but through Thy virtues and merit, I beseech Thee to inspire me with an ardent desire of knowing and following Thee. Grant, O my most amiable Saviour, that I may follow Thy maxims, practice Thy virtues and form myself upon Thine example, that my resemblance to Thee may make me worthy of Thy love, and cause me to find grace in the sight of Thy heavenly Father, who loves us only in proportion as we resemble Thee. Help me then to become imbued with Thy sentiments and conformed to Thine inclinations. Grant that, after Thy example, I may become meek, humble, patient, charitable, and submissive in all things to Thy Father's will. I hope that, presenting myself to Him in and by Thee, I shall not be rejected, and that the attachment which I desire to have for Thee may secure Thy love for me, and my ultimate salvation. Amen.

Imitation of Christ, Book II, Chapter 11:
Of the Small Number of the Lovers of the Cross of Jesus

JESUS has now many lovers of His heavenly Kingdom but few that are willing to bear His Cross.

He has many that are desirous of comfort, but few of tribulation.

He finds many companions of His table, but few of His abstinence.

All desire to rejoice with Him, few are willing to suffer with Him.

Many follow Jesus to the breaking of bread, but few to the drinking of the chalice of His Passion.

Many reverence His miracles, but few follow the ignominy of His cross.

Many love Jesus as long as they meet with no adversity.

Many praise Him and bless Him as long as they receive consolation from Him.

But if Jesus hide Himself, and leave them for a little while, they either fall into complaints or excessive dejection.

2. But they that love Jesus for Jesus' sake and not for any comfort of their own, bless Him no less in tribulation and anguish of heart than in the greatest consolation.

And if He should never give them His comfort, yet would they always praise Him and always give Him thanks.

3. Oh, how much is the pure love of Jesus able to do when it is not mixed with any self-interest or self-love.

Are not all those to be called hirelings who are always seeking consolation?

Are they not proved to be rather lovers of themselves than of Christ who are always thinking of their own profit and gain?

Where shall we find a man that is willing to serve God gratis?

4. Seldom do we find anyone so spiritual as to be stripped of all things.

For who shall be able to find the man that is truly poor in spirit and stripped of all affection to all created things? His price is from afar and from the uttermost coasts. (*Prov.* 31:10).

251

If a man give his whole substance it is yet nothing. (*1 Cor.* 13:3).

And if he do great penance it is yet little. And if he attain to all knowledge he is far off still.

And if we have great virtue and exceeding fervent devotion there is still much wanting to him, to wit, one thing which is chiefly necessary for him. (*Luke* 10:42).

And what is that? That, having left all things else, he leave also himself and wholly go out of himself and retain nothing of self-love.

And when he shall have done all things which he knows should be done, let him think that he has done nothing.

5. Let him not make great account of that which may appear much to be esteemed, but let him in truth acknowledge himself to be an unprofitable servant, as Truth itself has said: "When you shall have done all the things that are commanded you, say: We are unprofitable servants." (*Luke* 17:10).

Then may he be truly poor and naked in spirit and may say with the Prophet: "I am alone and poor." (*Ps.* 24:16).

Yet no one is indeed richer than such a man, none more powerful, none more free, who knows how to leave himself and all things and place himself in the very lowest place.

Practical Reflections

How many Christians adore Jesus, poor in the manger, and suffering upon the Cross, who will neither submit to privation, nor endure tribulation for His sake! Yet He was born, and lived, and died in poverty and sufferings, to teach us to renounce all things, and to bear our crosses with patience; to teach us by His preaching and example the virtues necessary for salvation, and to merit for us the grace to practice them. What will it avail thee to adore Jesus Christ, thy Saviour and thy model, if thou dost not imitate Him and place thy whole confidence in Him? Take, then, the generous resolution of renouncing all things by depriving the senses of all dangerous or unprofitable gratifications; by discarding from thy mind all vanity and self-complacency, and all malignity in condemning others; and by stripping thy heart of all attachment to self-satisfaction and self-seeking, on all occasions. Carry this interior poverty and deprivation even so far as to renounce thine own will in all things, to desire only and to accomplish the will of God. It is by thus giving up thy whole self to God that thou wilt constitute Him the sole master and proprietor of thy heart, and by stripping thyself of all things here, make Him thine inheritance forever hereafter.

Prayer

I conceive, O my Saviour, an exalted idea of the bereavement Thou requirest of a Christian heart, since Thou dost oblige it to yield itself up entirely to Thee, and to substitute Thy love in place of the love of itself. But how far am I from practicing it, how incapable of it of myself! Help me, O Lord, to renounce and to die to myself in all things. Suffer not my heart to seek itself, since Thou designest it to be entirely Thine. Grant that whenever it is tempted to live for, or to seek itself in anything, it may immediately renounce and die to itself, to live only in and for Thee. Then may I say with Thine Apostle: Jesus Christ is my life, and it is gain for me to die to all, that I may live only in Him, and by Him, and for Him. Amen.

Imitation of Christ, Book II, Chapter 12: Of the Royal Way of The Holy Cross

TO MANY this seems a hard saying: "Deny thyself, take up thy cross, and follow Jesus." (*Matt.* 16:24).

But it will be much harder to hear that last word: "Depart from me, ye cursed, into everlasting fire." (*Matt.* 25:41).

For they that at present willingly hear and follow the word of the cross shall not then be afraid of eternal condemnation.

This Sign of the Cross will be in Heaven when the Lord shall come to judge.

Then all the servants of the cross, who in their lifetime have conformed themselves to Him that was crucified, shall come to Christ their judge with great confidence.

2. Why then art thou afraid to take up thy cross, which leads to a kingdom?

In the cross is salvation; in the cross is life; in the cross is protection from thine enemies.

In the cross is infusion of heavenly sweetness; in the cross is strength of mind; in the cross is joy of spirit.

In the cross is the height of virtue; in the cross is the perfection of sanctity.

There is no health of the soul nor hope of eternal life but in the cross.

Take up, therefore, thy cross and follow Jesus, and thou shalt go into life everlasting.

He is gone before thee carrying His own Cross; and He died for thee upon the Cross that thou mayest also bear thy cross and love to die on the cross.

Because if thou die with Him thou shalt also live with Him, and if thou art His companion in suffering thou shalt also partake in His glory. (*2 Cor.* 1:7).

3. Behold the cross is all and in dying to thyself all consists, and there is no other way to life and to true internal peace but the holy way of the cross and of daily mortification.

Go where thou wilt, seek what thou wilt, and thou shalt not find a higher way above, nor a safer way below than the way of the holy cross.

Dispose and order all things according as thou wilt and as seems best to thee, and thou wilt still find something to suffer, either willingly or unwillingly, and so thou shalt still find the cross.

For either thou shalt feel pain in the body, or sustain in thy soul tribulation of spirit.

4. Sometimes thou shalt be left by God, other times thou shalt be afflicted by thy neighbor, and what is more, thou shalt often be a trouble to thyself.

Neither canst thou be delivered or eased by any remedy or comfort, but as long as it shall please God thou must bear it.

For God would have thee learn to suffer tribulation without comfort, and wholly to submit thyself to Him, and to become more humble by tribulation.

No man hath so lively a feeling of the Passion of Christ as he who hath happened to suffer suchlike things.

The cross, therefore, is always ready and everywhere waits for thee.

Thou canst not escape it, whithersoever thou runnest; for whithersoever thou goest thou carriest thyself with thee and shalt always find thyself.

Turn thyself upwards, or turn thyself downwards; turn thyself without, or turn thyself within thee, and everywhere thou shalt find the cross.

And everywhere thou must of necessity have patience if thou desirest inward peace and wouldst merit an eternal crown.

5. If thou carry the cross willingly, it will carry thee and bring thee to thy desired end; to wit to that place where there will be an end of suffering, though here there will be no end.

If thou carry it unwillingly thou makest it a burden to thee and loadest thyself the more, and nevertheless thou must bear it.

If thou fling away one cross, without doubt thou shalt find another and perhaps a heavier.

6. Dost thou think to escape that which no mortal ever could avoid? What saint was there ever in the world without his cross and affliction?

Our Lord Jesus Christ Himself was not one hour of His life without suffering: "It behooved Christ to suffer," saith He, "and rise again from the dead, and so enter into his glory." (*Luke* 24:46).

And why dost thou pretend to seek another way than this royal way, which is the way of the holy cross?

7. The whole life of Christ was a cross and a martyrdom, and dost thou seek rest and joy?

Thou errest, thou errest, if thou seekest any other thing than to suffer tribulations; for this whole mortal life is full of miseries and beset on all sides with crosses.

And the higher a person is advanced in spirit the heavier crosses shall he often meet with, because the pain of his banishment increases in proportion to his love.

8. Yet this man, thus many ways afflicted, is not without some allay of comfort, because he is sensible of the great profit which he reaps by bearing the cross.

For whilst he willingly resigns himself to it, all the burden of tribulation is converted into an assured hope of comfort from God.

And the more the flesh is brought down by affliction the more the spirit is strengthened by inward grace.

And it sometimes gains such strength through affection to tribulation and adversity, by loving to be conformable to the Cross of Christ, as not to be willing to be without suffering and affliction; because it is confident that it is so much the more acceptable to God, as it shall be able to bear more and greater things for Him.

This is not man's power, but the grace of Christ, which can and does effect such great things in frail flesh, that what it naturally abhors and flies, even this, through fervor of spirit, it now embraces and loves.

9. To bear the cross, to love the cross, to chastise the body, and bring it under subjection; to fly honors, to be willing to suffer reproaches, to despise one's self and wish to be despised; to bear all adversities and losses, and to desire no prosperity in this world, are not according to man's natural inclination.

If thou look upon thyself, thou canst do nothing of this of thyself.

But if thou confide in the Lord, strength will be given thee from Heaven, and the world and the flesh shall be made subject to thee.

Neither shalt thou fear thine enemy, the devil, if thou be armed with faith and signed with the Cross of Christ.

10. Set thyself then like a good and faithful servant of Christ, to bear manfully the Cross of thy Lord, crucified for the love of thee.

Prepare thyself to suffer many adversities and divers evils in this miserable life; for so it will be with thee wherever thou art, and so indeed wilt thou find it wheresoever thou mayest hide thyself.

It must be so, and there is no remedy against the tribulation of evil and sorrow but to bear them patiently.

Drink of the chalice of thy Lord lovingly if thou desire to be His friend and to have part with Him. (*Matt.* 20:22).

Leave consolations to God, to do with them as best pleaseth Him.

But prepare thou thyself to bear tribulations, and account them the greatest consolations; for the sufferings of this life bear no proportion to the glory to come (*Rom.* 8:18), although thou alone couldst suffer them all.

11. When thou shalt arrive thus far, that tribulation becomes sweet and savory to thee for the love of Christ, then think that it is well with thee, for thou hast found a paradise upon earth.

As long as suffering appear grievous to thee and thou seek to fly from it, so long will it be ill with thee, and the tribulation from which thou fliest will everywhere follow thee.

12. If thou set thyself to what thou oughtst, that is to suffer and die to thyself, it will quickly be better with thee and thou shalt find peace.

Although thou shouldst have been rapt up to the third heaven with St. Paul (*2 Cor.* 12:2), thou art not thereby assured that thou shalt suffer no adversity. "I" said Jesus, "will show him how great things he must suffer for my name." (*Acts* 9:16).

To suffer therefore, is what waits for thee, if thou wilt love Jesus and constantly serve Him.

13. Would to God thou wert worthy to suffer something for the name of Jesus! how great a glory would be laid up for thee, how great joy would it be to all the saints of God and how great edification to thy neighbor.

All recommend patience, but alas! how few there are that desire to suffer.

With good reason oughtst thou willingly to suffer a little for Christ, since many suffer greater things for the world.

14. Know for certain that thou must lead a dying life and the more a man dies to himself the more he begins to live to God.

No man is fit to comprehend heavenly things who has not resigned himself to suffer adversities for Christ.

Nothing is more acceptable to God, nothing more wholesome for thee in this world than to suffer willingly for Christ.

And if thou wert to choose, thou oughtest to wish rather to suffer adversities for Christ than to be delighted with many comforts, because thou wouldst thus be more like unto Christ and more conformable to all the saints.

For our merit and the advancement of our state consist, not in having many sweetnesses and consolations, but rather in bearing great afflictions and tribulations.

15. If, indeed, there had been anything better and more beneficial to man's salvation than suffering, Christ certainly would have showed it by word and example.

For He manfully exhorts both His disciples that followed Him and all that desire to follow Him to bear the cross, saying: "If any one will come after me, let him deny himself and take up his cross and follow me." (*Luke* 9:23).

So that when we have read and searched all let this be the final conclusion, that "Through many tribulations we must enter into the kingdom of God." (*Acts* 14:21).

Practical Reflections

Can we read, believe, and ponder seriously the wonderful advantages of the cross, and the great merits of suffering, as here described, and not love to suffer, to receive crosses from the hands of Jesus Christ, and to submit to endure whatever He pleases, and as much as He pleases, since to suffer much, and in a proper manner, is absolutely requisite for salvation, and is the most tender and efficacious effort of the goodness of God towards us, who will not spare us the pains of time, that He may spare us those of eternity? It is to bear the visible character of the predestinate, which, according to St. Paul, consists in our resemblance to Jesus Christ, an humble, suffering, and persecuted God; it is to render ourselves worthy of His life of glory by participating in His life of suffering; it is to efface the punishment due to our sins by perfect repentance; it is to gain the heart of Jesus Christ, merit His love, avenge Him, and punish ourselves, honor Him by our destruction, and prefer His good pleasure before our own satisfaction. Shall not all this console thee under affliction, and animate thee to bear it with becoming resignation? Say, then, in the time of suffering, in order not to fail: "Hell, which I have deserved, is something more horrible than anything I can now endure; my Saviour has suffered much more for me; and Heaven is worth infinitely more than I can undergo."

Prayer

Penetrate my heart, O Jesus, with these sentiments when Thou sendest me pains, and support me in all my afflictions; for, alas! Thou knowest how naturally I hate and fly from the cross, although I am persuaded that it was by the cross Thou didst save me, and that I cannot gain salvation, nor enter into Heaven, but by the way of Calvary. Inspire me with that patience, that strength, and that courage which Thou didst impart to Thy martyrs: and since I cannot better evince my love and gratitude towards Thee than by suffering for Thee, nor render myself more worthy of Thy grace and glory than by carrying the cross, vouchsafe to support me when sinking under its burden by the desire of pleasing Thee, and the hope of eternal happiness. Amen.

Imitation of Christ, Book III, Chapter 5: The Wonderful Effects of Divine Love

Disciple
I BLESS Thee, O heavenly Father, Father of my Lord Jesus Christ; because Thou hast vouchsafed to be mindful of so poor a wretch as I am.

O Father of mercies and God of all comfort (*2 Cor.* 1:3), I give thanks to Thee, who sometimes art pleased to cherish with Thy consolation, me who am unworthy of any comfort.

I bless Thee and glorify Thee forevermore, together with Thine only-begotten Son and the Holy Ghost, the Comforter to all eternity.

O Lord God, my holy Lover, when Thou shalt come into my heart all that is within me will be filled with joy. (*Prov.* 23:5).

Thou art my Glory and the Joy of my heart.

~~Thou art my Hope and my Refuge in the day of my trouble.~~ (*Ps.* 58:17).

2. But because I am as yet weak in love and imperfect in virtue, therefore do I stand in need of being strengthened and comforted by Thee. For this reason visit me often and instruct me in Thy holy discipline.

Free me from evil passions and heal my heart of all disorderly affections, that being healed and well purified in my interior, I may become fit to love, courageous to suffer and constant to persevere.

3. Love is an excellent thing, a great good indeed, which alone maketh light all that is burdensome and equally bears all that is unequal.

For it carries a burden without being burdened and makes all that which is bitter sweet and savory.

The love of Jesus is noble and generous; it spurs us on to do great things and excites us to desire always that which is most perfect.

Love will tend upwards and is not to be detained by things beneath.

Love will be at liberty and free from all worldly affections, lest its interior sight be hindered, lest it suffer itself to be entangled with any temporal interest or cast down by losses.

Nothing is sweeter than love; nothing stronger, nothing higher, nothing more generous, nothing more pleasant, nothing fuller or better in Heaven or on earth; for love proceeds from God and cannot rest but in God above all things created.

4. The lover flies, runs and rejoices, he is free and not held.

He gives all for all and has all in all, because he rests in one sovereign good above all, from whom all good flows and proceeds.

He looks not at the gifts, but turns himself to the giver above all goods.

Love often knows no measure, but is inflamed above all measure.

Love feels no burden, values no labors, would willingly do more than it can; complains not of impossibility, because it conceives that it may and can do all things.

It is able therefore to do anything and it performs and effects many things where he that loves not faints and lies down.

5. Love watches, and sleeping, slumbers not.

When weary is not tired; when straitened is not constrained; when frighted is not disturbed, but like a lively flame and a torch all on fire it mounts upwards and securely passes through all opposition.

Whosoever loveth knoweth the cry of this voice.

A loud cry in the ears of God is the ardent affection of the soul, which saith, O my God, my love, Thou art all mine and I am all Thine. (*Cant.* 2:16).

6. Give increase to my love, that I may learn to taste with the interior mouth of the heart how sweet it is to love and to swim and to be dissolved in love. (*Ps.* 33:9).

Let me be possessed by love, going above myself through excess of fervor and ecstasy.

Let me sing the canticle of love, let me follow Thee my Beloved on high, let my soul lose herself in Thy praises, rejoicing exceedingly in Thy love.

Let me love Thee more than myself and myself only for Thee, and all others in Thee, who truly love Thee as the law of love commands, which shines forth from Thee.

7. Love is swift, sincere, pious, pleasant, and delightful; strong, patient, faithful, prudent, long-suffering, courageous, and never seeking itself.

For where a man seeks himself there he falls from love.

Love is circumspect, humble, and upright, not soft, not light, not intent upon vain things; is sober, chaste, stable, quiet, and keeps a guard over all the senses.

Love is submissive and obedient to superiors, in its own eyes mean and contemptible, devout and thankful to God; always trusting and hoping in Him, even when it tastes not the relish of God's sweetness, for there is no living in love without some pain or sorrow.

8. Whosoever is not ready to suffer all things and to stand resigned to the will of his Beloved, is not worthy to be called a lover.

He that loveth must willingly embrace all that is hard and bitter, for the sake of his Beloved, and never suffer himself to be turned away from Him by any contrary occurrences whatsoever.

Practical Reflections

Who shall ever conceive or explain the wonderful effects of the love of God in a soul that is faithful to its impressions, and firm in the time of trial? It is much better to feel them than to speak of them; and it is more perfect to practice them than to feel them. What does not the love of God effect when it is active, solid, and constant, in a soul that is captivated with the beauty and goodness of its God, and inflamed with the ardor of His holy charity! It often thinks of Him, for we cannot forget what we love; it does all to please Him; it suffers all for His sake; it carefully avoids the slightest faults; for how can we love God and be willing to offend Him? It desires for God all the good which He is and possesses; it would that all the hearts of men were but one, and this the heart of a seraph; it rejoices in all the glory that is given to Him in Heaven and on earth; it invites all creatures to love and praise Him; it would procure for Him, at the expense of its very life and being, if it were possible, any addition of happiness and delight; it cannot be consoled for His absence; it sighs incessantly for the happiness of seeing Him; it considers this life an exile, which the will of God alone makes supportable; it looks upon death with joy, as being the only means of coming to the possession of Him, and of no more offending Him; it burns with a secret fire, which with lively ardor consumes it before God, in God, and for God; it lives no longer for itself, but for Him whom it loves more than itself; it seeks, it finds, it beholds, everywhere its God. Its joy and its felicity in this world is to suffer, to renounce, and to annihilate itself; and to die to all sensible objects in order to gain the love of Jesus. It believes, it hopes, it loves with a sovereign love, through the respect, esteem, and attachment which it has for the Author of its faith, hope, and charity. God exists, it says, and that is enough for my happiness, my consolation, and my joy. God deserves to be served; He wills that I should do or suffer this for Him; Jesus Christ was most willing to do and to suffer all for me. It is not satisfied with submitting itself in everything to the orders of its God; it seeks but to know His inclinations, and His good pleasure is its law. In a word a soul that loves its God no longer lives by its own life, but it is God who lives within it.

Prayer

Is it possible, O Lord, that Thou Who art infinitely amiable, and Who lovest us with an infinite love, shouldst find in us so little love for Thee? Revive in our hearts that fire of divine charity which Thou, my Saviour, didst bring from Heaven upon the earth, and which Thou desirest should glow within us. Grant that, becoming insensible and indifferent to all creatures, we may feel neither ardor nor attachment but for Thee alone; and that, being ever disposed to suffer all, and to lose all, rather than Thy love, but for one moment, we may love Thee in preference to all things else, and esteem our whole self of infinitely less consideration than Thee. Preserve us in that habitual love of Thee which is Sanctifying Grace; inspire us with an active love to animate us in all our actions. Give us that perpetual love which, causing us to do all for and by Thee, may procure for us the happiness of dying in the exercise of Thy love, to continue it throughout a blessed eternity. Amen.

Imitation of Christ, Book III, Chapter 6:
The Proof of a True Lover

Christ
MY SON, thou art not as yet a valiant and prudent lover.

Disciple
Why, O Lord?

Christ
Because thou fallest off from what thou hast begun, upon meeting with a little adversity and too greedily seekest after consolation.

A valiant lover stands his ground in temptations and yields not to the crafty persuasions of the enemy.

As he is pleased with Me in prosperity so I displease him not when I send adversity.

2. A prudent lover considers not so much the gift of the lover as the love of the giver.

He looks more at the good will than the value, and prizes his Beloved above all His gifts.

A generous lover rests not in the gift, but in Me above every gift.

All is not lost if sometimes thou hast not that sense of devotion towards Me or My saints which thou wouldst have.

That good and delightful affection, which thou sometimes perceivest, is the effect of present grace and a certain foretaste of thy heavenly country, but thou must not rely too much upon it, because it goes and comes.

But to fight against the evil motions of the mind which arise, and to despise the suggestions of the devil is a sign of virtue and of great merit.

3. Let not, therefore, strange fancies trouble thee, of what kind soever they be that are suggested to thee.

Keep thy resolution firm and thine intention upright towards God.

Neither is it an illusion that sometimes thou art rapt into an ecstasy and presently returnest to the accustomed weakness of thy heart.

For these thou rather sufferest against thy will than procurest, and as long as thou art displeased with them and dost resist them it is merit and not loss.

4. Know that the old enemy strives by all means to hinder thy desire after good and to divert thee from every devout exercise, namely from the veneration of the saints, from the pious meditation of My Passion, from the profitable remembrance of thy sins, from keeping a guard upon thine own heart and from a firm purpose of advancing in virtue.

He suggests to thee many evil thoughts that he may weary thee out, and frighten thee that he may withdraw thee from prayer and the reading of devout books.

He is displeased with humble confession, and if he could he would cause thee to omit Communion.

Give no credit to him, value him not, although he often lays his deceitful snares in thy way.

Charge him with it when he suggests wicked and unclean things and say to him:

Begone, unclean spirit; be ashamed, miserable wretch; thou art very filthy indeed to suggest such things as these to Me.

Depart from me, thou wicked imposter, thou shalt have no share in me, but my Jesus will be with me as a valiant warrior and thou shalt be confounded.

I would rather die and undergo any torment whatsoever than yield to thy suggestions.

Be silent, I will hear no more of thee, although thou so often strivest to be troublesome to me. "The Lord is my light and my salvation, whom shall I fear? The Lord is the protector of my life, of whom shall I be afraid?" (*Ps.* 26:1).

"If armies in camp should stand together against me, my heart shall not fear. The Lord is my helper and my Redeemer." (*Ps.* 69:6).

5. Fight like a good soldier, and if sometimes thou fallest through frailty rise up again with greater strength than before,

confiding in My more abundant grace, but take great care thou yield not to any vain complacency and pride.

Through this many are led into error and sometimes fall into incurable blindness.

Let this fall of the proud, who foolishly rely on their own strength, serve thee for a warning and keep thee always humble.

Practical Reflections

I know that the true love of God may consist more in suffering, for His sake, dryness, disgust, and the most grievous temptations, without yielding to them, than in the enjoyment of interior delights, sweetnesses, and consolations; for in the one instance we receive much from God, in the other we give much to Him. In the one we love the gifts of God, in the other we love Himself and His holy will preferably to all His gifts; and the love by which we love God for what He is, is much more perfect than that by which we love Him for what He bestows upon us. Ah, how pleasing to Almighty God to behold a soul ever watchful over itself to keep its heart free from the least faults, ever attentive to its duties, in obedience to His orders, and in resignation to His holy will, and ever willing generously to resist the demands of nature and the temptations of the devil! A soul which neither allows nor pardons itself anything, but endeavors to correspond with the holy designs of God in its regard, to destroy in itself everything human, and to overthrow self-love, takes for the rule of its conduct that rule of true love: All to please God, and nothing to gratify myself. But what most pleases God is to see that this soul, really clothed with the strength and grace of His spirit in all its contests with itself and its passions, can endure nothing contrary to His good pleasure; to see that it neither asks, nor seeks, nor finds any consolation or sensible support, its delight being the delight which God takes in seeing it suffer, even without being sensibly assured that He takes pleasure in it. Its submission and its self-renunciation are its consolation and support, happy in becoming a victim of immolation to the love of God.

Prayer

Abandon me not, O Lord, to the sensitiveness of self-love, which will suffer nothing; nor to the inefficacy of my desires, by which I ever will what I never perform. Penetrate my heart with a conviction of the happiness and obligation of suffering all for Thee, and as Thou didst suffer. Grant that, having no other interest but Thine, and willing only what Thou willest, I may receive pains of mind as cheerfully as consolations of spirit; and hoping that, punishing me here, Thou wilt spare me hereafter, I may often say to Thee, in the time of suffering, may Thy justice be satisfied whatever I may have to endure in this life. The less I enjoy Thee, the more will I love Thee; the more will I resist the irregular desires of my heart, that I may ultimately deserve the more to possess Thee. O my God! My Saviour! I am willing to be deprived of all consolation here below, provided I never offend Thee. What a happiness to become a victim of Calvary, a martyr to Thy crucified Heart, and entirely devoted to Thy good pleasure! Amen.

Imitation of Christ, Book III, Chapter 56: We Ought to Deny Ourselves, and Imitate Christ by the Cross

Christ

SON, as much as thou canst go out of thyself, so much wilt thou be able to enter into Me.

As desiring nothing abroad brings peace at home, so relinquishing thyself joins thee interiorly to God.

I will have thee learn the perfect renunciation of thyself, according to My will, without contradiction or complaint.

Follow Me (*John* 21:19): I am the way, the truth, and the life. (*John* 14:6). Without the way there is no going; without the truth there is no knowing; without the life there is no living.

I am the way which thou must follow; the truth which thou must believe; the life for which thou must hope.

I am the way inviolable, the truth infallible, and the life interminable.

I am the straightest way, the sovereign truth, the true life, the blessed life, and uncreated life.

If thou continue in My way thou shalt know the truth, and the truth shall deliver thee (*John* 8:32), and thou shalt attain to life everlasting. (*Matt.* 19:29).

2. If thou wilt enter into life, keep the Commandments. (*Matt.* 19:17).

If thou wilt know the truth, believe Me. (*John* 14:17).

If thou wilt be perfect, sell all things. (*Matt.* 19:21).

If thou wilt be My disciple, deny thyself. (*Matt.* 16:24).

If thou wilt possess a blessed life, despise this present life. (*Matt.* 16:25).

If thou wilt be exalted in Heaven, humble thyself in this world. (*Matt.* 18:4).

If thou wilt reign with Me, bear the cross with Me.

For none but the servants of the cross find the way of bliss and true light.

Disciple

3. Lord Jesus, forasmuch as Thy way is narrow, and despised by the world, grant that I may follow Thee, and be despised by the world.

For the servant is not greater than his lord, neither is the disciple above his master. (*Matt.* 10:24).

Let Thy servant meditate on Thy life, for there is my salvation and true holiness.

Whatever I read or hear besides does not recreate nor fully delight me.

Christ

4. Son, now thou knowest these things and hast read them all, happy shalt thou be if thou fulfill them.

"He that hath my commandments, and keepeth them, he it is that loveth me; and I will love him, and will manifest myself unto him" (*John* 14:21), and "I will make him sit with me in the kingdom of my Father." (*Matt.* 19:28).

Disciple

5. Lord Jesus, as Thou hast said and hast promised, so may it be indeed, and may it be my lot to merit it.

I have received the cross, I have received it from Thy hand; I will bear it, yea, I will bear it until death, as Thou hast laid it upon me.

Indeed the life of a good religious man is a cross, but it is a cross that conducts him to Paradise.

We have now begun, it is not lawful to go back, nor may we leave off. (*Luke* 9:62).

6. Take courage, my brethren, let us go forward together, Jesus will be with us. (*Heb.* 12:1).

For the sake of Jesus we took up His cross; for the sake of Jesus let us persevere on the cross.

He will be our helper, who is our captain and our leader.

Behold our King marches before us, who will fight for us.

Let us follow Him manfully; let no one shrink through fear; let us be ready to die valiantly in battle, and not stain our glory by flying from the standard of the cross. (*1 Mach.* 9:10).

Practical Reflections

If any man will come after Me, says our Divine Redeemer, let him deny himself, and let him take up his cross daily, and follow Me. In this is included the whole practice of a Christian life, and the way marked out by which we may securely go to eternal salvation, for Jesus is the way, the truth, and the life; the way we must follow, the truth we must believe, and the life we must hope for. To live as Christians, and to secure salvation, we must begin by renouncing and dying to ourselves; for this renunciation—this spirit of self-denial, is the first principle of the Gospel, the fundamental law of Christianity, our most essential duty, and the most effectual means of obtaining salvation. It is this interior mortification, this circumcision of the heart, this retrenchment of all criminal, dangerous, or useless indulgences, which constitutes the difference between the elect and the reprobate. The character of our present sinful state should be that of penance, which is the end of Christianity and the assurance of salvation.

To carry our cross with Jesus Christ is to suffer from all, while we are careful not to become the cause of suffering in others; it is to receive all pains of body and mind as coming from above; it is to endure with patience all the evils which happen to us from the justice of God or the injustice of man; it is to accept of contempt as our due, and to consider it our greatest misfortune to suffer nothing for God, but our sovereign happiness to suffer always for His love.

Prayer

O Divine Saviour, how few are willing to be with Thee on Calvary, yet how gladly would all accompany Thee on Thabor and in Heaven! While each one desires and seeks exemption from the cross, to live in tranquillity and ease, no one chooses to suffer for Thee; although the only sure proof we can give Thee of our love is to be willing to suffer with Thee, and to copy Thy painful example.

O cross of Jesus! how patiently do we bear Thy sorrows in our hearts! How shall I be able to behold Thee with confidence at the last day, if now I look upon Thee with horror? How shall I be able to give up my soul in the embraces of the crucifix, if now I live an enemy to that emblem of mercy? Permit it not, O Jesus, and since Thou hast saved me by the cross, grant that I may be ever willing to live in its practice, that I may die in its salvation. Amen.

Imitation of Christ, Book IV, Chapter 1: With How Great Reverence Christ Is to Be Received

Disciple

THESE are Thy words, O Christ, the eternal truth, though not all delivered at one time, nor written in one place.

Since, therefore, they are Thy words, and true, they are all to be received by me with thanks and with faith.

They are Thine, and Thou hast spoken them; and they are also mine because Thou hast delivered them for my salvation.

I willingly received them from Thy mouth, that they may be more inseparably ingrafted in my heart.

These words of such great tenderness, full of sweetness and love, encourage me; but my sins terrify me, and my unclean conscience keeps me back from approaching such great mysteries. The sweetness of Thy words invites me, but the multitude of my offenses weighs me down.

2. Thou commandest me to approach to Thee with confidence if I would have part with Thee; and to receive the food of immortality if I desire to obtain life and glory everlasting.

"Come," sayest Thou to me, "all you that labor and are burdened, and I will refresh you." (*Matt.* 11:28).

O sweet and amiable word in the ear of a sinner, that Thou, O Lord my God, shouldst invite the poor and needy to the Communion of Thy most sacred Body!

But who am I, O Lord, that I should presume to come to Thee?

Behold, the Heaven of heavens cannot contain Thee (*3 Kgs.* 8:27); and Thou sayest, "Come you all to Me."

3. What means this most loving condescension, and so friendly invitation?

How shall I dare to approach, who am conscious to myself of no good on which I can presume?

How shall I introduce Thee into my house, who have oftentimes provoked Thine indignation?

The angels and the archangels stand with a reverential awe; the saints and the just are afraid; and Thou sayest, "Come you all to Me." Unless Thou, O Lord, didst say it, who could believe it to be true?

And unless Thou didst command it, who would dare attempt to approach?

4. Behold Noe, a just man (*Gen.* 6:9), labored a hundred years in building the ark, that he with a few might be preserved; and how shall I be able in the space of one hour to prepare myself to receive with reverence the Maker of the world?

Moses Thy servant, Thy great and special friend, made an ark of incorruptible wood, which he also covered with the most pure gold, that he might deposit therein the tables of the law; and shall I, a rotten creature, presume so easily to receive Thee, the Maker of the law, and the Giver of life?

Solomon, the wisest of the kings of Israel, employed seven years in building a magnificent temple for the praise of Thy name:

And for eight days together celebrated the feast of the dedication thereof; he offered a thousand victims as peace offerings, and brought the Ark of the Covenant in a solemn manner into the place prepared for it, with sound of trumpet and jubilee. (*3 Kgs.* 8:6).

And I, a wretch, and the vilest of men, how shall I bring Thee into my house, who can hardly spend one half hour devoutly? And would I had even once spent one half hour itself as I ought!

5. O my God, how much did they endeavor to do to please Thee!

Alas! how little is what I do! How short a time do I spend when I prepare myself to communicate, being seldom wholly recollected, very seldom free from all distraction!

And yet, surely in the life-giving presence of Thy Deity, no unbecoming thought should occur, nor anything created take up my mind; for it is not an angel, but the Lord of angels that I am to entertain.

6. And yet there is a very great difference between the Ark of the Covenant with its relics, and Thy most pure Body, with its unspeakable virtues; between those sacrifices of the law, which were figures of things to come, and the true sacrifice of Thy Body, which is the accomplishing of all those ancient sacrifices.

7. Why then am I not more inflamed, considering Thy venerable presence?

Why do I not prepare myself with greater care to receive Thy sacred gifts, seeing that these ancient holy patriarchs and prophets, yea kings also and princes, with the whole people, have shown so great an affection of devotion towards Thy divine worship?

8. The most devout King David danced before the ark of God with all his might (*2 Kgs.* 6:14), commemorating the benefits be-

stowed in times past on the fathers. He made musical instruments of sundry kinds; he published psalms, and appointed them to be sung with joy; he himself likewise often sang them, playing upon his harp, inspired with the grace of the Holy Ghost. He taught the people of Israel to praise God with their whole heart, and to join their voices in blessing and magnifying Him every day.

If such great devotion was then used, and such remembrance of the praise of God before the Ark of the Covenant, how great ought to be the reverence and devotion which I and all Christian people should have in the presence of this Sacrament, and in receiving the most excellent Body of Christ!

9. Many run to sundry places to visit the relics of the saints, and are astonished to hear their wonderful works; they behold the noble church buildings and kiss their sacred bones, wrapt up in silk and gold.

And behold I have Thee here present on the altar, my God, the Saint of saints, the Creator of men, and the Lord of angels.

Oftentimes in seeing these things men are moved with curiosity, and the novelty of the sight, and but little fruit of amendment is reaped thereby; especially when persons lightly run hither and thither, without true contrition for their sins.

But here, in the Sacrament of the Altar, Thou art wholly present, my God, the man Christ Jesus; where also the fruit of eternal salvation is plentifully reaped, as often as Thou art worthily and devoutly received.

And to this we are not drawn by any levity, curiosity, or sensuality; but by a firm faith, a devout hope, and a sincere charity.

10. O God, the invisible Maker of the world, how wonderfully dost Thou deal with us! How sweetly and graciously dost Thou order all things in favor of Thine elect, to whom Thou offerest Thyself to be received in this Sacrament!

For this exceeds all understanding of man; this in a particular manner engages the hearts of the devout, and enkindles their love.

For Thy true faithful, who dispose their whole life to amendment, by this most worthy Sacrament, frequently receive a great grace of devotion and love of virtue.

11. Oh, the wonderful and hidden grace of this Sacrament, which only the faithful of Christ know; but unbelievers and such as are slaves to sin cannot experience.

In this Sacrament is conferred spiritual grace; lost virtue is repaired in the soul; and beauty disfigured by sin returns again.

And so great sometimes is this grace that from the abundance of the devotion that is bestowed, not only the mind, but the frail body also feels a great increase of strength.

12. Yet it is much to be lamented and pitied that we should be so lukewarm and negligent as not to be drawn with greater affection to the receiving of Christ, in whom consists all the hope and merit of those that shall be saved.

For He is our sanctification and our redemption; He is our comfort in our pilgrimage, and the eternal beatitude of the saints.

It is therefore much to be lamented that many esteem so lightly this saving mystery which rejoices Heaven and preserves the whole world.

Oh, the blindness and hardness of the heart of man that doth not more highly prize so unspeakable a gift; and from daily use falls into a disregard of it.

13. For if this most holy Sacrament were only celebrated in one place, and consecrated by only one priest in the world, how great a desire would men have to go to that place, and to such a priest of God; that they might see the divine mysteries celebrated?

But now there are made many priests, and Christ is offered up in many places, that the grace and love of God to man may appear the greater, the more this sacred Communion is spread throughout the world.

Thanks be to Thee, O good Jesus, our eternal Shepherd, Who hast vouchsafed to feed us poor exiles with Thy precious Body and Blood, and to invite us to the receiving these mysteries with the very words of Thine Own mouth, saying, "Come to me all you that labour and are burdened, and I will refresh you." (*Matt.* 11:28).

Practical Reflections

Who can conceive or explain the excellence of the all-divine gift which Jesus Christ bestows upon us in giving us His blessed Body and Blood in the Holy Eucharist, in which we receive God with all His perfections, the plenitude of His divinity, all the virtues and grace of His humanity, and all the merits of a Man-God? We may say, with St. Augustine, that God, though all-powerful, cannot bestow upon us anything greater than Himself, whom He here gives us; though most rich and liberal, yet He cannot dispense to us anything more from the treasures of His bounty than this one gift of His Body and Blood, His whole self; and though the uncreated and incarnate Wisdom of the Father, yet He cannot invent a more efficacious means of gaining our hearts than to enter into them by the Holy Communion, and thus unite and transform us into Himself.

But what should delight our minds and hearts is that in the sacred Host which we receive, and even in its smallest part (that we may lose nothing of so precious a gift), He has included all the riches of His bounty, wisdom, and love, to communicate them all to us, and by communicating them to us, to enable us to live in a supernatural and divine life by feeding and nourishing us with God; for it is to this end that He assumes a new life upon our altars, to impart it to us in the Holy Communion by which, says the Council of Trent, He infuses into our souls all the riches of His love. Yes, my Saviour, after having bestowed upon us all the goods of nature and of grace Thou addest still more to Thy gifts—Thy whole self in the blessed Eucharist. After having been liberal of Thy gifts in our regard, which, although most precious, are still much less than Thyself, in this adorable Sacrament Thou art prodigal even of Thy very self. Who then can refuse and withhold his heart from God, who comes thus to take possession of it, as belonging to Him upon so many titles?

Prayer

What return can I make Thee, O Lord, for all Thy gifts and favors? What can I give Thee in exchange for Thyself, Whom Thou bestowest upon my soul, to become to me the principle of a truly Christian life and the pledge of my salvation? As often as I have the honor of receiving Thee, my most amiable Saviour, I may say that Thou art all mine, and yet, alas! after having received Thee so frequently, I cannot as yet say that I am all Thine. Come, O Jesus, and take full possession of my ungrateful and unfaithful heart, which is so little devoted to Thee, and so much given to the world and to itself. Conquer its perversity, O Lord, and oblige it to love Thee, that it may hate itself and, recalling its affections, devote them entirely to Thee. It is Thine, O God, as the work of Thy hands and the price of Thy blood; it is Thy purchased inheritance, which Thou comest to take possession of. Permit it not to depart from Thee to become the slave of its passions, but, being come to me, establish Thy reign entirely and forever over me.

Suffer me not, O Jesus, when I receive Thee, Who art my all, both now and forever, to be so unhappy, like many Christians, as to be Thine only in appearance and exteriorly, only in desires and wishes, or to be but half Thine, so as to wish to reconcile God and the world, vanity and devotion; which Thou declarest in the Gospel is impossible and incompatible with salvation. Suffer me not to be so miserable as to belong to Thee only for a time, by almost immediately after Communion falling again into voluntary habitual faults, which Thy presence should correct, or at least diminish; for the fruit of a good Communion is strength, courage, and constancy to resist and conquer ourselves.

Receive, O Jesus, my most humble thanks for Thine institution of this adorable Sacrament, in which Thy love triumphs over all Thine other attributes, to feed and nourish me with Thine own Body and Blood. In gratitude for so great a favor, for so wonderful and divine a benefit, I beseech Thee to accept of the sincere, perfect, and irrevocable offering which I now make of my whole self to Thee, for time and eternity. Amen.

Imitation of Christ, Book IV, Chapter 8:
Of the Oblation of Christ on the Cross, And of our own Resignation

Christ

AS I willingly offered myself to God My Father, for thy sins, with My hands stretched out upon the cross, and My body naked, so that nothing remained in Me which was not turned into a sacrifice, to appease the divine wrath:

Even so must thou willingly offer thyself to Me daily in the Mass, for a pure and holy oblation, together with all thy powers and affections, as heartily as thou art able.

What do I require more of thee, than that thou endeavor to resign thyself entirely to Me?

Whatsoever thou givest besides thyself I regard not; for I seek not thy gift, but thyself.

2. As it would not suffice thee if thou hadst all things but Me, so neither can it please Me whatever thou givest, as long as thou offerest not thyself.

Offer thyself to Me, and give thy whole self for God, and thine offering will be accepted.

Behold, I offered My whole self to the Father for thee, and have given My whole Body and Blood for thy food, that I might be all thine, and thou mightest be always Mine.

But if thou wilt stand upon thine own self, and wilt not offer thyself freely to My will, thine offering is not perfect, nor will there be an entire union between us.

Therefore, before all thy works, thou must make a free oblation of thyself into the hands of God, if thou desire to obtain liberty and grace.

For the reason why so few become illuminated and internally free is because they do not wholly renounce themselves.

My sentence stands firm: "Unless a man renounce all he cannot be my disciple." (*Luke* 14:33). If, therefore, thou desire to be My disciple, offer up thyself to Me with all thine affections.

Practical Reflections

Be not of the number of those who, when they communicate, give themselves entirely to God, and immediately after return to themselves; whose lives, being a constant succession of good desires and frail relapses, are never firmly established either in the fear or love of God. It is of such souls, who are thus mean and ungenerous towards a God who is so prodigal of Himself towards them, that the Prophet speaks when he says: "On account of the iniquity of his covetousness I was angry, and I struck him; I hid my face from thee, and was angry; and he went away wandering, in the way of his own heart." (*Is.* 57:17).

Prayer

Yes, O Lord, Thou art now the God of my heart, for Thou comest to take possession of it, and to give me Thyself to repose within it. Mayest Thou be such in all things and forever; mayest Thou alone be the God of my soul in time, that Thou mayest be my portion for eternity. Unite me to Thyself, by making me like to Thee, meek, humble, patient, and charitable. Suffer not the union with which I am now honored to remain ineffective, like that of a dry branch with the sap of the vine, or languid, like that of a paralyzed arm with a vigorous body; but grant that it may become lively, vivifying and perpetual, like that of food with the body which it cherishes. Amen.

Imitation of Christ, Book IV, Chapter 13:
That a Devout Soul Ought to Desire, With Her Whole Heart,
to Be United to Christ in This Sacrament

Disciple
WHO will give me, O Lord, that I may find Thee alone, that I may open my whole heart to Thee and enjoy Thee as my soul desireth; and that now no man may despise me (*Cant.* 8:1), nor anything created move me or regard me, but that Thou alone speak to me, and I

to Thee; as the beloved is wont to speak to his beloved, and a friend to entertain himself with his friend. (*Ex.* 33:11).

This I pray for, this I desire, that I may be wholly united to Thee, and may withdraw my heart from all created things, and by the Holy Communion, and often celebrating, may more and more learn to relish heavenly and eternal things.

Ah! Lord God, when shall I be wholly united to Thee, and absorbed in Thee, and altogether forgetful of myself.

Thou in me, and I in Thee; and so grant us both to continue in one. (*John* 15:5).

2. Verily Thou art my beloved, the choicest amongst thousands (*Cant.* 5:10), in whom my soul is well pleased to dwell all the days of her life.

Verily Thou art my peacemaker (*Cant.* 8:10), in Whom is sovereign peace and true rest; out of Whom is labor and sorrow and endless misery.

Thou art, in truth, a hidden God (*Is.* 45:15), and Thy counsel is not with the wicked; but Thy conversation is with the humble and the simple. (*Prov.* 3:32).

Oh, how sweet is Thy spirit, O Lord, Who, to show Thy sweetness towards Thy children, vouchsafest to feed them with the most delicious bread which cometh down from Heaven! (*John* 6:50).

Surely, there is no other nation so great, that hath gods so nigh them as Thou our God art present (*Deut.* 4:7) to all Thy faithful; to whom, for their daily comfort, and for the raising up of their hearts to Heaven, Thou givest Thyself to be eaten and enjoyed.

3. For what other nation is there so honored as the Christian people?

Or what creature under Heaven so beloved as a devout soul, into whom God cometh, that He may feed her with His glorious Flesh?

O unspeakable grace! O wonderful condescension! O infinite love, singularly bestowed upon man!

But what return shall I make to the Lord for this grace, and for so extraordinary a charity? (*Ps.* 115:12).

There is nothing that I can give Him that will please Him better than if I give up my heart entirely to God, and unite it closely to Him. (*Prov. 23:26*).

Then all that is within me shall rejoice exceedingly when my soul shall be perfectly united to my God; then will He say to me: If thou wilt be with Me, I will be with thee: and I will answer Him: Vouchsafe, O Lord, to remain with me, and I will willingly be with Thee.

This is my whole desire, that my heart may be united to Thee.

Practical Reflections

Of the ends for which Jesus Christ is present upon our altars,
and the pious dispositions with which we should visit
the Blessed Sacrament, and assist at Mass and Benediction.

The Son of God remains upon our altars not only during Mass, but likewise at other times, first to hear and favorably to receive our prayers, and to continue the same mediation between God and man which He exercised upon the cross; secondly, to receive our visits, our homage, and adorations; hence, those Christians who visit Him seldom, coldly, through custom, or with indifference, are highly blameable for thus appearing before their God, their Saviour, and their Judge, without either reverence, love, or fear; thirdly, to console us under afflictions, to support us in difficulties, and to resolve and dissipate our doubts, according to what is written. Let us go to the Son of Joseph, and He will console us;* and as a prophet said to a prince, who sent to consult a false god: Is it because there is no God in Israel? fourthly, to be our nourishment during life, and our viaticum at the hour of death.

How should a Christian who has recourse to Jesus Christ in the Blessed Sacrament with assiduity, respect, and gratitude, as to his King, his God, and his Saviour, who never omits hearing Mass but from necessity, and when he assists at it, or at Benediction, endeav-

* St. Joseph passed for the father of Jesus Christ, but was only His foster parent.

ors to attend with a spirit of religion, that he may depart affected, converted, and a better man—how, I say, should a Christian, who is faithful in the discharge of all pious duties towards Jesus Christ immolated for him on the altar, repose his confident hope in His bounty and mercies, both in life and in death? Will not, however, the Son of God have reason one day to reproach multitudes of Christians who either neglect to visit Him in the Most Holy Sacrament, or do so with very little devotion; will He not have reason to reproach them with their irreverence and want of faith; saying to them, "There hath stood one in the midst of you whom ye knew not"? You have neglected to know and visit God, who was in the midst of you. In vain have I performed prodigies of power, wisdom, and bounty in the blessed Eucharist, that I might gain your hearts; you would not interrupt your employments, nor even your pleasure to come and pay Me your homage.

To answer the ends therefore for which Jesus Christ is always present in the Most Holy Sacrament, we should visit Him, hear Mass, and attend at Benediction with all the respect and submission of courtiers before their king, with the recollection and fervor of angels before their God, with the humble fear of criminals before their judge, and with the confidence and love of children before their father.

Prayer

Which may be recited either during Mass or at the Benediction, or when visiting the Blessed Sacrament.

1. I adore Thee, O Sovereign Majesty, Who residest upon our altars, to receive our homage, and dost there annihilate and immolate Thyself in honor of Thine eternal Father, to come and reign in our hearts. I profoundly pay Thee all the homage due to a God who is to decide my eternal doom. I prostrate myself before Thee. I desire to join in the profound adorations of the seraphim who assist around the altar, and I beseech Thee to accept their recollection and their love to supply the wanderings of my mind, and the indifference of my heart.

2. Penetrated with sorrow and confusion for the irreverences and indecencies which I have dared to commit in Thy presence, and for those also of all other Christians, I most humbly crave pardon for them, and am resolved to make amends for them, by appearing before Thee with all that modesty, all that reserve, all that respect, and all that spirit of religion with which I ought to present myself before Thee. I desire to satisfy Thy justice for all the outrages Thou hast received from impious libertines and heretics in the Most Holy Sacrament. Forgive them, O Lord, for they know Thee not; and cause me to suffer the temporal punishment which they have deserved, rather than abandon and punish them forever.

Grant, O adorable Victim of Thy love and of our salvation, grant that faith may immolate my mind, charity consecrate my heart, and religion sacrifice my whole being to Thee; and that so long as I shall be in Thy house, my eyes may behold only Thee, my heart overflow with Thy love, and my tongue proclaim Thy praise in prayer and supplication.

3. While the angels lie prostrate before Thee, O great God! and, struck with humble fear, fervently pay Thee their tribute of profound respect and ardent love, shall we mortals, who are the works of Thy hands and the price of Thy blood, appear in Thy presence with wandering eyes and dissipated minds, with cold and indifferent hearts, without addressing Thee, and almost without thinking of Thee? O my Saviour, suffer me not to be thus wanting in the respect and love which I owe to Thy greatness, and which Thou dost so much the more deserve as Thou dost the more humble Thyself for the love of me.

4. Inspire me with the sentiments of the publican, who dared not lift up his eyes towards God, penetrated with sorrow and confusion for his sins, and of the prodigal son, when he returned to his father's house; and grant that, like them, I may be restored through Thy bounty and my sorrow, to Thy grace and favor.

5. O my soul, behold thy God who died for thee, and of whose death thou wert the cause; how canst thou refrain from testifying thy love and gratitude towards Him? O my heart! be thou before Jesus

Christ like the lamp* which burns before Him, and be thou in like manner consumed in His presence. No, I desire not to depart from before Thee, my Saviour, without being truly converted and entirely Thine. Amen.

---

* In Catholic countries a lamp is kept continually burning in the churches, before the altar on which the Blessed Sacrament is kept.

THE CONSECRATION

The Day of Consecration

"At the end of the three weeks," says St. Louis De Montfort, "they shall go to confession and to Communion, with the intention of giving themselves to Jesus Christ in the quality of slaves of love, by the hands of Mary. After Communion, which they should try to make according to the method given further on [See no. 266], they should recite the formula of their consecration, which they will also find further on. They ought to write it, or have it written, unless they have a printed copy of it; and they should sign it the same day they have made it. It would be well also that on that day they should pay some tribute to Jesus Christ and our Blessed Lady, either as a penance for their past unfaithfulness to the vows of their Baptism or as a testimony of their dependence on the dominion of Jesus and Mary. This tribute ought to be according to the devotion and ability of everyone, such as a fast, a mortification, an alms or a candle. If they had but a pin to give in homage, yet gave it with good heart, it would be enough for Jesus, who looks only at one's good will. Once a year at least, on the same day, they should renew the same consecration, observing the same practices during the three weeks. They might also once a month, or even once a day, renew all they have done, in these few words: 'I am all Thine and all that I have belongs to Thee, O my sweet Jesus, through Mary, Thy holy Mother.'"

The Act of Consecration

Consecration to Jesus Christ, the Incarnate Wisdom,
through the Blessed Virgin Mary

O Eternal and Incarnate Wisdom! O sweetest and most adorable Jesus! True God and true man, only Son of the Eternal Father, and of Mary, always virgin! I adore Thee profoundly in the bosom and splendors of Thy Father during eternity; and I adore Thee also in the virginal bosom of Mary, Thy most worthy Mother, in the time of Thine Incarnation.

I give Thee thanks for that Thou hast annihilated Thyself, taking the form of a slave in order to rescue me from the cruel slavery of the devil. I praise and glorify Thee for that Thou hast been pleased to submit Thyself to Mary, Thy holy Mother, in all things, in order to make me Thy faithful slave through her. But, alas! Ungrateful and faithless as I have been, I have not kept the promises which I made so solemnly to Thee in my Baptism; I have not fulfilled my obligations; I do not deserve to be called Thy child, nor yet Thy slave; and as there is nothing in me which does not merit Thine anger and Thy repulse, I dare not come by myself before Thy most holy and august Majesty. It is on this account that I have recourse to the intercession of Thy most holy Mother, whom Thou hast given me for a mediatrix with Thee. It is through her that I hope to obtain of Thee contrition, the pardon of my sins, and the acquisition and preservation of wisdom.

Hail, then, O Immaculate Mary, living tabernacle of the Divinity, where the Eternal Wisdom willed to be hidden and to be adored by angels and by men! Hail, O Queen of Heaven and earth, to whose empire everything is subject which is under God. Hail, O sure refuge of sinners, whose mercy fails no one. Hear the desires which I have of the Divine Wisdom; and for that end receive the vows and offerings which in my lowliness I present to thee.

I, (Name), a faithless sinner, renew and ratify today in thy hands the vows of my Baptism; I renounce forever Satan, his pomps and works; and I give myself entirely to Jesus Christ, the Incarnate Wisdom, to carry my cross after Him all the days of my life, and to be more faithful to Him than I have ever been before.

In the presence of all the heavenly court I choose thee this day for my Mother and Mistress. I deliver and consecrate to thee, as thy slave, my body and soul, my goods, both interior and exterior, and even the value of all my good actions, past, present and future; leaving to thee the entire and full right of disposing of me, and all that belongs to me, without exception, according to thy good pleasure, for the greater glory of God, in time and in eternity.

Receive, O benignant Virgin, this little offering of my slavery, in honor of, and in union with, that subjection which the Eternal Wisdom deigned to have to thy maternity, in homage to the power which both of you have over this poor sinner, and in thanksgiving for the privileges with which the Holy Trinity has favored thee. I declare that I wish henceforth, as thy true slave, to seek thy honor and to obey thee in all things.

O admirable Mother, present me to thy dear Son as His eternal slave, so that as He has redeemed me by thee, by thee He may receive me! O Mother of mercy, grant me the grace to obtain the true Wisdom of God; and for that end receive me among those whom thou lovest and teachest, whom thou leadest, nourishest and protectest as thy children and thy slaves.

O faithful Virgin, make me in all things so perfect a disciple, imitator and slave of the Incarnate Wisdom, Jesus Christ thy Son, that I may attain, by thine intercession and by thine example, to the fullness of His age on earth and of His glory in Heaven. Amen.

THE LITTLE CROWN OF
THE BLESSED VIRGIN MARY

———•———

St. John the Evangelist saw a woman crowned with twelve stars, clothed with the sun, and the moon under her feet. According to the commentators, this woman is the Blessed Virgin Mary, with her virtues and her privileges, especially that of her divine maternity. Thus originated the *Little Crown of the Twelve Stars of the Blessed Virgin Mary*, which St. Joseph Calasanctius, St. John Berchmans and many other saints made it a practice to recite frequently.

In order to make this prayer more attractive, St. Louis De Montfort added to each *Hail Mary* one of the praises of the Blessed Virgin, with the invocation, "Rejoice, O Virgin Mary; rejoice a thousand times."

It is this prayer which St. Louis De Montfort gave to his religious families (The Montfort Fathers and the Daughters of Wisdom) as their morning prayer. He also recommends it to all those who embrace the devotion of the holy and loving slavery of Jesus through Mary.

Little Crown of the Blessed Virgin Mary

I. Crown of Excellence

(To honor the divine maternity of the Blessed Virgin, her ineffable virginity, her purity without stain and her innumerable virtues.)
1. *Our Father. Hail Mary.*

Blessed art thou, O Virgin Mary, who didst bear the Lord, the Creator of the world; thou didst give birth to Him Who made thee, and remainest a virgin forever.

Rejoice, O Virgin Mary; rejoice a thousand times!

2. *Hail Mary.*

O holy and immaculate Virgin, I know not with what praise to extoll thee, since thou didst bear in thy womb the very One Whom the heavens cannot contain.

Rejoice, O Virgin Mary; rejoice a thousand times!

3. *Hail Mary.*

Thou art all fair, O Virgin Mary, and there is no stain in thee.

Rejoice, O Virgin Mary; rejoice a thousand times!

4. *Hail Mary.*

Thy virtues, O Virgin, surpass the stars in number.

Rejoice, O Virgin Mary; rejoice a thousand times!

Glory be to the Father.

II. Crown of Power

(To honor the royalty of the Blessed Virgin, her magnificence, her universal mediation and the strength of her rule.)

5. *Our Father. Hail Mary.*

Glory be to thee, O Empress of the world! Bring us with thee to the joys of Heaven.

Rejoice, O Virgin Mary; rejoice a thousand times!

6. *Hail Mary.*

Glory be to thee, O treasure house of the Lord's graces! Grant us a share in thy riches.

Rejoice, O Virgin Mary; rejoice a thousand times!

7. *Hail Mary.*

Glory be to thee, O Mediatrix between God and man! Through thee may the Almighty be favorable to us.

Rejoice, O Virgin Mary; rejoice a thousand times!

8. *Hail Mary.*

Glory be to thee who destroyest heresies and crushest demons! Be thou our loving guide.

Rejoice, O Virgin Mary; rejoice a thousand times!
Glory be to the Father.

III. Crown of Goodness

(To honor the mercy of the Blessed Virgin toward sinners, the poor, the just and the dying.)

9. *Our Father. Hail Mary.*

Glory be to thee, O refuge of sinners! Intercede for us with God.

Rejoice, O Virgin Mary; rejoice a thousand times!

10. *Hail Mary.*

Glory be to thee, O Mother of orphans! Render the Almighty favorable to us.

Rejoice, O Virgin Mary; rejoice a thousand times!

11. *Hail Mary.*

Glory be to thee, O joy of the just! Lead us with thee to the joys of Heaven.

Rejoice, O Virgin Mary; rejoice a thousand times!

12. *Hail Mary.*

Glory be to thee who art ever ready to assist us in life and in death! Lead us with thee to the kingdom of Heaven!

Rejoice, O Virgin Mary; rejoice a thousand times!
Glory be to the Father.

Let Us Pray

Hail, Mary, Daughter of God the Father; Hail, Mary, Mother of God the Son; Hail, Mary, Spouse of the Holy Ghost; Hail, Mary, Temple of the most Holy Trinity; Hail, Mary, my Mistress, my treasure, my joy, Queen of my heart; my Mother, my life, my sweetness, my dearest hope—yea, my heart and my soul! I am all thine and all that I have is thine, O Virgin blessed above all things! Let thy soul be in me to magnify the Lord; let thy spirit be in me to rejoice in God. Set thyself, O faithful Virgin, as a seal upon my heart, that in thee and through thee I may be found faithful to God. Receive me, O gracious Virgin, among those whom thou lovest and teachest, whom thou leadest, nourishest and protectest as thy children. Grant that for love of thee I may despise all earthly consolations and ever cling to those of Heaven until, through the Holy Ghost, thy faithful Spouse, and through thee, His faithful spouse, Jesus Christ thy Son be formed in me for the glory of the Father. Amen.

THE HOLY ROSARY
ACCORDING TO THE METHOD OF
ST. LOUIS DE MONTFORT

Introductory Prayer

I unite with all the saints in Heaven, with all the just on earth and with all the faithful here present. I unite with Thee, O my Jesus, in order to praise worthily Thy holy Mother and to praise Thee in her and through her. I renounce all the distractions I may have during this Rosary, which I wish to say with modesty, attention and devotion, just as if it were to be the last of my life.

We offer Thee, O most Holy Trinity, this *Creed* in honor of all the mysteries of our Faith; this *Our Father* and these three *Hail Marys* in honor of the unity of Thy Essence and the Trinity of Thy Persons. We ask of Thee a lively faith, a firm hope and an ardent charity. Amen.

Apostles' Creed, Our Father, 3 Hail Marys, Glory Be.

The Five Joyful Mysteries

1. *The Annunciation*

We offer Thee, O Lord Jesus, this first decade in honor of Thine Incarnation in Mary's womb, and we ask of Thee, through this Mystery and through her intercession, a profound humility. Amen.

Our Father, 10 Hail Marys, Glory Be to the Father. O my Jesus, forgive us our sins, save us from the fires of Hell; lead all souls to Heaven, especially those in most need of Thy mercy. (Prayer to be said at the end of each decade in accord with Our Lady of Fatima's requests in 1917).

May the grace of the Mystery of the Annunciation come down into our souls. Amen.

2. *The Visitation*

We offer Thee, O Lord Jesus, this second decade in honor of the Visitation of Thy holy Mother to her cousin St. Elizabeth and the sanctification of St. John the Baptist, and we ask of Thee, through this Mystery and through the intercession of Thy holy Mother, charity toward our neighbor. Amen.

Our Father, 10 Hail Marys, Glory Be to the Father, O my Jesus.

May the grace of the Mystery of the Visitation come down into our souls. Amen.

3. *The Nativity*

We offer Thee, O Lord Jesus, this third decade in honor of Thy Nativity in the stable of Bethlehem, and we ask of Thee, through this Mystery and through the intercession of Thy holy Mother, detachment from the things of the world, contempt of riches and love of poverty. Amen.

Our Father, 10 Hail Marys, Glory Be to the Father, O my Jesus.

May the grace of the Mystery of the Nativity come down into our souls. Amen.

4. *The Presentation in the Temple*

We offer Thee, O Lord Jesus, this fourth decade in honor of Thy Presentation in the Temple and the Purification of Mary, and we ask of Thee, through this Mystery and through the intercession of Thy holy Mother, purity of body and soul. Amen.

Our Father, 10 Hail Marys, Glory Be to the Father, O my Jesus.

May the grace of the Mystery of the Presentation in the Temple come down into our souls. Amen.

5. *The Finding of Our Lord in the Temple*

We offer Thee, O Lord Jesus, this fifth decade in honor of Mary's finding Thee in the Temple, and we ask of Thee, through this Mystery and through her intercession, the gift of true wisdom. Amen.

Our Father, 10 Hail Marys, Glory Be to the Father, O my Jesus.

May the grace of the Mystery of the Finding of Our Lord in the Temple come down into our souls. Amen.

The Five Sorrowful Mysteries

1. *The Agony in the Garden*

We offer Thee, O Lord Jesus, this sixth decade in honor of Thine Agony in the Garden of Olives, and we ask of Thee, through this Mystery and through the intercession of Thy holy Mother, contrition for our sins. Amen.

Our Father, 10 Hail Marys, Glory Be to the Father, O my Jesus.

May the grace of the Mystery of the Agony in the Garden come down into our souls. Amen.

2. *The Scourging*

We offer Thee, O Lord Jesus, this seventh decade in honor of Thy bloody Scourging, and we ask of Thee, through this Mystery and through the intercession of Thy holy Mother, the grace of mortifying our senses. Amen.

Our Father, 10 Hail Marys, Glory Be to the Father, O my Jesus.

May the grace of the Mystery of the Scourging come down into our souls. Amen.

3. *The Crowning with Thorns*

We offer Thee, O Lord Jesus, this eighth decade in honor of Thy being crowned with thorns, and we ask of Thee, through this Mystery and through the intercession of Thy holy Mother, contempt of the world. Amen.

Our Father, 10 Hail Marys, Glory Be to the Father, O my Jesus.
May the grace of the Mystery of the Crowning with Thorns come down into our souls. Amen.

4. *The Carrying of the Cross*

We offer Thee, O Lord Jesus, this ninth decade in honor of Thy carrying of the Cross, and we ask of Thee, through this Mystery and through the intercession of Thy holy Mother, patience in bearing our crosses. Amen.

Our Father, 10 Hail Marys, Glory Be to the Father, O my Jesus.
May the grace of the Mystery of the Carrying of the Cross come down into our souls. Amen.

5. *The Crucifixion*

We offer Thee, O Lord Jesus, this tenth decade in honor of Thy Crucifixion and ignominious death on Calvary and we ask of Thee, through this Mystery and through the intercession of Thy holy Mother, the conversion of sinners, the perseverance of the just and the relief of the souls in Purgatory. Amen.

Our Father, 10 Hail Marys, Glory Be to the Father, O my Jesus.
May the grace of the Mystery of the Crucifixion come down into our souls. Amen.

The Five Glorious Mysteries

1. *The Resurrection*

We offer Thee, O Lord Jesus, this eleventh decade in honor of Thy glorious Resurrection, and we ask of Thee, through this Mystery and through the intercession of Thy holy Mother, love of God and fervor in Thy service. Amen.

Our Father, 10 Hail Marys, Glory Be to the Father, O my Jesus.
May the grace of the Mystery of the Resurrection come down into our souls. Amen.

2. *The Ascension*

We offer Thee, O Lord Jesus, this twelfth decade in honor of Thy triumphant Ascension, and we ask of Thee, through this Mystery and through the intercession of Thy holy Mother, an ardent desire for Heaven, our true home. Amen.

Our Father, 10 Hail Marys, Glory Be to the Father, O my Jesus.

May the grace of the Mystery of the Ascension come down into our souls. Amen.

3. *The Descent of the Holy Ghost*

We offer Thee, O Lord Jesus, this thirteenth decade in honor of the Mystery of Pentecost, and we ask of Thee, through this Mystery and through the intercession of Thy holy Mother, the coming of the Holy Ghost into our souls. Amen.

Our Father, 10 Hail Marys, Glory Be to the Father, O my Jesus.

May the grace of the Mystery of Pentecost come down into our souls. Amen.

4. *The Assumption*

We offer Thee, O Lord Jesus, this fourteenth decade in honor of the resurrection and triumphant Assumption of Thy holy Mother into Heaven, and we ask of Thee, through this Mystery and through her intercession, a tender devotion for so good a Mother. Amen.

Our Father, 10 Hail Marys, Glory Be to the Father, O my Jesus.

May the grace of the Mystery of the Assumption come down into our souls. Amen.

5. *The Coronation of the Blessed Virgin*

We offer Thee, O Lord Jesus, this fifteenth decade in honor of the Coronation of Thy holy Mother, and we ask of Thee, through this Mystery and through her intercession, perseverance in grace and a crown of glory hereafter. Amen.

Our Father, 10 Hail Marys, Glory Be to the Father, O my Jesus.

May the grace of the Mystery of the Coronation of the Blessed Virgin come down into our souls. Amen.

Concluding Prayer

Hail Mary, beloved Daughter of the Eternal Father, admirable Mother of the Son, faithful Spouse of the Holy Ghost, august Temple of the most Holy Trinity! Hail, sovereign princess, to whom all owe subjection in Heaven and on earth! Hail, sure refuge of sinners, Our Lady of Mercy, who hast never refused any request. All sinful though I am, I cast myself at thy feet and beseech thee to obtain from Jesus, thy beloved Son , contrition and pardon for all my sins, as well as the gift of divine wisdom. I consecrate myself entirely to thee with all that I have. I choose thee today for my Mother and Mistress. Treat me, then, as the least of thy children and the most obedient of thy servants. Listen, my princess, listen to the sighs of a heart that desires to love and serve thee faithfully. Let it never be said that of all those who have had recourse to thee, I was the first to be abandoned. O my hope, O my life, O my faithful and Immaculate Virgin Mary, defend me, nourish me, hear me, teach me and save me. Amen.

THE CONFRATERNITY OF MARY, QUEEN OF ALL HEARTS

———————————•———————————

It is recommended that persons making the consecration register as members of the Confraternity of Mary, Queen of All Hearts.

It is not necessary to join any religious group in order to make and live St. Louis De Montfort's consecration to Jesus through Mary. However, those who so desire may join the Confraternity of Mary, Queen of All Hearts (a religious group which the Church classifies as a "pious union" of the faithful).

The Confraternity of Mary, Queen of All Hearts was first established in Canada, by Archbishop Duhamel of Ottawa, on March 25, 1899. On April 28, 1913, Pope St. Pius X erected it as an Archconfraternity in Rome. Today there are branches of the Confraternity in various parts of the world: the United States, Canada, Haiti, South America, Europe, Asia and Africa. There are several hundred thousand members throughout the world.

Purpose

The purpose of the Confraternity of Mary, Queen of All Hearts is to help the members live and publicize the Marian way of life as the easier and more secure means to sanctify themselves. This Marian way of life is explained in the writings of St. Louis De Montfort; its object is to establish within us the reign of Mary as a means of establishing more perfectly the reign of Jesus in our souls.

In keeping with the specific purpose determined in its Constitutions as approved by the Holy See, the Company of Mary employs this Confraternity as an aid to restore the reign of Christ through Mary. The prescribed means to fulfill this purpose is the zealous promotion of the Consecration to Mary, Queen of All Hearts.

Admission

Any Catholic, including clerics and religious, may become a member of the Confraternity of Mary, Queen of All Hearts.

In accordance with the General Moderator's directives, the members may assume other obligations special to their spiritual life or their apostolate.

Membership in the Confraternity is acquired by entering the applicant's name in the official register. This is done by sending in one's name to the Father Director of the Montfort Fathers (see page 215) to be recorded in the official register; the Father Director will then send the new member a membership certificate.

Prior to enrollment, the applicant must consecrate himself to the Blessed Virgin (preferably on one of her feast days), using for this purpose the consecration of St. Louis De Montfort. (See page 197).

Obligations

In keeping with the purpose of the Confraternity, the members apply themselves zealously to live always in dependence on Mary and to perform all their actions in union with her—doing all things with Mary, through Mary, in Mary, and for Mary. By this means, they will more perfectly live and act with, through, in, and for Jesus Christ.

Thus they should renew their consecration faithfully and frequently, making a special practice of renewing it every morning at the beginning of each new day. Their donation of themselves can easily be renewed from time to time during the day by repeating the short formula: "I am all Thine and all I have is Thine, O most loving Jesus, through Mary, Thy holy Mother." The consecration can even be renewed by a mere interior act of the mind.

The members also have an obligation to publicize Marian teaching, especially that of St. Louis De Montfort, that all may come to acknowledge and honor the Blessed Virgin as their Mother and Queen.

Recommended Practices

It is commendable to make a small offering or to do a good work in honor of Our Lady on the day of Consecration. "It would be well," says St. Louis De Montfort, "that on that day they should pay some tribute to Jesus Christ and our Blessed Lady. . . . This tribute ought to be according to the devotion and ability of each one, such as a fast, a mortification, an alms or a candle."

It is also recommended to wear the medal of Mary, Queen of All Hearts.

Share in Good Works

The members share in all the good works and prayers of the members of the Company of Mary and the Daughters of Wisdom.

The Masses offered by the members of the Company of Mary (Montfort Fathers) on the first Monday of every month for the deceased of their Congregation are applied also to the deceased members of the Confraternity.

Feasts of the Confraternity

The Annunciation (March 25) is the principal feast of the Confraternity. On this feast, there is recalled to our minds the great truth of Our Divine Lord's Incarnation and that He came to us through Mary and willed to submit Himself to her, His holy Mother.

The feast of St. Louis De Montfort (April 28) is the second principal feast of the Confraternity.

Other special feasts of the Confraternity are the Immaculate Conception (December 8), Christmas (December 25), the Purification (February 2), the Visitation (July 2), the Assumption (August 15), the Immaculate Heart of Mary (August 22), the feast of Our Lady of Sorrows (September 15).

Indulgences

The members of the Confraternity may gain a plenary indulgence, under the usual conditions, on the day of their enrollment as well as for renewing their consecration on the anniversary of enrollment, on the universal feasts of Our Lord and the Blessed Virgin, on the feast of St. Louis De Montfort, and on the first Saturday of every month. (Sacred Penitentiary, July 2, 1956).

The "usual conditions" consist of Confession, Holy Communion, prayers for the intention of the Holy Father—for example, an *Our Father* and a *Hail Mary*—and being free from all attachment to sin, even venial sin.

They may also gain a plenary indulgence at the moment of death on condition that, having received the Sacraments of Penance and Holy Communion or, if this be impossible, being of contrite heart, they invoke the Sacred Name of Jesus verbally or mentally and patiently accept death as a punishment of and as coming from the hand of God.

The members may gain a partial indulgence each time they say with a contrite heart the invocation: "I am all Thine and all I have I give to Thee, my loving Jesus, through Mary, Thy most holy Mother."

They may also gain a partial indulgence each time they perform a work of piety or charity with a contrite heart and in the spirit of the Confraternity. (Holy Office, December 18, 1913).

For further information, one should write to:

Reverend Father Director
The Confraternity
Montfort Fathers
26 South Saxon Ave.
Bay Shore, N.Y. 11706